World Rock Art
REVISED EDITION 2010

Emmanuel Anati

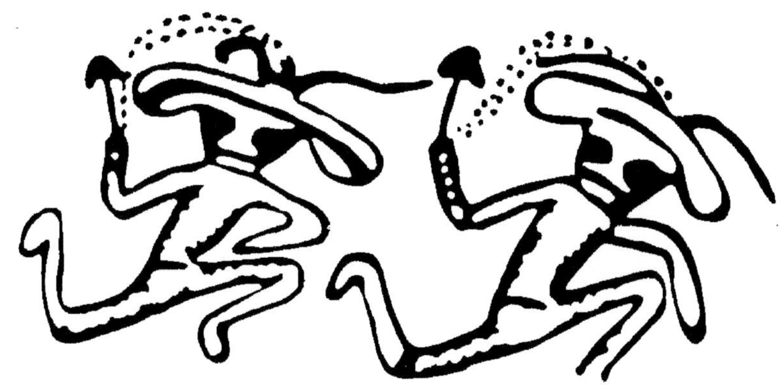

Above: see Fig. 17

Front cover:
Rio Pinturas, Santa Cruz, Patagonia, Argentina. Covacho de Las Manos Pintas.
Photo: G.C. Ligabue, WARA 88: X-7
Area Code: G-III. Cat.: A-II.

Back cover:
See Fig. 158

WORLD ROCK ART
THE PRIMORDIAL LANGUAGE

EMMANUEL ANATI

Director, Centro Camuno di Studi Preistorici
Professor of Paleo-Ethnology, University of Lecce (Ret.)

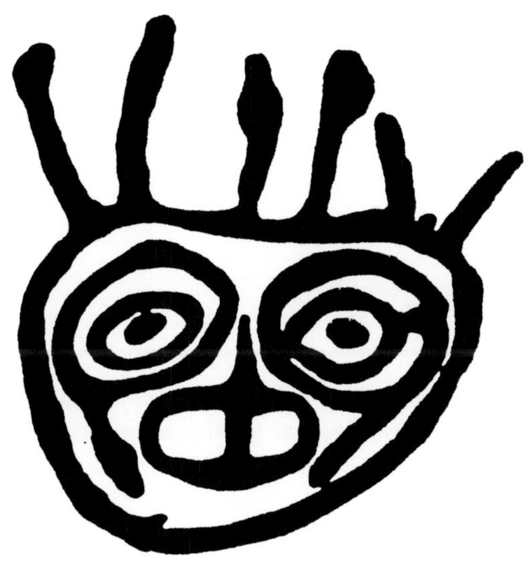

Fourth English Edition, 2010

Archaeopress
Gordon House
2776 Banbury Road
Oxford
OX2 7UP
www.archaeopress.com

WORLD ROCK ART: THE PRIMORDIAL LANGUAGE
By Emmanuel ANATI

ISBN 978-1-905739-31-8

Key words: *Aesthetics, Archetypes, Homo Sapiens, Ideograms, Intellect, Origins of Art, Paradigms of Art, Pictograms, Prehistoric and Tribal Art, Psychograms, Rock Art, Semiology of Art.*

Printed and bound in Great Britain by Marston Book Services Ltd, Oxfordshire

Contents

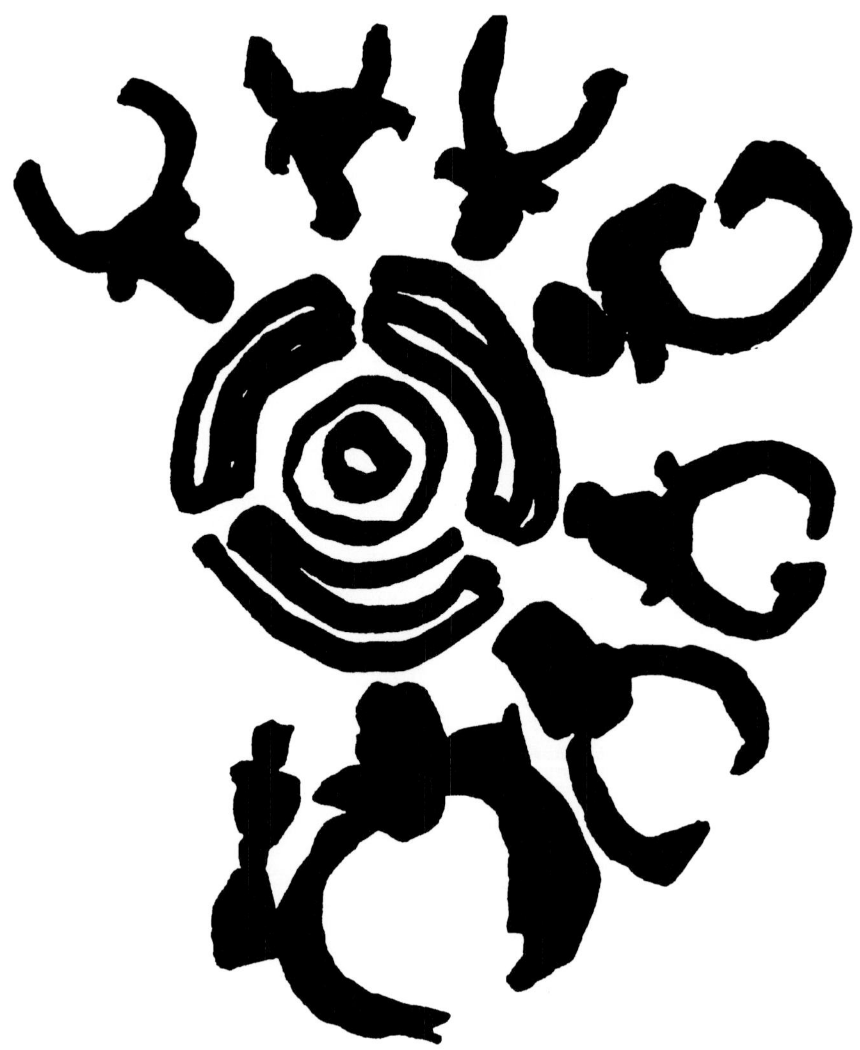

Fig. 1
Sujanpura, Bhanpura-Chambal, Inde. Rock painting describing the assembling of bovines around what has been interpreted as a water pond. The problem is the reading of the message: why it was made? What is the metaphoric meaning of bovine or cow? And what is the significance of water pond?
Source: drawing by CCSP, in E. Anati, 1995 (WARA Archive W00018)
Area Code: A-III; Cat. D-III.

PREFACE

The present volume is a new version of a set of university lectures given in 1989-1990 at the University of Lecce, Italy. It was distributed to students in a mimeographic form. It was then published by *Edizioni del Centro* under the title of *'**Arte Rupestre: il linguaggio dei primordi'*** and reprinted in a second Italian edition in 1994. *Edizioni del Centro* is the publishing branch of CCSP, the Italian research centre directed by the author. Its publications are addressed to fellow members and research institutions. They are not distributed or sold in bookshops. The first English edition came out under the present title: *'**World Rock Art: The Primordial Language'*** in July 1993 published by the *'Edizioni del Centro'*. A second English edition followed in October 1993 and a third edition in November 1994. The book spoke a new language, was appreciated and reached an audience of rock art specialists and amateurs. In the following years, more advanced publications by the same author, have caused the neglecting of this text which was never again reprinted until the present edition. Over fifteen years have now elapsed since the previous edition.

Its re-reading convinced the editor that it still remains a precious introductory text for students of rock art. This text, when it was first published, proposed a new and critical approach to rock art studies. It was the starting point of the new school of methodology, based upon typology and style, which was first developed by the author, at the Centro Camuno di Studi Preistorici (CCSP) and became widespread. It marked the beginning of a new discipline, the systematic study of world rock art.

One of the peculiarities of this study is its emphasis on the value of stylistic patterns in the visual arts as expressions of the human intellectual processes and as a diagnostic factor in defining the cultural setting of prehistoric art. It should be kept in mind that the concern about style in prehistoric art was demonised at the time when this text was conceived. And when it came out it marked a confrontation against a widespread tendency which was then proven to be wrong by this book. As such it has a historical value as a landmark. Further, after twenty years, its text is still readable, fresh and appealing.

The author was then requested to revise and update it. A few additions were made to the original text. The major change is that a new category of rock art had come to the awareness of scholars in the meantime and it is added here. The previous versions had one of the R.A. categories defined as the art of 'Hunters-Gatherers'. Since then the author has been able to separate the typology of rock art related to people having a prevailing early hunting economy and a prevailing carnivore diet, from that of gatherers and food collectors having a prevailing vegetarian diet. The present edition includes the new classification.

This volume is a basic introduction to rock art studies and it was decided that its original approach should be preserved. Having served students for twenty years, and having contributed to the formation of young scholars, this book is once more going to introduce the primary Anati view on rock art studies to new generations of students and scholars.

INTRODUCTION

In 1983, UNESCO (United Nations Educational, Scientific and Cultural Organization) commissioned a World Report on the State of Research in Rock Art: the paintings and engravings in caves and on rock surfaces. It was the first attempt at a world view on the most ancient art. After ten years, in 1993 another State of Research in Rock Art was commissioned by ICOMOS (International Council on Monuments and Sites). In 2008 UNESCO commissioned another World Report on rock art to update the previous ones and to advise on the strategies for nomination of new rock art sites in the World Heritage List.

Having been the author of these three reports, I had the opportunity of assessing the enormous progress made by rock art studies in the last quarter of a century. This book presents the main evaluations and messages of the world reports; and it goes beyond, exploring the meaning of symbols, identifying the main types of syntaxes in rock art and looking at the future, analysing what may be the uses of research in rock art and how rock art is contributing to world culture.

The Australian Aborigines say that rock art tells us the story of 'dreamtime'. This is probably true for rock art everywhere. Dreamtime is the time beyond our direct memory. For the Australians it includes true history. Recent events are chronicles rather than history. For people who have a written history, rock art is the record of whatever impressed and concerned their ancestors before they became able to write down their memories. For tribal people who did not learn as yet to write in a conventionally-accepted script, rock art is their writing. The pictographic and ideographic systems used are reminiscent of dreams. Written history came much later and concerns only a short time and a small part of humanity, that part which became urban and literate. Only 500 years ago, a large majority of humankind in five continents still used rock art as the main means of recording. And such a pattern had persisted for fifty thousand years.

Generation by generation, the focus of research has shifted. At the beginning of the twentieth century, after having established, in a rather vague way, the age of some rock art groups, the main interest of researchers concentrated on motivation. Most scholars dismissed the idea that rock art was produced to embellish the rock surfaces, but they proposed different motivations for making rock art. Hunting magic, shamanism, picture writing for communication purposes, initiation tutoring, worship of animals and other roles were all advocated and defended. None of them provides a complete answer; most of them had a role in the making of rock art.

Next, rock art research went through a period which was characterised by uses and abuses of comparisons between prehistoric and tribal art. With much curiosity, researchers were discovering that tribes from one part of the world would still represent something depicted in another part of the world centuries or even millennia earlier.

Then for over two decades, dating became the principal concern. Definition of styles took over as the main theme of debate. Some researchers displayed their acrobatic abilities in 'defining' ages, styles and sub-phases. All these issues were seen mostly at local levels. At that time attempts were often made to present overviews of local and national character but comparison between rock art expressions from different continents was often defined as a non-scientific approach.

In the 60s and the 70s the major trend tended to identify 'scientific' with 'technical' and the literature was subjected to an endless series of measurements, recorded details of specific sites and other issues which are today seen as means of research rather than its goals. The question of why was rock art made was hardly faced.

Research was still conducted in a rather geocentric way. Most of the studies concerned restricted geographical areas. Phenomenology was occasionally considered and then only by singling out isolated details. Most researchers had only local data at their disposal and the possibilities for discovering universal patterns was limited. All these studies however have been necessary steps and constitute the basis of present research.

When the first 'World Report' was compiled in 1982-83, the first world data bank on rock art was being established and the main issue was to demonstrate that rock art is a world wide phenomenon, a means of expression as well as a cultural trend of pre-literate people. In the second World Report, in 1993, the focus was on the presence of constants, archetypes and universal paradigms. Phenomenology was faced systematically and globally. The main focus of the third report was on the search for meaning and on the methods of deciphering rock art. It was made clear that rock art was a means of communication, a sort of pictographic writing used to convey, commemorate or memorise messages. Deciphering rock art meant making history out of prehistory.

A number of recurring elements, present in all continents, indicate that the basic grammar and syntax of rock art respond to universal patterns of cognition, logic and communication. Rock art appears as the expression of a primordial language, with different dialects, which can be read disregarding the language in which one thinks and communicates. It takes us back to a universal pictographic proto-script which, once deciphered, can be read and understood in any spoken and written language.

To reactivate the use of a method of pictographic and ideographic writing which can be read in any language would open up a new horizon for human communication and may appear as a sort of utopia. And yet our cultural heritage is providing examples of successful attempts in this direction. The system applied by the rock art makers is simple and follows some elementary principles. The same kind of logic is widespread both geographically and chronologically but each period and each culture have their own peculiarities. Such local features help us to detect the common denominators. Could we reactivate primordial picture writing? How should linguists and epigraphers contribute to the progress of such a concept?

The archetypes are still functioning and they convey immediate and deep messages. This is the kind of language that many artists, teachers, politicians, publicity people, public relations agents and prophets would like to master. No wonder that it awakens so much interest and curiosity in the general public as well.

The painted caves of Lascaux in France, and Altamira in Spain, are well known to the public because of their geographic location in western Europe and their inclusion in art history textbooks. The rock paintings of the Tassili in the Algerian Sahara, and the rock engravings of Valcamonica (Camonica Valley) in the Italian Alps, have been recorded and studied for decades. Only recently have they become part of general culture. Less known is the fact that these sites represent only a small fraction of the world heritage of rock art. Recent discoveries show, in many parts of the world, that early man chose to depict and engrave on rock surfaces. Although exploration has by no means been exhaustive, rock art is reported from thousands of sites. Scientific evidence, such as Carbon-14 dating, palaeo-climatic data and archaeological contexts, indicate that the oldest datable rock art known today was executed over 50,000 years ago.

Rock art reveals the human capacities of abstraction, synthesis and idealization. It describes economic and social activities, ideas, beliefs and practices and provides unique insight into the intellectual life and cultural patterns of man. Long before the invention of phonetic writing, rock art recorded the most ancient testimony of human imaginative and artistic creativity. It constitutes one of the most significant aspects of the common heritage of humanity.

The analysis of rock art on a world scale is a new field of research and it is at its beginning. The present study is based on data collected from about 200 major rock art areas selected from all the inhabited continents. Some general trends and a number of working hypotheses have emerged which are summarised in seventeen postulates. Rock art is subdivided into five categories which show different elements of style and content and refer to five different socio-economic backgrounds. A comparative study on the location of major rock art sites reveals some most interesting elements on the ecological setting of rock art. Recurring patterns indicate the presence of a relationship between environment and human creativity. Universal characteristics are identified by the comparative analysis of large concentrations of rock art around the world.

The presence of a basic grammar and of recurring syntax patterns in the visual art of non-literate societies unveils widespread patterns. It illustrates the presence of a human 'basic logic' and of elementary conceptual processes of sequences and associations. The systems of human cognitive processes are evidenced in 50,000 years of rock art. No other source provides so far such a broad, universal, uninterrupted expression of the human cognitive system. In this volume, paradigms and archetypes in the visual arts are sorted and illustrated, and a preliminary world vision of the phenomenon of rock art is attempted. Some of the universal patterns still survive in contemporary art and in present-day mental processes.

The world endowment of rock art is rapidly deteriorating due to such processes as deforestation, pollution, urban growth and the spread of roads and development areas. Vandalism and other human actions are by far the major causes of degradation. Most of this heritage has not yet been recorded or studied, and humanity is risking its loss for ever. It has become urgent to carry out the recording, inventory and salvage of whatever may still be preserved for future generations. It is not just a matter of saving an archaeological patrimony. It is a source for understanding the human mind, human logic and human behavior exhibited since the presence of our earliest direct ancestor, *Homo sapiens*. It is an essential source of research for understanding the mental behavior of the species.

The first step towards a broad participation is awareness. How can an intelligent person wish to protect a patrimony without being aware of its value? At the 10th International Symposium on Rock Art which took place in Valcamonica (Camonica Valley) Italy, in 1992, an appeal was addressed to governments and international organizations to promote the understanding of rock art, to develop educational programmes on its preservation and on its cultural value. Because of its paramount role for the development of human culture, it is important to make its messages accessible to world education and culture, especially to the indigenous people in whose territories rock art is found. Such a recommendation has been repeated ever since. Ultimately, something might start moving in the right direction.

Obviously, rock art may become a very valuable source of touristic and economic development. When such developments take place without an appropriate cultural and educational background, two major risks arise. The local population may be left aside, alienated from participation and uninspired to protect sites; inappropriate measures of protection may cause rapid deterioration of the rock art sites and of their environment. Enforcement of bureaucratic regulations can hardly replace the awareness and the concern of the people. As we have seen in Europe, in Australia and elsewhere, the patrimony of rock art can best be preserved if both the local population and the visitors seriously care for the sites.

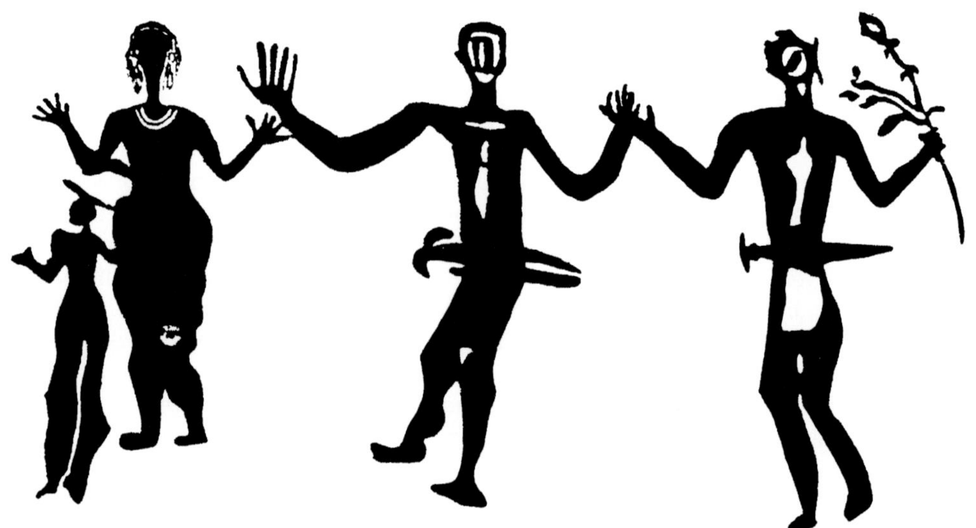

Fig. 2
Shaib Samma, Central Arabia. Dancing scene of the 'Oval Head People'. Men, a woman and a child dance together. The first figure to the right is holding a bush which may be some sort of narcotic plant, the reason for the feast.
Source: Tracing by Anati, E. after a photo by J. Ryckmans, 1952; in: Anati, E. 1968a vol I, p. 40, fi g. 18 (WARA Archive W00096)
Area Code: B-IV; Cat. D-II.

PART ONE

1
THE SURVEY

A preliminary survey of rock art, based on the existing documentation in the archives of the CCSP (Centro Camuno di Studi Preistorici, Italy) and on the reports received from researchers, has enabled us to locate some 820 areas of rock art in the world, including thousands of sites. At first there were discrepancies, among rock art specialists, about the definition of rock art groups. It was necessary to define what constitutes an 'area' and a 'site'. On the whole, there now seems to be general agreement on two points:

1. *Site*: A rock art site is any place where there is rock art. Its boundaries are traced 500 meters beyond the last decorated rock in every direction. Two clusters of depictions which are separated by a figureless distance of over 500 meters are considered two different sites. Over 68,000 sites are documented around the world. In Italy alone there are over 3,000.
2. *Area:* A rock art area may include several sites. It is defined primarily by its cultural and topographic characteristics. Rock art areas coincide with geographical features such as valleys, plateaus and mountain ranges. In order to be distinct from one another and form different *areas*, two assemblages of rock art should be at a distance of at least twenty kilometers from each other, a distance that requires about one day's walking. Over 820 *areas* have been located, but this figure depends primarily on the information that has been made available. The real number of rock art areas is likely to be much higher.

Rock art areas usually include other archaeological remains. They are vital for the understanding of the role played by the area, at the time in which the rock art was executed. Each area obviously has a landscape and topographic features. They should be preserved and protected as part of the patrimony as they are the natural setting in which the rock art was produced. The choice of men to produce rock art in a certain locality was usually motivated by the nature of the place.

A selection of areas was attempted in order to identify *major areas*. A *major area* provides an outstanding contribution to the knowledge of the intellectual identity of early man. Most of the major areas have over 10,000 figures in a zone of less than 1,000 km^2, but this is not a prerequisite. Surprisingly such areas are quite evenly distributed: in no continent are there less than ten major areas, or more than forty. 150 major areas had been identified in 1983, and are distributed as follows:

Africa:	24	Countries	31	Areas
Asia:	13	'	34	'
The Americas:	13	'	39	'
Europe:	14	'	31	'
Oceania:	6	'	15	'
Total:	**70**	'	**150**	'

This list was subsequently revised at least twice but the general picture on world distribution did not change. Some of these major areas of rock art have an enormous quantity of figures. The Drakensberg range in Lesotho and South Africa includes over 5,000 sites with an estimate of over three million figures. Kakadu, in the Arnhem Land, Australia, has over two million figures. The Tassili n'Ajjer, in Algeria, has over 400 sites with at least 600,000 figures. The Negev and Sinai, in Israel and Egypt, include seventeen areas with over 300 sites and at least 500,000 figures. The Alpine range in France, Italy, Switzerland and Austria, numbers sixteen areas. Just one of them, Valcamonica (Italy), includes twenty-six sites with over 250,000 figures recorded and with an estimated total of over 350,000 figures. Various areas in Arabia, India, Siberia and Central Asia, Brazil and Argentina may each contain as many figures, though precise surveys are not yet available.

The world production of rock art documented so far numbers over 75 million figures, but we may safely estimate that the total number of rock art figures still preserved should be well over 100 million. This constitutes an extraordinary documentation of man's intellectual adventures, an outstanding world heritage and a unique source for historical reconstruction and for understanding the human mind.

Each figure is part of an assemblage which was produced deliberately and which conveys some message. All together they make the raw material of a 50,000 year record. In the course of research some story is often being reconstructed. Each year keys are found to decipher the codes of some chapter, providing new light on the long history of mankind. This may become the most challenging task of the humanities in the coming generations.

The importance of carrying on an accurate world survey and in producing a world archive of rock art is evident. A new kind of world history would make available the intellectual adventures, the beliefs and the habits of many populations which have been so far ignored by world history. These peoples are represented by a unique database that records the intellectual development of *Homo sapiens* from the moment our species conceived the concept of art.

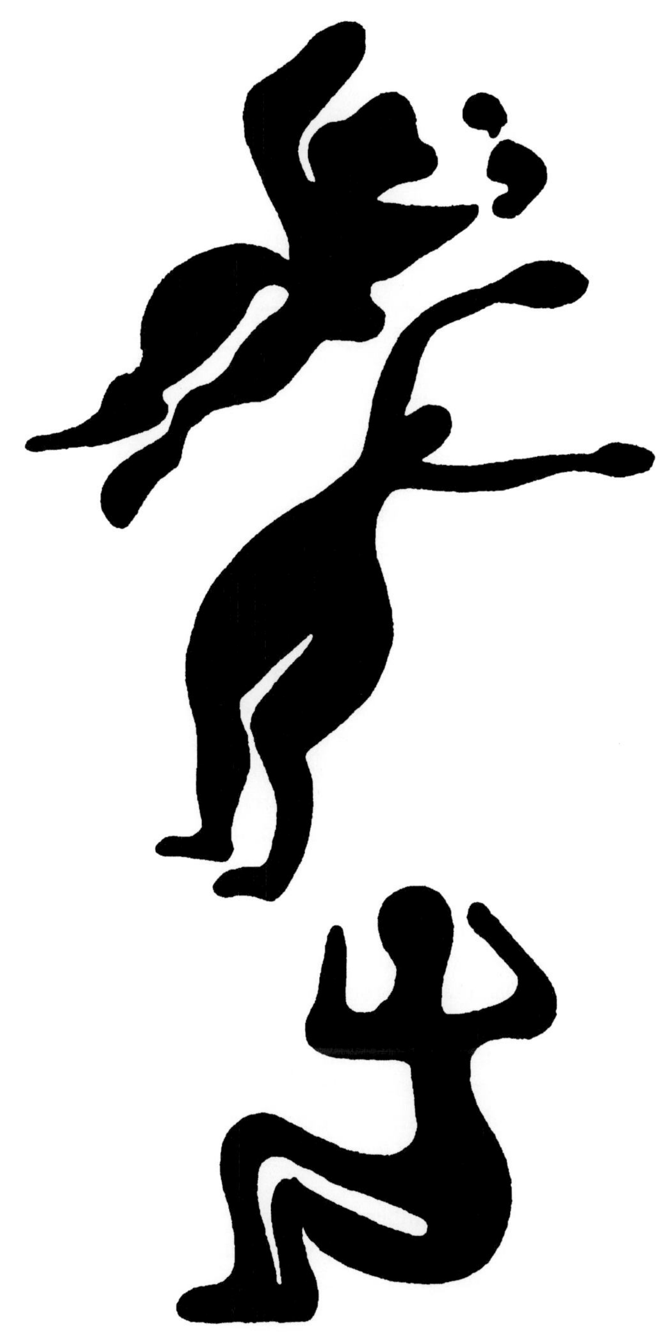

Fig. 3
Baraq, Siba, Central Saudi Arabia. Idealized feminine figures belonging to a style defined as the 'People with Oval Heads'. Pastoral tribes from the IVth and IIIrd millennia BC. Who are these images? What is the story behind?
Source: tracing by Anati, 1968 (WARA Archive W00108)
Area Code: B-IV; Cat. D-II.

2
THE BEGINNING OF RESEARCH

Rock art was often an attempt to understand and convey meanings and interpretations of nature. In itself it has the spirit of research. The conceptual structure of depictions that represent ideas imply the ability of synthesis and metaphoric expressions. Conceiving the graphemes is a result of research. The trials of reading their messages were expressions of research from the very beginning. Likely, rock art and rock art research started together. Not far from Dakhla, in Upper Egypt, an ideographic sequence of engravings of Early Hunters, at least 12,000 years old, was interpreted, after several thousand years, by a Neolithic artist of ca. 5000 BC, who added the figure of a woman near a female ideogram. In such a way he displayed his ability to decipher a symbol which was no more in use. His goal is likely to have been that of conveying its meaning to make the sequence understandable to his keens. Rock art research had started already.

At the site of Luine, in Valcamonica, Italy, a rock engraving of a dagger belonging to the Chalcolithic period, ca. 3000 BC, was recognized by a passer-by in the Roman period, 3000 years later, and below this image he engraved the word 'mucro' which in Latin means dagger. In the same Italian valley, Medieval shepherds engraved crosses on rocks with prehistoric engravings to neutralize their satanic power. At Bhimbetka, Madja Pradesh, India, Buddhist hermits in the last centuries before our era were living in the rock shelters decorated by prehistoric rock art, adding Buddhist images to renew the sacredness of the site. Generation after generation the makers of rock art have tried to understand, modify and adapt the messages of their predecessors. We may therefore consider that studying rock art is as old as rock art itself.

In 1627, the first tracings of prehistoric rock art were made in Bohuslaan (Sweden) by a Norwegian school teacher, by the name of Peder Alfsson. The study of rock art has since developed gradually to interest both scholars and laymen.

In the last century, the number of publications concerning the subject has steadily increased. Even so, the study of rock art is still a relatively young and undeveloped field of archaeological and anthropological research. Today the subject is awakening an ever-growing interest among researchers. However, well-tested recording systems and fully assimilated patterns of aims and purposes are still lacking in many regions of the world.

Sporadic reports on rock art appeared throughout the 18th and 19th centuries. In America, an invaluable book by G. Mallery, *Picture-writing of the American Indians*, was published by the Smithsonian Institution in 1893. From the beginning of the 20th century there have been significant reports and data collection on rock art in South Africa, the Sahara and Australia. In Sweden, rock art studies were pioneered by O. Almgren and in the Alps by the English clergyman Clarence Bicknell.

After the discovery of Altamira cave, in Spain, over one hundred years ago, a wealth of Palaeolithic cave art in France and Spain was brought back to light. Beginning in the early 1900s, recording and descriptions of rock art sites were conducted primarily by the Abbé Henri Breuil and by Hugo Obermaier.

These two scholars, followed by Teilhard de Chardin, created a challenging school of thought that contributed to a new cultural approach in rock art studies. A major cultural role of these clergymen dealing with prehistoric art and primary expressions of intellectual life was that of producing some sort of truce between creationists and evolutionists.

'Research' at that time consisted of a combination of descriptions and theories. Scholars attempted to establish dating for prehistoric paintings and to explain their meaning, relating them to tales and habits of present-day tribes. There were many more or less factual accounts, yet little analysis and no synthesis in these preliminary studies; however, they provided an astounding intellectual base that raised curiosity and stimulated further research.

More recently, valuable scholars such as Paolo Graziosi and André Leroi-Gourhan have brought order to the discoveries of Palaeolithic European cave art. They contributed to setting the bases for a structural analysis. In spite of this, a world-wide view was still missing. The study of rock art as a world phenomenon was created and developed by the Centro Camuno di Studi Preistorici (CCSP) in Italy from 1964 on. As a result the CAR, International Committee on Rock Art of the ICOMOS (International Council on Monuments and Sites) came to exist in 1982 And CISENP (Commission Internationale Scientifique pour l'étude des Expressions Intellectuelles et Spirituelles des Peoples sans Ecriture) came into existence in 2007, as an organ of UISPP (Union Internationale des Sciences Prehistoriques et Protohistoriques).

The CCSP has developed a World Archive of Rock Art (WARA), a Who's Who in Rock Art, world reports and international symposia. The data that is being collected grows constantly; scholars and students from different countries join efforts to give vitality to a new-born discipline: Rock Art Studies.

Methods of recording and analysis have been, and still are, continually being refined. There is no doubt that they will further evolve. The growth of research itself generates ever deeper aspects of study, with a consequent need for new systems of documentation and analysis.

Until universal methods are established for a world data bank, methods must be adapted for each project to ensure that the basic data required for analysis can be obtained: analysis must be planned according to the specific questions which the project addresses. To record paintings calls for different techniques from recording engravings; where both occupy the same surface, still other considerations must be made. In addition, the dimensions of figures and decorated surfaces, their state of preservation, the type of rock, the presence or lack of various techniques of execution and stratigraphic superimpositions, irregularities in the rock surfaces, and differences in patination (that is, the colour of the naturally oxidized rock surface that changes hue with age) demand, in each case, specific approaches of study and research. Today the methods of recording developed in Italy by the CCSP have been adapted for use at several major rock art sites in Europe, the Near East and Africa, yet there is still no recording method that is universally applicable.

Recording is the first step to enable research. It requires a concern with superimpositions and stratigraphy, quantitative analyses of subject matter, evaluation of stylistic patterns, the study of raw materials and the tools used by the artists, and numerous other items that enable an in-depth understanding of rock art technical aspects.

Differences obviously exist in the methods used by researchers due to variations in approach and training. Nevertheless it is imperative to develop and establish a conventional, universal system which will enable researchers to understand each other, to compare results and to identify common elements and particularities in each area. Any recording of rock art should make available a representation as reliable as possible of what the makers of rock art intended to represent

Once an area is accurately recorded, the main question that arises is what should be done with the collected data: in other words, what are the aims and purposes of rock art studies. As with methods of recording, the goals of research are also developing. In the last few years wider scopes and new implications have emerged within this field. Once a message is identified, it should be decoded. Once it is decoded, it should be understood to whom it was addressed and why.

Matters changed when it was understood that rock art, like writing, is a vital source for historical reconstruction. Because of this consideration research in rock art has grown both in dimension and in outlook. In the last generation it has ceased to be just a descriptive subject and has become a research discipline.

The term 'beautiful' which is often used to stress the importance of a site, is a subjective evaluation reflecting the taste of the evaluator. Nevertheless the beauty of a site or of a painting is certainly relevant as a mean of attraction to the object. Most of primary human relations are influenced by aesthetic evaluations. But what is mainly relevant in cultural and historical terms is our ability to read the message and to understand why it was formulated, and to whom it was addressed. Rock art is the major archive on 50,000 years of the history of mankind and should be considered as such.

Thirty years ago there were very few specialists in rock art, and these few were concentrated in a few countries. Today there are over 300 professional specialists in over 100 countries throughout the world; many general archaeologists develop interest in rock art and numerous amateurs cooperate. Thousands of laymen make 'pilgrimages' to rock art sites. In thirty years the number of visitors to rock art sites such as Valcamonica in Italy, Har Karkom in the Israeli Negev Desert, Kakadu in Australia Northern Territories, Bhimbetka in Madja Pradesh, India or the Tassili in Algeria, has multiplied thirty times. Rock Art is being discovered by the public at large, and yet scholars have still to define the broader aims and purposes of their research. Time is running short. Surveys should provide data base on inventory. Decoding should provide contents. Research should convey knowledge and disseminate culture. Visitors should be able to know the meaning of what they are looking at. Rock art should acquire its role in culture and education.

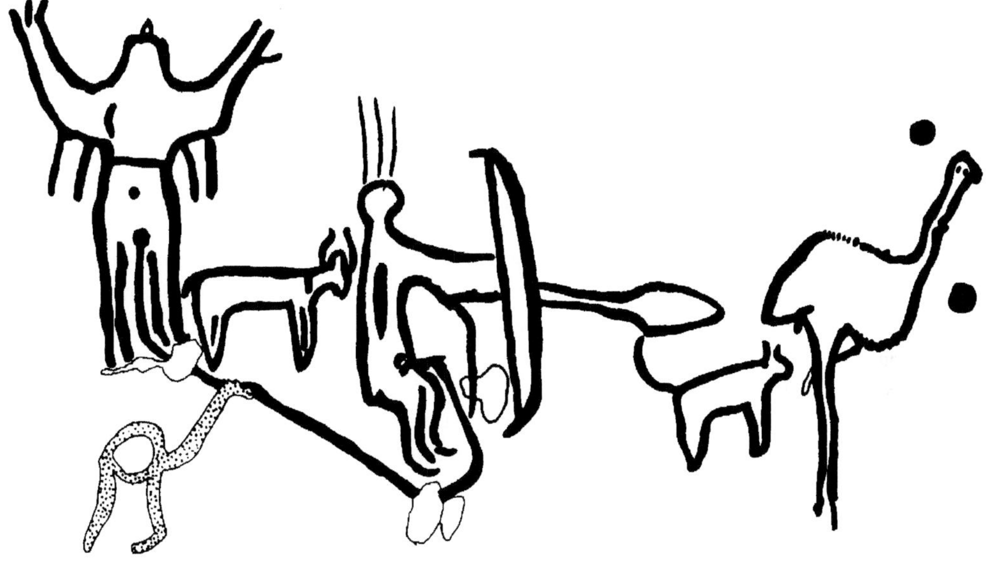

Fig 4
Relationship between hunting and sex. Rock engravings of Tiout, Atlas Range, Sahara, Algeria. An ostrich hunter is using the bow and an arrow with a large head. He is helped by a dog. His penis and his arm are related by a line to the pubis of the female figure behind him. Between the woman and the hunter there is a caprine with a triangular symbol between the horns. The same symbol is repeated on the head of the woman and probably is an indicator. The animal, plus the ideogram, may indicate the identity or the name of the woman. The object of the hunt, the ostrich, has, in its vicinity, two cup marks. They indicate the ostrich as the object meaning 'to do' or, in this case, 'subject to be hunted'.
Source: Drawn from a photograph of G. Camps, 1975, p. 328. (WARA Archive W00160)
Area Code: C-II. Cat.: C-I

3
HISTORICAL BACKGROUND

The appearance of *Homo sapiens* on earth marks the emergence of a new species: one able to communicate thoughts and ideas through a complex assemblage of vocalizations that we call language. This species spread across the planet, and we are its issue. Early vocalizations, gestures and other communicative expressions, either oral or visual, were not preserved. But their graphic messages did reach us. While art objects have been unearthed in early archaeological sites, over 90% of prehistoric creative expressions are preserved in the form of rock art. Its study and evaluation provides unique insight into man's intellectual life during the last 50,000 years, and reveals his imagination and conceptual adventures. The consistency of subjects and figures exhibited in rock art throughout the world testifies to the common origin of the human intellect.

In every territory which was inhabited by human beings, concentrations of rock art provide new perspectives into the history of mankind. All prehistoric groups are represented; from Paleolithic hunter-gatherers to contemporary collectors, fishermen and pastoral societies. As a result of the information gleaned from these creative registers, we have gained a greater historical awareness of the remote past of peoples in many countries of Asia, Africa, the Americas, Europe and Oceania.

Because it falls before the advent of conventional writing, rock art constitutes a major testimony of early man's expression of himself and of his world view. While even the most ancient script is just over 5,000 years old, rock art provides a record of the way man lived many thousands of years earlier. Yet despite its value as a source of cultural, social and historical information, in most regions of the world this expression of human creativity has been sorely neglected. For one reason or another much of the knowledge of regional scholars does not become available to the rest of the world. In order to establish a more co-operative and receptive forum for thought, it is vital that researchers share their information and their conclusions on the state of rock art studies. International symposia and congresses are of course very important but many researchers cannot attend them. A network is needed to grant permanent contact among specialists.

Technical aspects of culture progress in a more or less coherent evolution. New inventions and innovations constitute the bases of each step in the evolutionary sequence, and result from experiences which motivate subsequent progress. It is questionable, however, whether such logical evolution occurs in the artistic aspect of culture as well. Art creativity may follow trends which are not directly influenced by technological evolution. A wide range of factors influence artistic creativity. They operate on various levels, from the psychological reality of the artist to his social conditioning, from the kind of the available raw material to the conceptual function expected to be covered by the artistic output.

Current cultural standards influence the evaluation and appreciation of art and creativity. Aesthetics change from culture to culture, from generation to generation and from person to person according to fluctuations in style and taste. This concern should be kept in mind when rock art styles are described as realistic, descriptive, abstract or symbolic, for such terms reflect our own degree of comprehension and our own cultural criteria which are the result of complex, dialectical and individual capacities.The artist did not represent everything he saw or knew, but instead made specific choices. Although the subject matter varies consistently from one age to another, it is always rather circumscribed within each age or culture. Thus the frequency and the kind of assemblage of subjects allow us to construct a rudimentary hierarchy of the artist's values. The gamut of subject matter is always well-defined and consistent within specific cultural and tribal patterns. There have always been defined impulses to paint, draw or engrave in a certain way, and both subject matter and style are reflections of deep motivations.

Rock art may help in defining patterns of culture. When assemblages can be identified chronologically, each one represents a specific stage in the cultural sequence; hence, through subject matter and associations, rock art can divulge many aspects of human life. The depiction of the species of animal hunted and of the food gathered tells us much about the ecosystem in which man lived. The depiction of weapons, tools and other objects reveal his technical abilities. The illustration of his myths and beliefs bring back to our consciousness essential aspects of our intellectual roots and displays the existential relationship between Man, Nature and the 'Supernatural'.

Comparative studies help to identify similar kinds of societies around the world. Certain kinds of hunting societies, for example, tend to depict animals in a particular style and to use a consistent assemblage of symbols the world over. Pastoral societies from different regions have style characteristics in common and focus their representations on the animals they breed and on their social activities. The art of fishermen or of pastoral populations from areas which may be quite distant from one another may show similar traits of style. No doubt, daily concerns and specific patterns of activities have had parallel impacts on peoples with similar activities and backgrounds, resulting in similar trends of figurative or graphic output.

It appears therefore that patterns of style and subject matter in the visual arts indicate specific horizons of mentality and hence enable us to detect stages of culture. Thus it already seems possible to define the meaning of style in a general way. Of course the details of each figure may still reveal much more about the individual artist's state of mind, preoccupations and motivations within his cultural horizon. Rock art studies may have a tremendous impact in the near future on providing new insight into unexplored aspects of the history of mankind and of specific ethnic and cultural entities.

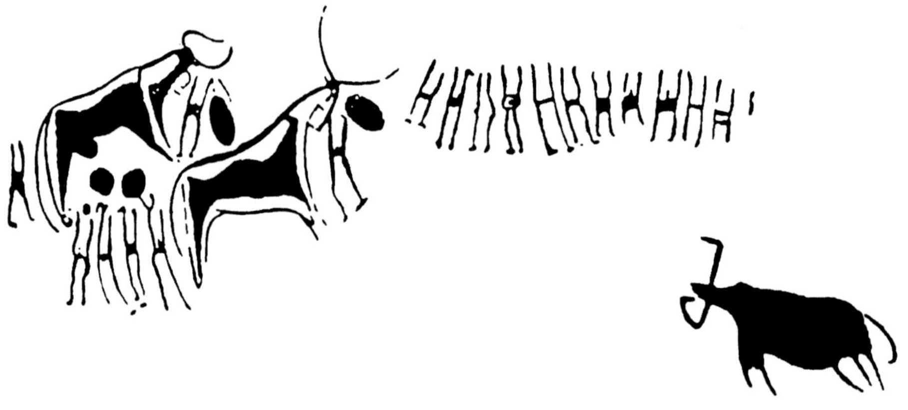

Fig. 5
Cattle and man. Rock paintings of Senda Bifton, Ethiopia. Men with shields seem to defend two bovines while a group of people approaches. The lower bovine is made by a different hand.
Source: A.R. Willcox, 1984, p. 58. (WARA Archive W00163)
Area Code: C-V. Cat.: D-II

4
WORLD DISTRIBUTION

The world distribution of prehistoric art indicates that early man viewed visual art as an integral and essential part of his daily life. In every inhabited region human groups painted and engraved rock art. Indeed, rock appears to have been the first canvas used by man, in every part of the world. This is the art that was preserved. Many other art forms, likely to have been as old, have not survived. Body paintings and decorations, as well as sand drawings and collections of stones of peculiar shapes or colours may have been practiced by man as early or even before the inception of rock art. Music and dance have left indirect traces only through depictions in rock art and some rare remains of musical instruments in archaeological layers.

The rock art heritage is immense. Millions of figures and signs make miles-long art galleries. Major concentrations of rock art are found more or less evenly distributed on earth's inhabited land. At the time of the Second World Report, in 1993, the world distribution of major sites involved seventy-six countries, six more than in 1983. We shall start our survey in southern Africa which, according to present knowledge, has the greatest concentration of rock art in the world. There are major concentrations in twelve countries: Angola, Botswana, Kenya, Lesotho, Malawi, Mozambique, Namibia, South Africa, Tanzania, Uganda, Zambia and Zimbabwe. In northern Africa the major concentrations are located in twelve countries: Algeria, Chad, Egypt, Ethiopia, Libya, Mali, Mauritania, Morocco, Niger, Nigeria, Somalia and the Sudan.

In Asia, major concentrations in the Near East are known in six countries: Iran, Israel, Jordan, Saudi Arabia, Sinai (Egypt) and Anatolia (Turkey). In Central Asia and the Far East significant concentrations are found in nine countries: Afghanistan, China, India, Kazakhstan, Mongolia, Pakistan, Russian Central Asia and Siberia, Turkmenistan, Uzbekistan.

Major rock art sites in North America are located both in Canada and the USA. In Latin America they are known in eleven countries: Argentina, Bolivia, Brazil, Chile, Colombia, Ecuador, Guatemala, Mexico, Peru, the Dominican Republic and Venezuela. In Europe, major concentrations are found in fifteen countries: Austria, Azerbaijan, Bulgaria, Denmark, Finland, France, Ireland, Italy, Norway, Portugal, Spain, Sweden, Switzerland, the United Kingdom and Russia. In Oceania, Major concentrations of rock art are known in seven countries. By far the major concentrations known are in Australia, including Tasmania; others are found in Easter Island (Chile), Hawaii (USA), New Guinea, New Zealand, Papua-New Guinea and the Solomon Islands. New criteria of evaluation for defining a 'major site' and newly available data will probably modify again the number of concerned countries.

Recent research indicates that the beginning of rock art on every continent goes back much farther in time than was believed a few years ago. In Africa the oldest figurative art dated so far is from the Apollo 11 cave in Namibia, where painted animal figures on stone slabs were found at an archaeological level defined by W.E. Wendt as 'Middle Stone Age', dated by three C-14 tests (not calibrated) to 28,400, 26,700 and 26,300 BP (Wendt, 1976). In Tanzania, the earliest figurative rock art is from the Kondoa and Singida districts, and may be older. In one of the painted rock shelters, coloring materials with marks of use as crayons, were found in archaeological levels dated by C-14 to over 40,000 years (Anati, 1986). A sequence of different styles of Early Hunters' rock paintings are likely to have started earlier than any other rock art dated so far in Africa and may well be over 40,000 years old (cf. *BCSP*, vol. 21, 1984). Non figurative markings are much older but they are not considered as 'art'.

In northern Africa, the earliest dates available so far for the beginning of rock art are much later than in southern Africa; they refer to Early Hunters' art from the Acacus range in Libya, going back to the late Pleistocene, and date according to F. Mori to over 12,000 BP (Mori, 1970; 1991). Similar stylistic assemblages are known from the Tassili n'Ajjer in Algeria and from the Ennedi in Chad.

In the Near East the earliest clues for dating are from Central Arabia (Dahthami Wells) and, because of the depictions of extinct animal species, are likely to belong to the Pleistocene epoch, before 12,000 BC (Anati, 1970). In Central Asia and the Far East chronological data so far are more limited than elsewhere. Mobiliary art from Malta and other sites in the Baikal region of Central Siberia has been dated (not calibrated) to ca. 34,800 BP (Abramova BCSP 25-26 1990, p. 81). By comparison, Aleksej P. Okladnikov has proposed a Pleistocene date for ancient rock art sites of similar styles in various parts of central Siberia. These datings are controversial. But Early Hunters rock engravings are widespread in Siberia, some of them include images of extinct fauna and may well go back to the Pleistocene.

In India, in Madhya Pradesh at Bhimbetka, V.S. Wakankar detected a series of rock paintings from the Stone Age which he located in the Pleistocene. Decorated ostrich eggshells from the same area have been dated by C-14 to 25,000 BP. There are several sites of Early Hunters' rock paintings which are likely to be of Pleistocene age.

In Europe, the earliest graphic signs are found in contexts of the Middle Paleolithic, before 70,000 years ago but the earliest figurative depictions are dated 34,000 to 30,000 years BP. They seem to coincide with the first presence on the continent of the Upper Paleolithic cultures of *Homo sapiens*. Nonetheless, the beautiful polychrome paintings from the caves of Altamira and Lascaux developed in the Magdalenian period, between 18,000 and 14,000 years ago. Some graphic markings have been attributed to the Mousterian period and are considered a 'pre-figurative' or 'pre-art' stage which has been attributed to Neanderthal Man. So far, no figurative images have been demonstrated to belong to that stage.

In the Americas, the earliest art dated so far comes from the southern continent where in the Piaui State, Brazil, rock art sites have been tentatively dated by Niede Guidon to over 40,000 years. Anthropic layers, connected with rock art and including fragments of painted rock surfaces, have been dated by C-14 to ca. 22,000 and 17,000 BP. Recently, much earlier dates have been proposed for rock art in Brazil but, so far, they have to be confirmed. In the far south of Argentina, at Rio Pinturas, in the province of Santa Cruz, C-14 datings have again enabled researchers to locate early representational assemblages as far back as 12,000 BP. By then the habit of making rock art had reached the 'end of the world', the southern tip of the South American continent. Peoples had been travelling around the world to bring with them the figurative tradition.

In Australia and Oceania the earliest reliable evidence of art so far, around 50,000 BP., is provided by G. Chaloupka in the Arnhem Land. Graphic non figurative markings at Koonalda Cave near the south-western edge of South Australia, West of Adelaide, dated by C-14 to ca. 20,000 BP. Early graphic patterns may have survived quite late in Australia, while some figurative trends may have been present quite early. Recent considerations propose dates older than 50,000 years for Australian rock art.

This brief summary of the earliest dates of rock art available so far seems to indicate that the earliest rock art we know of, may mark an early horizon of figurative depictions, between 50,000 and 30,000 BP, in different parts of the world. May we conclude that the figurative tradition arrived in the various continents with *Homo sapiens?* Was he the carrier of this tradition?

The production of art and therefore of rock art, seems to be a basic attribute of *Homo sapiens.* Our common direct ancestor is today believed to have originated in a 'primary home land' in Africa or in Asia. In Europe, America and Oceania there is no evidence for the presence of previous hominids from whom *Homo sapiens* may have emerged. All of the present day mankind derives from this primary core. Early groups of *Homo sapiens* reached the various continents as a result of a trend of migrations and diffusion. They carried with them their traditions of hunting and food collecting, their technological abilities to produce tools, their primordial mother language, their social and conceptual patterns, their ability and need to communicate, and their ability to produce art. Early *Homo sapiens* produced art and therefore we may find its traces wherever he arrived. Recent studies indicate that strong similarities in myths from different areas of the world may hint to the existence of a mythology previous to the dispersion of *Homo sapiens.* The core of art and religion may be older than so far believed. Their world distribution is likely to coincide with the world distribution of *Homo sapiens.*

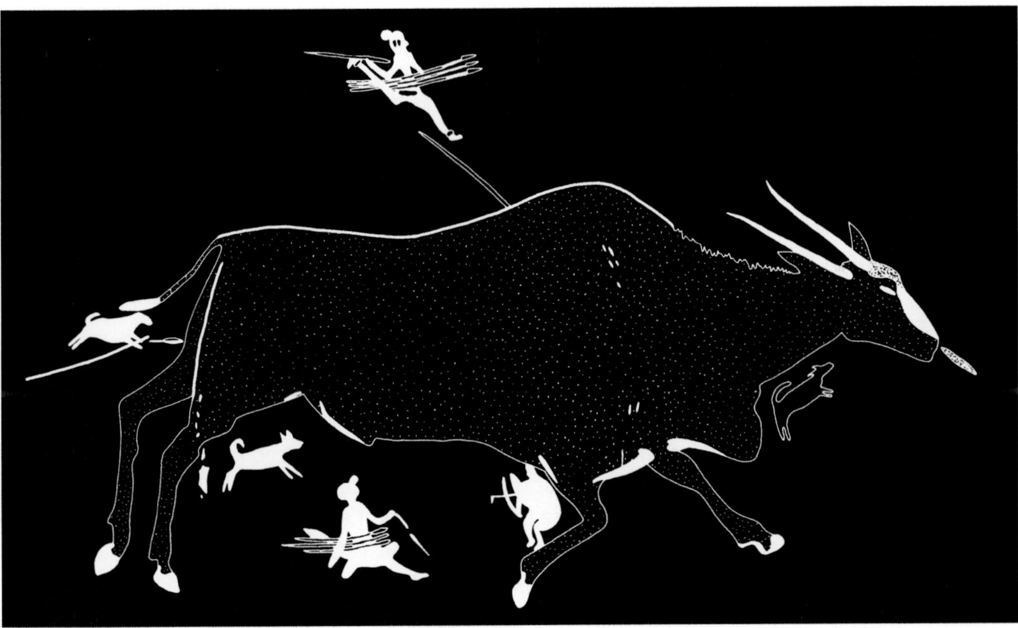

Fig. 6
Accumulation of figures. Hunters with spears and bow as well as domestic dogs are hunting an antelope depicted in a previous period. Rock painting of Martinsdale, Barkly East, South Africa
Source: J.D. Lewis Williams, 1983, p. 48. (WARA Archive W00169)
Area Code: D-IV. Cat.: C-I; C-II.

5
ECOLOGICAL SETTING OF ROCK ART

While over three quarters of the emerging lands in our planet are in the northern hemisphere, the richest concentrations of rock art, counting millions of graphemes, are located in the southern hemisphere, in Africa, Australia and South America. The southern hemisphere has always been less populated than the northern hemisphere. The northern hemisphere has been a ground of transfers, of intense human movements in different directions, the southern hemisphere has been a land of arrivals and of gradual penetration southward as far as it was possible. In such a context, surprising as it may be, the human species, *Homo abilis* and then *Homo sapiens,* and probably also the idea of visual art, are likely to have been born in the southern hemisphere. Well over three quarters of humankind, ever since rock art is being produced, has lived in the northern hemisphere. And yet rock art production has been more prolific in the southern hemisphere. It is not a pure coincidence.

A large percentage of the 'major areas' of rock art detected so far reside in what are now desertic or semi-desertic areas.

We may define these areas as peripheral or underpopulated zones in the present ecological situation. It may be assumed that they never had been extremely flourishing in the age of *Homo sapiens.* In the last 50,000 years the present-day deserts have never been more fertile than the present-day fertile zones. Rock art was mainly created in underpopulated regions.

This general pattern recurs, from the Dahthami Wells in Central Arabia to Tromso in Arctic Norway; from the Acacus in the Libyan Sahara to Ayres Rock in Central Australia; from the Kalahari Desert in southern Africa to San Ignazio in Baja California, Mexico; From Valcamonica in the Italian Alps to the Middle Yenisei River in Siberia; and from Rio Pinturas in Argentinean Patagonia to Har Karkom in the Israeli Negev desert.

On the other hand, the data available so far indicate that the less dense areas of rock art are confined to the regions covered today by large tropical forests. We have little evidence of rock art in the areas of tropical forest in Brazilian Amazonia, in the Congo and in other west-central African countries, and in south-eastern Asia. The few areas of rock art known in these regions are usually either poor or rather late or both. The most common habitat of major rock art localities is in marginal areas poor in natural vegetation. In Africa, the most populated regions are the poorest in rock art.

The major concentrations of Paleolithic cave art in Europe are located in the dead-end area which faces the Atlantic Ocean, in the Franco-Cantabrian region. In fact, man is likely to have

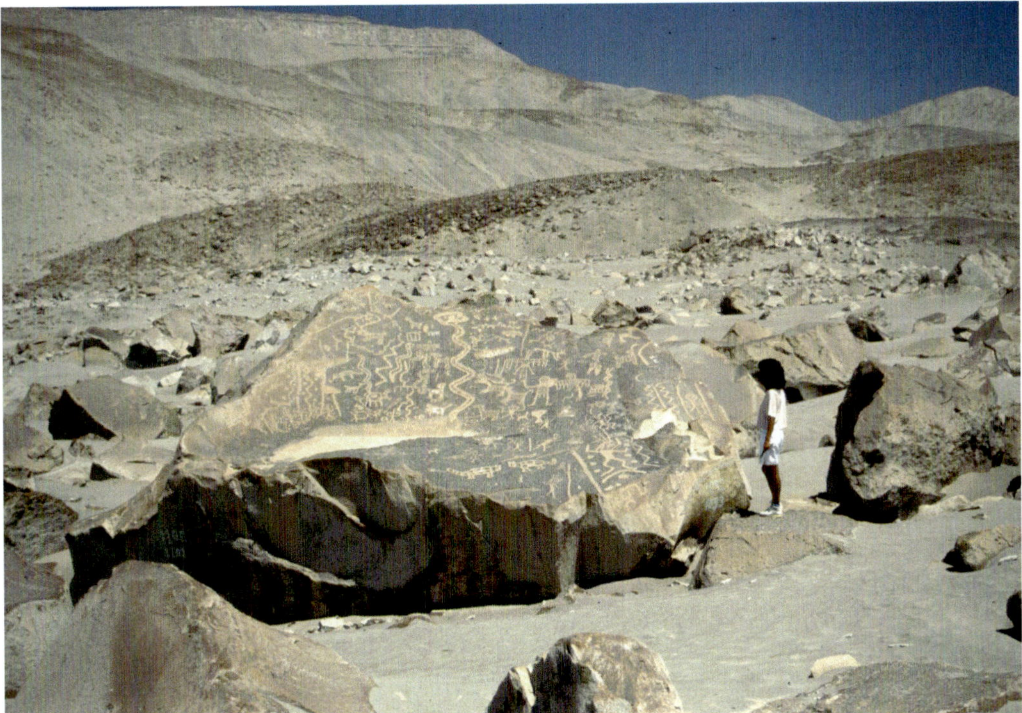

Fig. 8
The environment of Toro Muerto, a major rock art site in Peru, in a desert area.
Source: Photo G. Samorini. (WARA Archive W00165) WARA 9 0:V-40.
Area Code:G-II. Cat.:D-I.

moved about much less there than in Eastern Europe, the Balkans or the Mediterranean areas, where later civilizations flourished and where the presence of rock art is poor, or non-existent. In Australia this phenomenon repeats itself; although man must have arrived to the sub-continent from the north, populating that area before expanding southward, some of the most archaic known instances of rock art occur in the most far away regions from there, in the south, in dead-end regions facing the Southern Ocean, in Tasmania and elsewhere.

In Africa, once again, the major concentrations of the earliest figurative art horizons come from Tanzania and Namibia, both in mountainous, rather marginal areas in late Pleistocene human movements. The same may be said of places such as Rio Pinturas in southern Patagonia, or the peninsula of Baja California in Mexico. Such recurrent ecological and topographic environments for early rock art still demand an explanation. There is no doubt, however, that man arrived to these areas with the intellectual capacities for producing art; he found there the settings which were particularly favorable to artistic creation. Environment, landscape, natural shapes and colours are the setting of every living being. Man had to adapt to new settings. He turned out to be more creative in desolated areas then in thickly populated or exuberant environments. Is this teaching us something on the ideal setting for artistic creativity?

The ecological setting of rock art seems to fit the 'revelation pattern'. A common denominator of many faiths responds to the biblical concept that 'the prophet comes from the desert'. Medicine men in various parts of Africa go for long periods of isolation to the sacred caves, and shamans in Siberia choose to remain isolated for months at a time in the icy tundra. In many parts of the world the preparation for initiation into adulthood demands isolation away from populated areas.

Christian hermits choose lonely places. Buddha went to meditate on the mountain. Also revelations choose deserts. Islam was born in a desert oasis. Judaism was born on a desert mountain. Har Karkom, believed to be the biblical Mount Sinai, has also the richest concentration of rock art in the entire Sinai peninsula.

Many places around the world where rock art is still practiced are considered to be sacred and some of them are also secret where access is restricted to the initiated. No doubt many prehistoric rock art sites had a reason for their location. The landscape, the peculiar characters of the site, the environment, the topography, and other features may have been the source of the proper atmosphere for creating a communion between man and nature 'Why just here?' is the question that should be asked for every rock art site. Like the ecological setting, other common denominators may turn up.

At Har Karkom we know that the rock art was produced in a place which had a long tradition as a sacred site. In Malawi the Nyau traditions produce rock art in caves which are sacred because 'ancestral spirits live there'. The Paleolithic sanctuary caves of Western European were both sacred and secret and the same can be said for many Australian rock art sites. Just like the Nyau rock shelters, they were the receptacles of myths and traditions. One of their main roles was that of being schools where the instructors prepared the young generation for the initiation.

Nevertheless the geographic and topographic pattern of most of the major rock art sites in the world is rather puzzling. What is the meaning of the ecological setting of rock art? In all periods there have been places where art flourished more than elsewhere. These sites and the human relations with them favored and enhanced the artistic and creative abilities of men. How and why? The functioning of the relations between human cognition and environment is now acquiring some new hints but remains a field for further exploration.

6
THE DAWN OF ART

The hunting way of life has conditioned the human habits for over two million years and left profound marks on the intellectual nature of the species. Many aspects of human behavior, still today, reveal the nature of a hunter: Life still demands hunting, hunting for economic and social positions, hunting for mating partners, hunting for hunting ground. **The fundamental human processes of association and 'logic' developed throughout the ages in which the human species acquired its basic behavioral patterns** (*Postulate EA1*). These millennia are characterized by hunting bands who shared activities and refined communication. For hunting societies the basic unit is the clan, not the individual. The individual identifies himself as part of the clan. This way of life reached a high level of perfection and efficiency in the last 100,000 years with the diffusion of our direct forefather, *Homo sapiens.* He had a developed technological level, quite refined mental abilities, he was capable of producing precise and efficient implements. He was responsible for creating an ideology whose matrix is still present at the core of modern man's conceptuality, including a capacity for synthesis and abstraction which, among other things, led him to produce art and to develop an articulate and complex language.

The art of the Sapiens fossil population is the mirror of mind and spirit and constitutes a precious record of man's conceptual and psychological matrix. As we shall further elaborate, we come across archetypes and paradigms that are essential to our being and which are still deep within us.

Those populations whose livelihood is based on hunting and gathering are today almost extinct. They are confined to the most inhospitable parts of the world. These regions include the deserts of Australia and Southern Africa, the tropical forests of the Amazon basin, the Congo basin, Southeast Asia, the Arctic tundra of Lapland, Siberia, Alaska and the great Canadian North. They occupy territories which constitute more than 20% of the Earth's land surface and yet are less than 1% of the world's population. Only 500 years ago, at the time when America was reached by Columbus, 70% of the Earth's surface was populated by hunting and gathering people who then accounted for more than 20% of the world population. 12,000 years ago, at the end of the Pleistocene, the entire population of Earth pursued this means of subsistence which was gradually replaced by economies based on food production. It is only in the last 12,000 years that other ways of life have developed. Most of the rock art was produced by peoples who did not know cooking pots, the wheel, woven fabrics and the use of money. All these are among the recent acquisitions belonging to the new patterns of way of life.

Tribal societies around the world have the common characteristic of producing art, especially rock art. Their visual output is recorded in millions of figures, in thousands of zones distributed in 120 countries on all inhabited continents. Over 70% of all known rock art was produced by hunting and gathering societies while less than 30% is the work of Pastoralists and Agriculturalists. The growing interest in this art is caused by the light it projects on the collective memory and on universal conceptual processes.

Each assemblage of rock art has a story behind, the account of a myth, the memory of an event, the quest for help to an ancestral spirit or to a god, the magic formula for rain-making or for obtaining a good hunt. These are our own expressions, some thousand years ago. Through these ancient expressions of the human mind a wide range of submerged memories come back to consciousness, reviving stored chapters of our intellectual heritage. But as important is rock art's historical relevance. Rock art is a sort of pictographic writing. It constitutes humanity's largest and most significant historical archive for 50,000 years, from the beginning of visual art to the advent of conventional modern writing. New discoveries almost daily increase the record. Even in Valcamonica, where we have been working for fifty years, the 300,000 figures and signs recorded so far are only a part of the cultural patrimony that has yet to be surveyed.

Other examples are from Lesotho. For over twenty years, Lukas A. Smits has catalogued thousands of pictures from around 500 caves and rock shelters. There are still about 5,000 sites that have yet to be catalogued (L.A. Smits 1988). In the Negev desert about 200 rock art sites have been recorded. Preliminary surveys indicate that there are likely to be twenty times as many. Analogous situations exist in most countries (E. Anati 1989).

Recent surveys reveal the size of this heritage that is being re-appropriated by human culture in such disparate regions as the Americas or the Far East (C. Grant 1982; J. Schobinger & C. Gradin 1985; Chen Zhao-Fu 1988). Countries like Italy, Sweden, Spain and France, claiming to have complete inventories are rare and even in these countries there are new discoveries every year demonstrating that the exploration is not yet concluded (A. Beltran 1988). The recording, study and comprehension of the rock art patrimony is still in its infancy.

So far, cataloguing and making inventories of rock art have been mainly the private work of students and amateurs occasionally supported by universities and museums. It is only in the last few years that some governments have become aware of the importance of this documentation as an immense cultural and historical heritage, as an outstanding source of education, and are now embarking on systematic inventories. This came about largely as a result of an information campaign conducted by the CCSP (Centro Camuno di Studi Preistorici, Italy) and CAR (ICOMOS International Committee on Rock Art), with the support of UNESCO (United Nations Educational, Scientific and Cultural Organization) and ICOM (International Council of Museums). When a site is being recognized by UNESCO as belonging to the 'World Heritage', governments wake up and try to develop it, but often for tourism and economic development, rather than for culture, education and research.

At the same time, it was deemed necessary to stimulate individual scholars to make the results of their research available to the scientific world. For this purpose we promoted a monographic series of books on rock art, 'The Imprint of Man', published by Jaca Book in Italy and by the Cambridge University Press in England. Following the recommendation of a UNESCO consultancy held in 1981, the periodical BCSP has become the *'World Journal of Prehistoric and Tribal Art'* and devotes much space to current studies and discoveries of rock art.

Without the private initiative of a few scholars nothing would have developed. However, the task of making history out of rock art, of decoding millenary records, of adding new chapters to the history of mankind, should be the concerns of national and international organizations. The work must be done by scholars, but the support and the incentive should be the concern of the institutions appointed to promote culture and society supported by public funding. Considering the increasing process of deterioration, the most urgent task is that of recording. A world data base would be a major contribution to culture and to the preservation of chapters of the history of mankind that have to be decoded. And yet, both international organizations and national governments are neglecting this fundamental and urgent task.

Mobiliary art: figurines, plaquettes and decorated objects, have received different treatment. Once they are found they usually end up in museums and collections which draw up the inventory more for the institution than for humanity. A single world inventory is also necessary in the sector of mobiliary art. However, both in terms of the immensity of existing documentation and of world distribution, rock art appears to be a global phenomenon which constitutes more than 90% of the known prehistoric art. It is found in all inhabited continents, it remained in situ, in the spots where it was created. It is even possible, sometimes, to reconstruct the movements made by the prehistoric artists to produce their art.

In order to reach a valid global vision of rock art a world data bank is urgently needed and it should be a cleaver and functional tool. Data should be classified using universal standards so that comparisons can be made. This would require collecting the same type of data having the same cataloguing procedures in different countries and creating a fluid and open exchange of information. With this aim in mind CAR has produced, since 1984, standard forms which can enter a world data base in different languages and can be read and printed in any language. This data bank is being compiled in various countries such as Canada, Ireland, Israel, Italy, Malawi and Tanzania (E. Anati 1984). Despite such welcome private cooperation, it is unthinkable that a world data bank on rock art of high scientific standard might be realized with success without the active support of the international organizations and the participation of the official national institutions responsible for the sites.

The rock engravings in Alto Adige, Italy and those only a few kilometers away in Austria are analyzed and catalogued in different ways each being ignorant of the other's methods and criteria. This sort of situation signifies that systematic research is impossible. Co-ordination should be pushed for by international organizations encouraging regional and local institutions as well as individual scholars and giving them concrete support and guidelines.

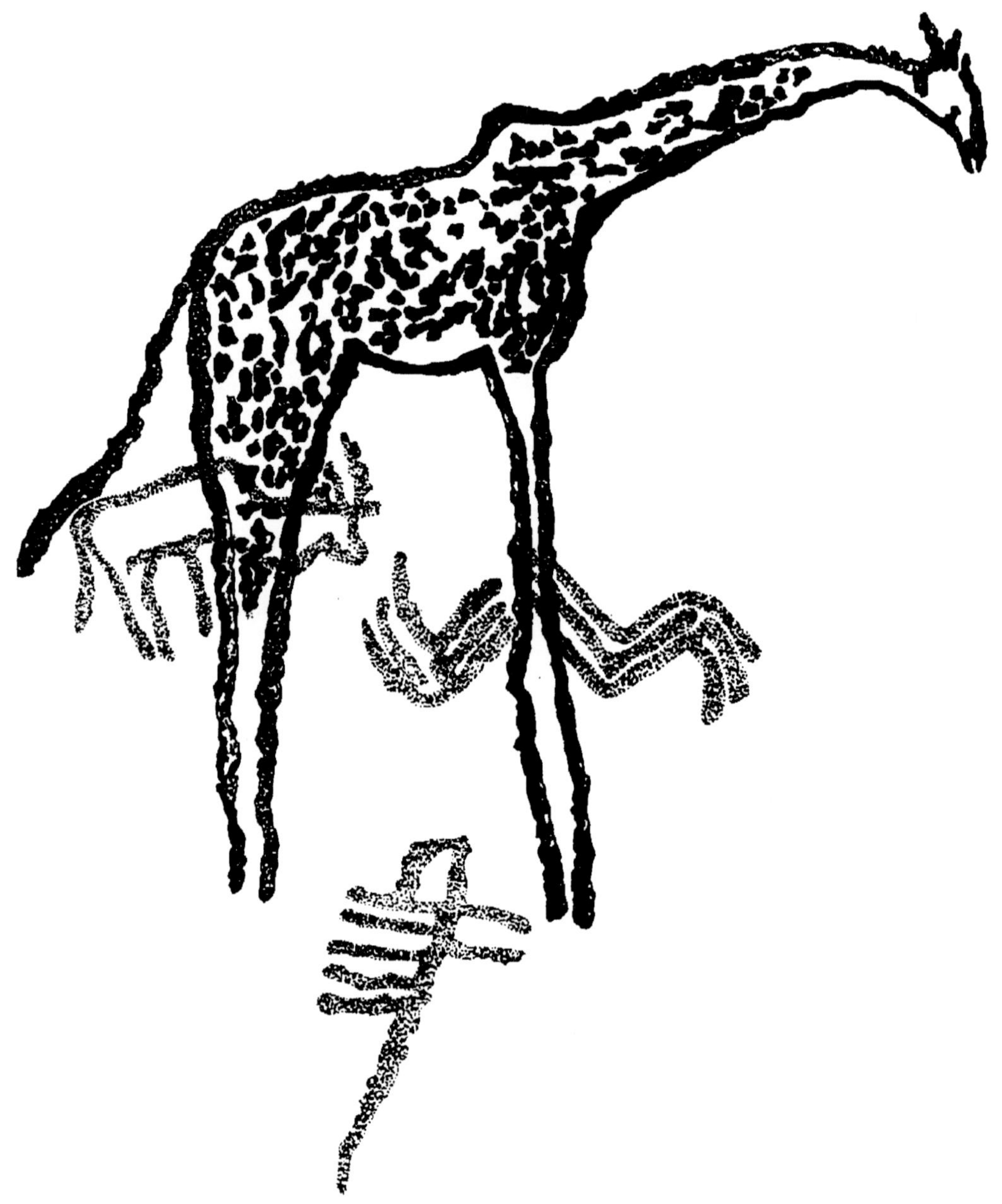

Fig. 9
Two phases of rock engravings of Early Hunters. Rocklands, Pomfret, South Africa. Two phases display different approaches. The later artist invested much time and energy to decorate the body of the giraffe with dots. The earlier artist engraved a quadruped, probably a kudu, a zig-zag pattern and another ideogram, in essential lines. For the artist, the association of the animal with the ideograms was the essential point.
Source: Drawn from a frottage by G.J. &.D. Fock, 1984, p.142. (WARA Archive W00168)
Area Code: D-IV. Cat.: A-II and A-IV.

7
ECONOMIC AND SOCIAL CONTEXTS

A number of elements of style, subject-matter, syntax and content have been shown to be constant on a world level and we have been able to distinguish five categories of rock art each responding to universal typological characteristics (E. Anati 1981). How can we define these categories and how can we explain the formation of different typologies on a world scale?

Visual art is a mirror of the artist's cognitive system and rock art is a fundamental source for understanding the conceptual setting of early and tribal societies. Social and economic background is strongly determining ideology and ideology is conditioning art.

The five categories of prehistoric and tribal art reflect, respectively, 1. Archaic (or Early) Hunters; 2. Food Gatherers (or Collectors); 3. Evolved Hunters; 4. Pastoralists and Animal Breeders; and 5. Populations with a Mixed Economy which includes agriculture.

At first figurative art displays a great similarity in different regions of the world. Diverse manners developed out of these primary styles. Toward the end of the Pleistocene, between 30,000 and 12,000 years ago, one begins to recognize regional styles, markedly different from one another, though all of them are still within the context of Archaic Hunters or of Early Food Collectors.

With the beginning of the Holocene, about 12,000 years ago, the first nuclei of Evolved Hunters (using bow and arrow) emerged in various parts of the world. Still later there developed artistic expressions characterizing Pastoralists and Animal Breeders and of populations with Complex Economies professing agriculture. Visual art is the mirror of a gradual cognitive and conceptual diversification of the species *Homo sapiens*.

I. **Early Hunters** (also named **Archaic Hunters**):
    The art of hunting populations which do not know the use of bow and arrow. Figures and signs are associated but true descriptive scenes are practically absent. The style tends to display a tendency to the idealization of outlines and spaces, Animal figures receive more care than human figures. Associations are simple and appear to refer to an allegoric system giving additional meaning, besides the figurative one, to figures and signs. The main subject is animals, often related to symbols. Anthropomorphized animals or zoomorphized humans reflect a specific animistic conceptual vision.

II. **Food Gatherers** (also named **Food Collectors**):
    The art of populations having a way of life based on gathering. Their diet is prevailing vegetal and the use of hallucinogenic plants produces a deformed vision which is reflected in their art. They depict scenes with metaphoric senses. The style is often characterized by a high sense of aesthetic. The main subjects are anthropomorphic beings and vegetal themes such as fruits,

leaves and tubers. Anthropomorphized plants and tubes reflect a specific animistic conceptual vision.

III. Evolved Hunters (also named **Bow-and-Arrow Hunters**):
The art of hunting populations which use the bow and arrow. Descriptive and anedoctal scenes are present. The main subjects are human and animal figures in interplay. Realistic hunting scenes and other descriptions of daily lige show both men and animals moving in dynamic postures.

IV. Pastoralists (also named **Animal Breeders**):
The art of populations whose primary economic activity is the rearing of livestock. The main interest of the artist focuses on domesticated animals and on scenes of daily life. Scenes describe moments and anecdotes, and tend to be rather static.

V. Complex Economy (also names **Agriculturalists**):
The art of populations having a diversified economy including farming activities. Several typologically different groups are present, displaying various types of style, from naturalistic, to schematic, to abstract. Schematic groupings of signs are repetitive. Mythical and commemorative scenes describe memorable beings and events.

Only a small percentage of the documented rock art can not be put into any of the five categories and this in itself indicates that almost all of the world's rock art belongs to one of these categories.

In the first edition of the present study, only four categories had been considered. Archaic Hunters and Food Gatherers had been considered as one category defined as Hunters-Gatherers. Subsequent analyses have shown the presence of consistent differences between the art and way of thinking of peoples relying primarily on hunting and having a prevailing carnivore diet and food collectors mainly supported by a vegetal diet.

A sub-category concerns the collectors of shells and other mollusks. They have been included among the Food-Gatherers. Their rock art has a peculiar schematic typology and a syntax frequently consisting in sequence association, which are quite different from those of other food collectors.

Between Early Hunters and Food Gatherers, both the gamut of subject-matter and the type of associative syntax are fundamentally different. The most evident factor consists in the major concern of hunters on depicting the potential animal preys. Food Collectors tend to have less care and less interest in animal depictions and more care and interest for anthropomorphic beings. They include in their repertoire figures of vegetal elements such as fruits, plants, yams and roots. Such depictions are practically absent in the other categories. They also display the narrative-anecdotal nature of their depictions, scenes are common; on the other hand Early Hunters tend to use a type of syntax defined as 'symbolic associations'; scenes are practically absent. Different diets and ways of life have different visual outputs.

These subdivisions present a schematic synthesis, nevertheless they allow to define the economic and social background of the rock art makers and this is a necessary step for an in-depth analysis of rock art. There are transitional phases and groups with mixed characteristics; within each category there are considerable and meaningful variations that enable the definition of sub-categories. At the present state of research and given the immensity of the material already recorded and available for research, it is necessary to create general lines of analysis on themes and style which go beyond the limits of regional definitions. Categories must be well defined and as few as possible. The methodology requires further sophistication but even now it is producing results. A preliminary order has been established for the larger assemblages of rock art.

Clear definitions of typological identification of categories have concerned rich concentrations in various European regions such as Iberian Galicia, south-west France, the Alpine range, Southern Scandinavia, as well as in Central Tanzania, Madhya Pradesh in India, the Kimberley region in North-western Australia, Central Arabia, Anatolia, the Negev and Sinai deserts, Baja California in

Mexico, The Pecos and Seminole Canyon in Texas.

Criteria based on themes and typology, the nature of the associations and the presence of scenes, figurative, schematic and abstract styles, the importance given to certain wild or domestic animals, the presence or absence of certain symbols which act as 'fossil guides' have all led to the discovery of significant recurrent elements. This has brought us to the working hypothesis that: **universal reflections conditioned by the way of life influence behavior, thought, ideology, associative processes, and consequently artistic manifestations** (*Postulate EA2*).

A thorough analysis of the essential elements of rock art groups at a world level is necessary to determine universal factors and to identify and distinguish them from local factors. Five elements have been taken into consideration: 1-Subject matter. 2-Syntax, that is types of associations, compositions and scenes. 3-Stylistic trends. 4-Technical patterns. 5-Type of location on rock surface.

In Valcamonica, in Northern Italy, the Proto-Camunian period (ca. 10000-6000 BC) is Category I (Early Hunters) while all the successive periods belong to Category V (Complex Economy) (ca. 6000-16 BC). Cat. II (Gatherers), III (Late Hunters) and IV (Pastoralists) are not represented in Valcamonica (E. Anati 1976).

For some groups of rock art in Spain we may make quite clear attributions: Cat. I for Cantabrian cave art (ca. 30,000-8000 BC); Cat III (Late Hunters) for large parts of Levantine rock art (tentatively dates ca. 8000-2000 BC); Cat IV (Pastoralists) for some assemblages of schematic art and for others Cat V (Complex Economy) (both present since ca. 4500 BC). A small group of peculiar paintings defined as 'macroschemathic' is likely to be the work of peoples from Cat. II (Gatherers).

The rock art of Mount Bego (France), until recently, had been considered by many to be the work of an agricultural population. In fact, the Mount Bego rock art belongs to Cat. IV (Pastoralists). It is the work of peoples having animal rearing as their main activity (ca. 3500-1000 BC). It is only in a later phase that the marks and images, including figures of plows appear to reflect a partly agricultural mentality (after 1500 BC).

The rock art of the Negev and Sinai deserts shows successions of categories I, III and IV while no rock art of Cat. II has been recorded; Cat. V has been detected in an isolated case. (This region of rock art displays a sequence of seven main stylistic horizons from 10,000 BC to the present. Four of them, making the bulk, belong to Pastoralists and display marked typological and stylistic differences between each other), (E. Anati, 1979).

It is likely that more specific definitions and subdivisions can be made within the Categories. The basic structure of Categories can be further detailed For the time being it seems advisable to keep it as simple and as schematic as possible. Further subdivisions can always be made for specific studies.

In various parts of the world there are schematic groups of paintings and engravings which, at first appearance, seem abstract. Nevertheless, marks with numerical value, repetitive associations of dots and lines and network motifs actually follow repetitious patterns and conceptual rules. In Europe, various groups of Mesolithic art, the La Cocina type in Spain, Azilian art in France, Magelmoisian art in Germany and Scandinavia, and the Romanellian art in Italy, are very close to styles encountered in Turkey and the Near East, North Africa, Malawi and Zambia in Southern Africa, along the Murray river in Southern Australia and in various Polynesian Islands. These assemblages from different areas of the world belong to different ages and were made by peoples that did not even suspect of the existence of each other.

Several of these groups produced either mobiliary art or rock art or both. Many of these groups have two main recurrent features: a certain amount of specific associations of lines and dots which are repeated using similar associative syntaxes in various parts of the world, and constant proximity to escargotières or shell mounds. These are sites where human groups camped and where heaps of shells and other mollusk remains are to be found, revealing a particular diet and economy based on the collection of river or marsh small size animals. Thus it appears that a specific graphic style reflects a way of life with more or less uniform consistency, at different ages, in various parts of the world. We tend to find this type of art by present day or fossil rivers, lakes, marshes and the sea-shore. It appears to reflect a gathering mentality, rather than a hunting mentality, of people who survived on gathering mollusks. Such activity, for reasons that are not entirely clear, seems to have aroused a particular interest in arithmetic and a tendency for schematism. Such style is in contrast with that of the Early Hunters, with their spirit of observing large animals in great detail. It is also contrasting with the dreamy style of other kinds of Food Gatherers.

In two different occasions, on UNESCO's assignment, we have attempted to single out the rock art zones of 'primary importance'. It was necessary to establish objective criteria and even if these criteria are modified for future evaluation the attempts have been useful.

The list which was published in the *BCSP* vol. 21 (1984) included about half of the 120 countries where rock art is known to exist. It recognized others as having more than one zone of primary importance. Each of these zones may include numerous sites such as the Franco-Cantabrian zone or the areas rich in cave-painting of Central Tanzania, or the Lesotho Drakensberg western range. Based on a series of criteria already pointed out in the UNESCO report (1983) we selected 150 areas which, from the available information, are to be considered of primary importance. Since then this list has been updated several times and recently (2008) the list of major sites has been reduced to 100. Upon studying their distribution we came to realize that all the various lists are more or less homogeneously diffused on all continents. Indeed, rock art appears to be a truly universal phenomenon.

Since the early attempts the criteria of evaluation of 'major sites' has changed, giving more weight to contents and decoding results, and less to aesthetic and monumental aspects which were then the main aspects of evaluation.

In almost all cases recorded so far **rock art is a phenomenon of non-urban, non-literate societies** (*Postulate EA3*). **In all the examined zones there are areas of great concentration of rock art which do not reflect an analogous concentration of people** (*Postulate EA4*). On the contrary, it seems to be a universal pattern of rock art that it is scarce where the population is more concentrated. There appear to be many zones the world over, where people went for artistic or other ritual and social activities, where little or no trace of living and daily activities have been found besides rock art.

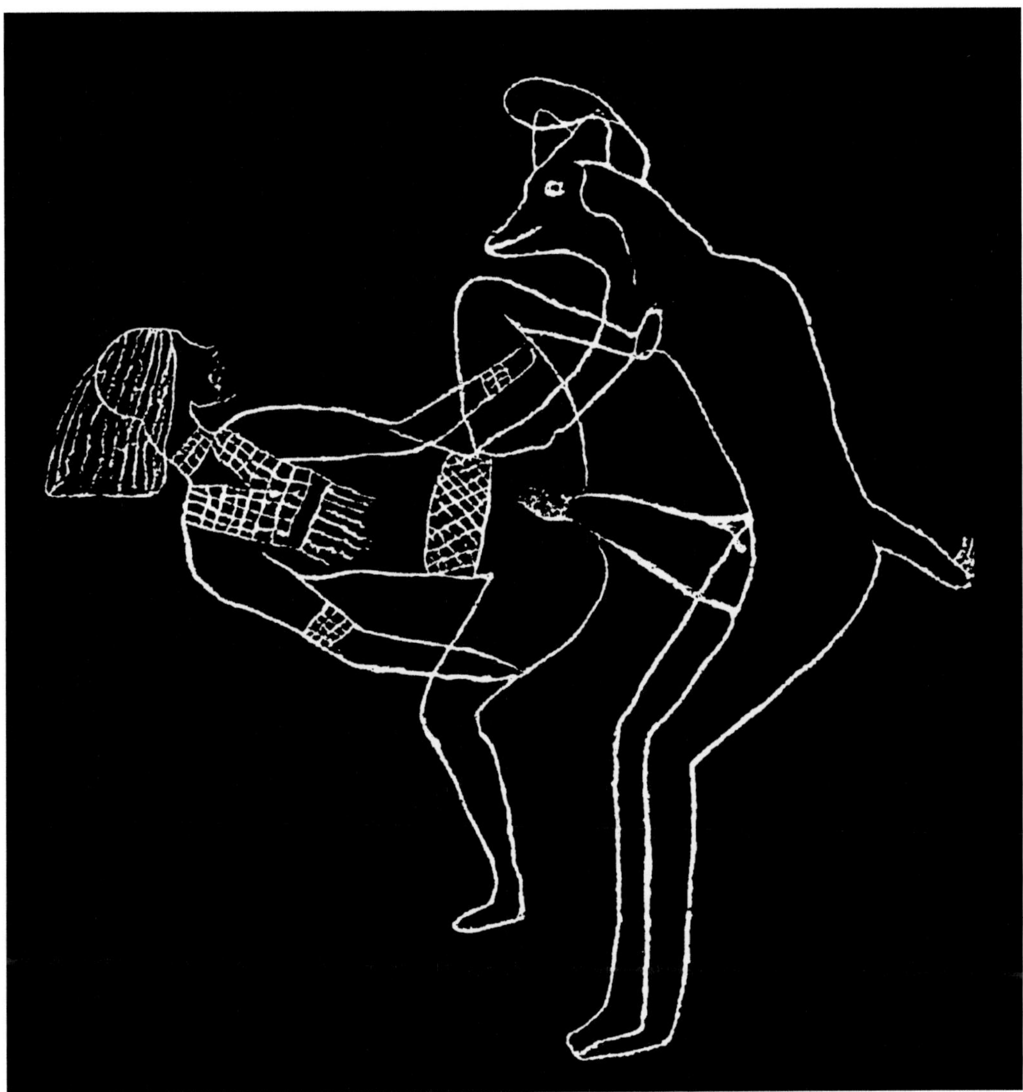

Fig. 10
The animal spirit brings fertility on Earth. Pastoral rock engraving from Ti-n-Ialan, Tadrart Acacus, Libya. The woman is using her hands to keep her legs wide open so that the animal spirit or divinity can easily penetrate her. The garments suggest the woman's status or her beauty. Pastoralists often have animal divinities and spirits in their Olympus. Early phase of Pastoral Neolithic; size of tracing 1.65 by 1.70 meters.
Source: F. Mori, 1975, p. 356. (WARA Archive W00164)
Area Code: C-II. Cat.: C-II.

8

PICTOGRAMS, IDEOGRAMS AND PSYCHOGRAMS

Each category of rock art (representing respectively the production of Archaic Hunters, Early Gatherers, Evolved Hunters, Pastoralists and people with a Complex Economy) displays a limited typological range of subjects which recurs in the rock art of all continents (*Postulate EA5*).

Three types of signs are to be found grammatically different from each other. They are pictograms, ideograms and psychograms (*Postulate EA6*). They recur not only in rock art but also in mobiliary art. The same three types of conceptual expressions are present in other fields of artistic creations such as music and dance. The associations and combinations of the three types reflect an elementary pattern of the human cognitive system.

Pictograms (and mythograms): Are figures in which we may recognize identifiable forms of real or imaginary objects, anthropomorphic and zoomorphic figures. They often are the subject of sentences in which the ideograms are the verb and the adjectives.

Ideograms: Are repetitive and synthetic signs that are sometimes named as zoomorphic and anthropomorphic schemes, sticks, tree-shapes, phallic and vulval signs, discs, groups of dots and lines. **Repetitiveness and constants of association indicate the presence of conventional concepts in a number of ideograms** (*Postulate EA7*).

Psychograms: Are signs which are not recognizable as and do not seem to represent either objects or symbols. They are strokes; violent outputs of energy that perhaps express sensations or even more subtle perceptions. They often appear to be conceptual exclamation marks.

Pictograms are images whose shapes we may identify. They may have metaphoric meanings **In the rock art of non-literate people, pictograms are of four main themes:**

1. **Anthropomorphic;**
2. **Zoomorphic;**
3. **Topographic and Tectiforms;**
4. **Implements and Weapons**
5. **Other** (*Postulate EA8*).

Only very rarely do 'other' themes occur such as vegetation, landscapes or realistic portraits and only in very specific contexts. Therefore we add the fifth denomination: 'Other'.

Next to the above we often find associated ideograms. The meaning of the figures themselves and of these associations has been studied and discussed by many scholars and various theories have been suggested (H. Breuil 1952; A. Leroi-Gourhan 1982; A. Lommel 1970; G.G. Luquet 1926; A. Marshack 1972). Nowadays no one is satisfied with the mere identification of the animal species represented or other technical details since this is only a prelude to definition of raw material for further study. The metaphoric meaning may emerge from the comparative analysis of repetitive types of associations. The cognitive system is the same that still survives today and it is based on both, associative processes and conventional cultural acquisitions.

For Renaissance painters the dove was undoubtedly a dove. However, as in Fra' Angelico's Annunciation Scene, to say, 'There is a dove in the painting', does not convey the meaning of the work. When we know the Christian theme that inspired the artist and when we are familiar with his methodological and conceptual equipment the dove takes on a metaphoric content and meaning as the Holy Ghost. Similarly Picasso uses the dove not merely as a dove. He combines this pictogram with the ideogram of the olive branch that we recognize as such only because we are initiated. Twenty thousand years hence, perhaps someone will ask what could be meant by the ideogram near the beak of that strange pictogram that vaguely resembles a bird. It may not be easy then to read it as a metaphor for 'peace'.

The metaphorical associative system still represents a common cognitive pattern which is practiced by tribal and urban societies alike. A host of other examples could be cited such as the eagle in Roman times. *Homo Supersapiens* in a few thousand years will say: 'Yes, the bird represented does seem to be an eagle'. Tests will prove this from the shape of the beak or from the wing-span. But what does this eagle mean? Sometimes, when the pictogram is accompanied by four ideograms that nowadays we are able to read as SPQR, some inkling of the conceptual content of the figure will perhaps emerge as a sort of 'totemic animal' of the Senate and the People of Rome.

But then, other eagles will be found, dating nearly two thousand years later, excavating the remains of a town on the shores of the Danube River, from the Austro-Hungarian Empire, or in a monumental house with white columns, in a town believed to have been the Capital of the United States of America; and in the ruins of a princely palace in the Middle East which, the finds will show, had been used by both a Shah and an Ayatollah.

Different ideograms will accompany the eagle in each case and, no doubt, the eagle as a symbol will cause debate. The meaning of pictograms is not always obvious, but common denominators will show researchers that in these various cases the eagle is connected with power or leadership.

The quantitative analysis shows drastic numeric relative differences between pictograms, ideograms and psychograms in different periods and groups. In the Early Hunters' assemblages, there is a more even balance between the three types of graphemes which is more or less constant around the world; almost in even proportions between pictograms and ideograms and the sporadic presence of psychograms. In the Evolved Hunters and in the Pastoral groups, usually there is a predominance of pictograms.

In the Gatherers' groups, ideograms are usually prevailing, while in groups with complex economies, the possible variations have a larger range, from assemblages with a high majority of pictograms to assemblages with a high majority of ideograms. Throughout the range there may be assemblages with or without psychograms.

Thus, the splendid pictograms of the Hunters frequently accompanied by their ideograms must have been clearly legible to anyone who was familiar with their conceptual content. Today there has been a breach in the direct tradition. The work of the archaeologist, or of the art historian, or of the linguist, is now to assemble the components and observations that may enable us to approach an understanding of the content. In prehistoric art there are no meaningless images. Depictions were not produced to embellish the rock surfaces but to convey messages. The goal of research is that of decoding the messages.

Ideograms in ancient writings and in many groups of rock art are signs that convey ideas from the writer to the reader, from the painter to the real or imaginary beings to whom the message is addressed. We have recognized three main types of ideograms which tentatively have been named:

1.   **Anatomic** (such as phallic, vulvas signs or hand prints);
2.   **Conceptual** (such as the cross or the disk);
3.   **Numeric** (such as groups of dots or of lines).

These terms are invented and used for the benefit of present day communication. They do not necessarily imply their literal significance.

Most of the ideograms used for millennia by prehistoric groups are later found as characters in the first writings in various parts of the world: in China, the Near East and Central America. **In the cases in which the meaning of an ideogram can be traced back to a single common core in more than one continent a universal pattern is established** (*Postulate EA9*). Some ideograms appear to have a universal meaning and may be considered as archetypes.

The rectangle or the square mean land, site or territory in most early scripts as well as in most areas of rock art. Two or more wavy lines mean water or liquid; the rayed disk means sun, light or day; the non rayed disk means sky or air. In more than one continent it may mean also hut or site or water source. In some early ideographic scripts from different continents, and in rock art, (of complex economy), the triangle with a point turned downward means the pubic triangle, sex, fertility or birth. In some cases it appears to indicate the ctonic world, the world of the dead, the residence of the ancestors, but in more than one continent it may also signify reincarnation or rebirth.

In many instances, in the rock art of Late Hunters, Pastoralists and of human groups with Complex Economies, in Europe, the Near East, North Africa and beyond, the dot, near an anthropomorphic being, is a verb of action, like 'to do'. Then if it is near the foot of a person it may mean 'to go' or 'to walk', if it is near the penis or the vulva - 'to have intercourse', if it is near the bow and arrow - 'to shoot', if it is near the head, 'to think'. or 'to decide'. Such significance of the 'accompanying dot' emerged from the rock engravings of Helan Shan in northern China, of Southern Scandinavia, of the Moroccan Atlas, of the Negev and Sinai, and of Valcamonica, Northern Italy. Tentatively it might be tested on a global level.

In the rock art of the Plain Indians, in New Mexico and Arizona, a line near the foot of a human figure, indicates the direction of a trail. Similar lines appear to have the same significance in the rock engravings of later periods in Central Asia, the Near East and North Africa. There are several other ideograms that appear to have a universal or a widespread common meaning. Obviously they become an essential mean for the decoding of rock art. Their possible reading must be always tested in any new attempt at decoding. The fact that the reading of a specific sign has been proved to be correct in five previous cases is a good hint but, alone, it does not give any certainty that the meaning must be exactly the same in the next case.

Psychograms are signs that convey sensations from him/her who depics to him/her/it which observes. For us this level may appear to be more abstract than the symbolic level which still has its own well-defined meaning. The psychogram works at a subconscious level as do certain archetypal signs that our conscious memory is no longer able to define but which, deep within the self, release associative and sensory processes on wavelengths that escape the bands of ordinary transmission. They are remarkable for their immediacy.

Psychograms do not seem to be intellectualizations but signs that have the power to stir the mind without conjuring up any specific associations. They are the quintessence of something hard to consciously define but which resonates deep within us. Sometimes they seem to have the role of exclamation marks. They may result to be expressions of pleasure, of desire, of wonder, of gratification or else.

In the rock art of all continents landscapes are extremely rare as are images of plants. They are either completely absent or indicative of some particular characteristic if they do exist. The rare cases of depictions of naturalistic landscapes in the rock art of Europe, Africa, Australia, Central Asia and the Near East appear to be, all of them, recent and result of contact with urban and literate cultures.

The Tanzanian rock art sequence spans over at least 40,000 years and is considered one of the longest continuous sequence in the world. Yet all the images of the vegetal world are concentrated in one phase which is tentatively dated to the end of the Pleistocene and the beginning of the Holocene (ca. 12,000-8,000 BC). From the data at our disposal it appears to be a phase of food gathering populations rather than of hunting, even though it was defined as a Hunting-Gathering period (E. Anati, 1986).

After having isolated and defined this kind of rock art assemblage in Tanzania, comparative studies led to the identification of similar presence of assemblages of vegetal depictions in the rock art of the Pecos River and Seminole Canyon in Texas, of the Tassili and the Acacus in Central Sahara, of the Kimberley, in North Western Australia and elsewhere. All these displayed a peculiar interest for the vegetal themes along with other common characters in style and typology.

The subjects represented indicate the range of interests expressed throughout the ages. It is significant that the quantitative proportion of the four main themes of pictograms varies from period to period. In some contexts, the anthropomorphic beings are the overwhelming majority while elsewhere they may be practically absent. The same happens with the other three main themes; zoomorphic, topographic and implements. In the rich sequence of Valcamonica, Italy (Rock engravings), the relative percentage of the four themes varies drastically from period to period. The same is true for the sequence of the Seminole Canyon in Texas (rock paintings), for the Yenisei sequence in Siberia (rock engraving), for the sequence of Gobustan, Azerbaijan (rock engravings) and for the Tassili sequence in Algerian Sahara (rock paintings and engravings).

Likewise, the type of assemblage in rock art, with associations of pictograms, ideograms and psychograms, varies from period to period. The frequent association of the three types is widespread among Early Hunters. When the scene becomes the main type of syntactic association, psychograms tend to disappear or to turn up as attributes of the pictograms. Among Evolved Hunters and Pastoralists pictograms are the dominating grammatical form. But in the rock art of people with Complex Economies, ideograms are again common. And in some cases they are far more numerous than pictograms. Such variations in the relative frequency of the three grammatical forms reflect changes in the cognitive dynamics.

If, as it seems, pictograms, ideograms and psychograms make the grammatical structure of rock art, the variations in the recurring patterns of their associations and combinations are likely to be diagnostic elements for the identification of the associative processes and the conceptual context of the human groups that produced the rock art.

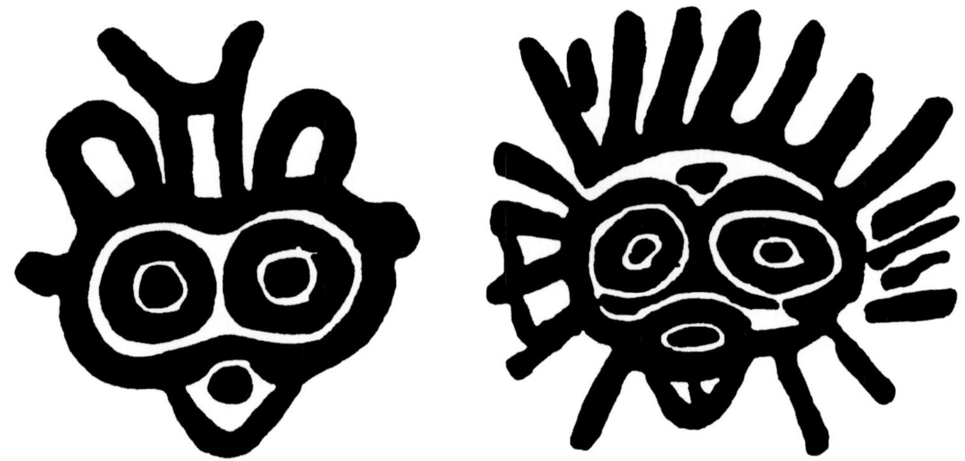

Fig 11 e 12
Masks and spirits of people with Food Producing economy. Rock engravings from Port Neville and Venn Passage, British Columbia, Canada. Resembling masks have been produced in wood for cult and evocative performances by coastal tribes until a few generations ago. Their tradition in partially persisting.
Similar masks are depicted in the rock art of Northern China and Eastern Siberia. Those have been connected to pottery decorated with mask figures belonging to a Neolithic culture of 7000 to 5000 years ago.
Source: B. & R. Hill, 1974, p. 266
Area Code: F-I. Cat.: D-II

9
PARADIGMS

In each of the aforementioned categories elements exist that we call 'paradigms'. They illustrate standards of behavior which are likely to have a meaning. In each category there are preferences for the type of place: cave, shelter or open air rock surface. There are also preferences for the type of surface, be it horizontal, oblique, vertical, floor or ceiling. For all five categories there seem to be precise choices made in the surface on which the painting or engraving is done. The chosen surfaces have preferential characteristics of colour and form that seem to mean that the 'support' (or background) has been taken into account by the maker of rock art.

Every assemblage of rock art appears to reflect choices of the artists concerning the place, the inclination of support and the selection of the surface to decorate, according to recurring criteria. In tested areas of important concentrations of rock engravings, rock painting or both, some surfaces have been intensely decorated, others have remained untouched. It is evident that a selection has been made on the choice of the surface and that such a choice may have been confirmed and reconfirmed for ages. Some of the major rock art areas in the world correspond to such patterns. Systematic evaluations in this respect have been made in the Camonica Valley, Italy; Bohuslaan, Sweden; Gobustan, Azerbaijan; the Negev Desert, Israel; Tataouine, Tunisia; Singida and Kondoa, Tanzania; Central Malawi; La Pileta Cave, Spain. Usually one type of choice is prevailing over the others:

I. Choice of Place:
    A.   Open-air rock
    B.   Rock shelter (rock art visible with natural light)
    C.   Deep cave (Rock art visible only with artificial light)

II. Inclination of support (or rock surface):
    A.   Vertical (approximation of 10°)
    B.   Oblique
    C.   Horizontal - Floor
    D.   Horizontal - Ceiling

III. Natural shape of decorated surface
    A.   Surface completely flat: no shape detectable
    B.   Shapes of surface visible only with directional lighting
    C.   Natural shapes visible with any light

From the analysis of a random sample of 1,000 surfaces it appears that a high percentage (over

85% of paintings and engravings) correspond to recurring criteria. However exceptions exist and both, prevailing patterns and exceptions require explanation.

In many cases, precise technical methods appear to have been used whether for painting, engraving, pecking, graffiti, or for the various types of relief work. **Certain rock art techniques are broadly repeated throughout the world although they do not seem to reflect processes of acculturation or diffusion** (*Postulate EA10*).

In some cases it seems to be simply the result of a given technological level or way of thinking or both. **A few basic colours are used in rock paintings all over the world, red being by far the most common in all continents** (*Postulate EA11*).

We may postulate that: **Even in the absence of direct communication between different populations, similar outcomes were reached in places far apart** (*Postulate EA12*). It cannot, therefore, be a question of external influence in all cases. We may thus hypothesize that certain convergences exist. These paradigms bring us into contact with behavioral imperatives which appear as 'fossilized cultural standards'. They belong to our own submerged memory and may open the way to a fresh understanding of the functioning of the human mind.

In the following chart we see summarized the main universal factors:

DOMINANT CHARACTERISTICS OF ROCK ART

Analysis Criteria	A. Archaic Hunters	B. Food Gatherers	C. Evolved Hunters	D. Pastoral Breeders	E. Complex Economy
Thematics	Ideograms, Psychograms, Pictograms, Large wild animal figures. Anthropomorphic and zoomorphic images. Human figures are often masked. Presence of anthropo-zoomorphic images.	Pictograms, ideograms and psychograms. Pictograms represent mainly anthropomorphic beings, probably mythological figures Ideograms and psychograms are often included in the pictograms.	Pictograms, animal and human figures. Few ideograms. Psychograms are rare Constant presence of imaginary beings	Pictograms, domesticated animals and anthropomorphic figures. Images of huts and other structures. Sporadic ideograms Absence of Psychograms.	Human, animal, structures, implements and weapons; schemes and ideograms. Pictograms more varied than in previous categories. Psychograms only in some cultures.
Associative	Simple associations. Complex compositions exist but are rare. Hermetic and synthetic syntax. Scenes are rare. or non-existent	Complex associations. Scenes are synthetic and illustrate concepts rather than anecdotal moments . Sequences of graphemes convey messages.	Descriptive and anecdotal scenes are widespread. Simple syntax defined by the associations in the scenes and compositions.	Scenes and compositions. Prevalence of descriptive anecdotal scenes.	Compositions and scenes. Complex syntax with vernacular characteristics. Mythological scenes are widespread.
Stylistic	Naturalistic figures , mainly of animals and ideographic sequences.	Idealized and stylized figures, mainly of anthropomorphic beings. Depictions of flora. Geometric compositions.	Naturalistic and realistic ensembles .and scenes. Realistic-dynamic styles	Realistic groups with frequent tendency to generalization. Idealization of forms.	Schematic and abstract graphemes. Special interest in details. Vast use of metaphoric depictions.

Analysis Criteria	A. Archaic Hunters	B. Food Gatherers	C. Evolved Hunters	D. Pastoral Breeders	E. Complex Economy
Technical	Prevalence of paintings over engravings. Monochromatic ensembles. Polychromy's restricted to specific regional phenomena.	Prevalently paintings, .mainly monochrome. Rare engravings	Prevalently painting but also engravings. Most paintings in Eurasia are monochromatic. Polychromy widespread in Africa and S. America.	May be painting or engraving. Varies from zone to zone.	Engravings prevail but paintings are preferred in some zones.
Location	Normally on vertical surfaces, and on roof or plafonds, with exceptions.	Mainly on vertical surfaces	Normally on vertical surfaces.	On vertical or oblique surfaces.	On horizontal, oblique or vertical surfaces. Location more varied than in other categories.

In Europe, Asia, Africa, the Americas and Australia the same range of figures may be found. Certain aspects of the environment, economy and social life simply do not enter into the artist's thematic range. The artists, hunters or otherwise, made precise choices in terms of the themes they chose to represent, they did not paint or engrave just anything. And their choices follow similar standards in different continents. As mentioned already, over 90% of the entire repertory of millions of prehistoric pictograms from five continents is made of four subjects: anthropomorphic, zoomorphic, topographic and implements. Anthropomorphic and zoomorphic figure make together more than 75% of them all. This is what has interested man ever since he became 'sapiens'.

Sometimes we may come upon themes of preference: The large representations of animals, life-size or more, are almost exclusive to the hunting populations, primarily with Early Hunters. With Pastoralists, they are only to be found in certain zones that today are deserts, and among populations that practiced hunting along with animal rearing. They are especially present in Arabia and the Sahara where breeders practiced hunting as well. They are rare or non-existing in the rock art of Complex Economy populations. On the other hand, there are phases in both Archaic and Evolved Hunters' art in which medium size or even miniature animal representations are found. An interesting phenomenon has been noted: When large animals are prevailing human figures are rare. When the animals are smaller the percentage of anthropomorphic figures is usually higher. In cases where large size and small size animal figures appear to belong to different phases on the same rock surfaces, as is the case in South African San rock art, or in that of the 'Levante' rock art from Spain, the majority of the human figures belong to the phases in which the animal figures are small size.

In all categories primary and secondary subjects are to be found.

There is an initial choice of the main subject and then minor complementary themes are added. **There are repetitive elements, ideograms and pictograms, which appear to accompany the dominant figures** (*Postulate EA13*). It is frequently stated in the professional literature that the animal is the most commonly represented figure in European Paleolithic art and that throughout the world animals are the main feature of Archaic Hunters' art. However, contrary to what is normally believed, isolated animal figures are practically non-existent. Animals are almost always accompanied by ideograms. Frequently, animals occupy the largest space on the painted surface simply due to their size and of their being the main subjcd. But symbols (ideograms) vary in number and they frequently exceed the number of animal figures with which they are associated.

Animals, like other figures, both in prehistoric and in tribal art, often have metaphoric significance.

They may have a totemic meaning, representing tribal groups or specific human beings. (See 'La Ferrassie Style' 2008), or they may represent qualities or attributes. We know that a group of American Indians used to refer to their chief Black Bison by depicting his name rather than his profile, they depicted a black bison to represent their chief. Others used to indicate a liar by representing a snake with a forked tongue. Even in our current language, qualities and attributes are represented by animals. When referring to a man, everybody would understand the different meanings of 'he is a ...' dog, pig, shark, lion, eagle, jackal, monkey, snake, chicken. Or, referring to a woman, 'she is a ...' gazelle, elephant, cat, bird, rabbit, bitch, rat, butterfly, ...'

Myths, all over the world, have always included animals. The deer as messenger from the underworld and the dove as messenger from the sky, the scorpion as source of evil and the snake as a tempter, have been represented in Europe for centuries. The frog in China as a symbol of courage or the elk in Siberia as a symbol of plenty, are likely to go back to prehistoric origins.

Such kinds of metaphors are used by people from different regions, different cultures and languages all over the world. They are likely to represent primordial trends of the associative processes. They are living survivals of the primordial paradigms

As was already brought to evidence by A. Laming (1962) and A. Leroi-Gourhan (1965), in the Upper Paleolithic cave art of Western Europe there are frequent cases of animal figures of different species being associated with each other.

There are two animal species, the bison and the horse, which are more frequently than others represented one in front of the other as the main theme; that is to say that they are preferred to other wild animals, repeated more frequently and would seem to imply something quite specific in the dialectic of associations. In the art of Early Hunters in Gobustan, Azerbaijan, the dominant association is between ox and horse. The ox is replacing the bison of Western Europe.

In Tanzania, the Early Hunters' art contains representations of the elephant and giraffe which play a similar role, in terms of associations and quantitative proportion to other animals, as the horse and bison in Europe. They are frequently associated with each other and are by far the most commonly represented animals (E. Anati 1986). Quite probably they played the same role within the conceptuality of the Tanzanian Early Hunters as the horse and bison did in the Franco-Cantabrian art in Europe. These are premises for yet another paradigm: **In the art of hunters there is the presence of dominant animal species with dialectic relationships between them** (*Postulate EA14*).

As for the meaning of such associations A. Laming and A. Leroi-Gourhan had proposed a possible connection to the concept of male-female interplay, one of the animals representing the male or male attributes, the other, the female or female attributes. Other theories have been proposed but no final conclusions have been reached. It is not unlikely that they reflect metaphors of binary relations. Whatever the case may be there can be little doubt that the European association of horse-bison shows grammatical and syntactic parallels to the African association of elephant-giraffe. It is therefore likely that they may reflect also conceptual analogies.

Such paradigms reveal the existence of 'logic constants' which are, or have become, part of the human nature and are widespread the world over. The identification of constant patterns of constants is one of the future goals of research. It is a matter of concern for a vast range of disciplines, from neurology and psychoanalysis to art history and history of religions, to general linguistics. A World Archive of Rock Art would provide a unique raw material to do multi-disciplinary research, and to obtain meaningful results.

If we were to carry out a detailed analysis of rock art syntax on a world scale a great deal of progress would be made on the study of paradigms. It is particularly important to develop a systematic analysis that defines the patterns of associations, compositions and scenes; that is to say the system of relationship between one grapheme and another in any given context. A few recurring patterns are widespread and can be easily detected. But a better knowledge of the whole structure of associations between graphemes, and between natural forms and man-made graphemes, could open up new perspectives in the understanding of elementary cognitive processes.

A general tendency of research in the humanities has focused on the identification of exceptions and on the definition of aberrant cases. It is a natural tendency of the human mind to identify exceptions. Paradigms and other universal common denominators are sometimes so obvious that they can be ignored. They are however fundamental for understanding standard cognitive processes of the human mind. The study of rock art is based on row material which covers the entire age of *Homo sapiens*. A perspective of 50,000 years, covering the entire planet, offers a unique opportunity for understanding universal patterns and the development of widespread tendencies in the minds of our species.

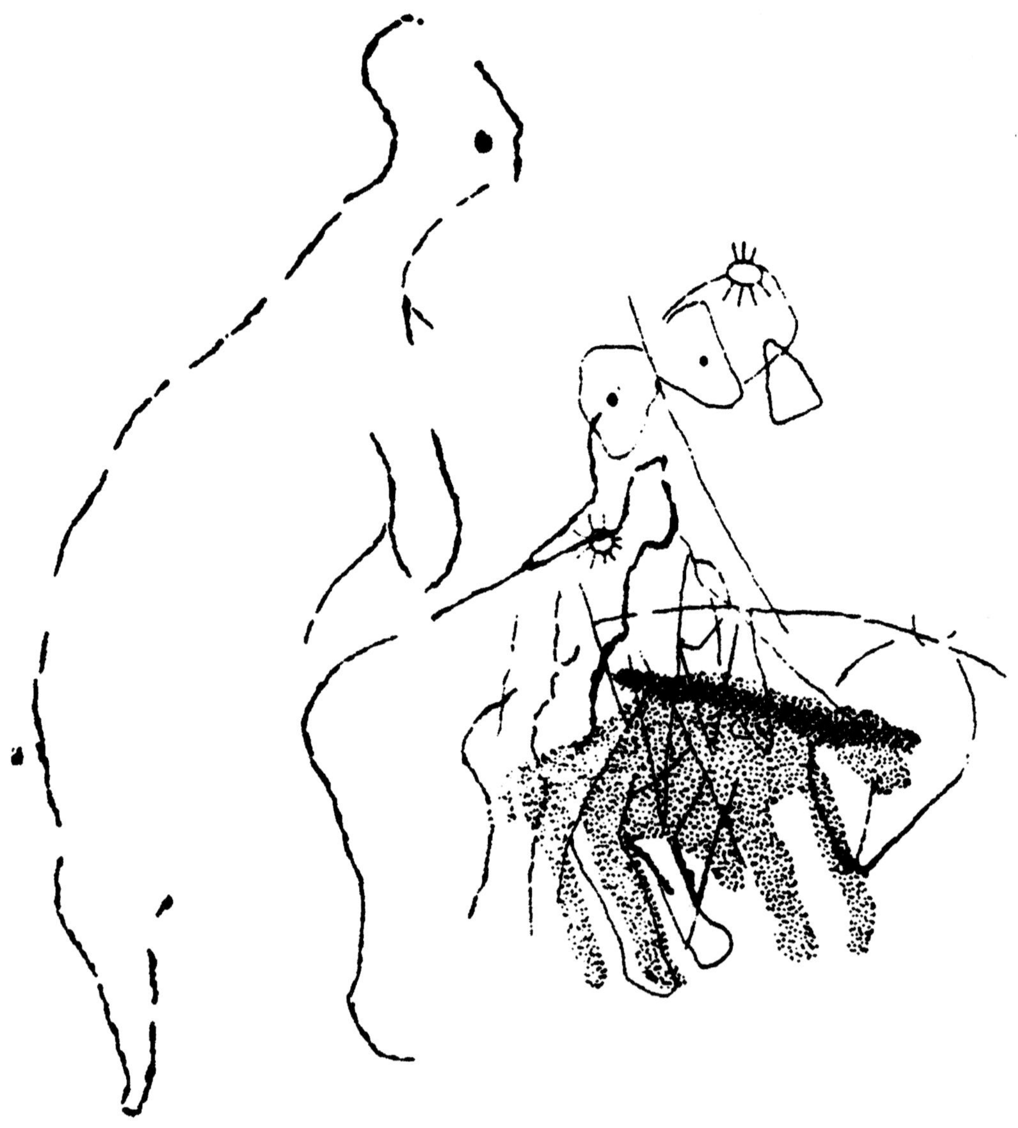

Fig. 13
Sequence of superimpositions. Rock engravings of Palanli Cave, Anatolia, Turkey. 1-two female outlines, one quadruped, and other signs Food Gatherers style. 2- Pecked animal figure from Evolved Hunters. 3- Non-figurative line drawings. 4- Line drawings of solar disks, 'butterfly' , axe and other signs of Incipient Agriculturists (Chalcolithic or Bronze Age).
Source: E. Anati, 1972, p.32. (WARA Archive W00173)
Area Code: B-I. Cat.: B-I; C-I; E-II.

10
ARCHETYPES

The system of association of graphemes varies consistently between different categories of prehistoric and tribal art. Assemblage of graphemes without an apparent order, sequences of graphemes, simple associations, associations in sequence, spot-scenes, anecdotal and descriptive scenes, reflect different ways of associating ideas and concepts. The definition of the type of syntax applied by the art-makers is revealing of their cognitive system. Intentional superimpositions are another way of association having a specific cognitive concept. The syntactic structure of any group of signs or images is the mirror of a mental process. A point of interest for various disciplines is that different ways of life and social organizations produce predictable recurring patterns of syntactic structure in their visual expressions. Such graphic reflections are a major source for detecting archetypes.

The presence or absence of the scene as a syntactic system, and the definition of its typology, are diagnostic aspects of the way of thinking of the art-makers. In the art of Early Hunters descriptive scenes are practically non-existing. Metaphoric associations have sometimes been considered as 'symbolic scenes' but they are not: they do not reflect the nature of the scene which intends to present the record of a moment or of an event.

Spot-scenes provide syntheses of absolute events or of recurring or eternal moments. Classical and widespread spot-scenes are the depiction of a worshipper, with upraised arms, in front of the sun disk or some other object of worship. They are common in the art of the early phases of Complex Economy. Other types of spot-scenes represent the association between an animal and a human being. They are common in the art of pastoralists. They represent recurring or eternal moments.

Anecdotal and descriptive scenes of events may represent hunting, fights, dances, ceremonies, intimate relations, and other specific moments. They are a common syntactic structure of Evolved Hunters and of Pastoral groups living in nomadic clans. Hunting scenes, scenes of meetings, both friendly and unfriendly, scenes of events and happenings represent moments that have impressed the maker and that have to be remembered. Stereotyped hieratic scenes are present among Food Collectors. They may represent dream-like imaginary events. Various types of scenes describing mythological accounts and commemorations of special events are present among societies with Complex Economy.

There are certain types of associations that resemble one another in different regions. The association between pictograms and ideograms is present in the art of hunters all over the world. An animal that has been added in a certain way in the context of other associated figures does not necessarily reflect a naturalistic reality as our present-day thinking would like to suggest. The animals are to be found repeatedly in similar relationships in accordance to rules that made sense for 'them' but which do not correspond to the type of composition and vision of our contemporary culture.

There is apparently no concept of a 'base' or 'ground level' in most of the art of the Early Hunters. The large animals are placed on cave walls or on rock surfaces as if they were levitating or suspended in mid-air. It has often been asked if they are not the spirits of the animals rather than the animals themselves. We find this in Europe as well as in Tanzania, Australia and elsewhere.

The association between animal and symbol recurs with analogies in all Early Hunting populations. The animals appear to be the subject or the object, often having a metaphoric meaning. The ideograms (the symbols) are types of logic reasoning around the subject which give a sense, a meaning and a purpose to the composition. There are no direct descriptions of hunting although the animal prey is the main subject-matter.

The Evolved Hunters use the bow and arrow which may be a conditioning factor in determining the dynamic style of their depictions. With the Evolved Hunters we find scenes which show a completely different mentality. Both human hunters and animal preys are depicted in action, running, fighting, reacting. According to our way of thinking the associations of the Evolved Hunters are more narrative, naturalistic and less abstract. But is it correct to consider the mentality of Early Hunters as more 'abstract' than that of more evolved cultures?

Sometimes the transition between the two is unpredictable. The tradition may be upset at a certain point and something new begins, as it happens in the rock art of Tanzania. In other contexts, however, the evolution is gradual and we may therefore detect the transitional phases, as it happens in the rock art of Gobustan, Azerbaijan, or in that of Northern Scandinavia.

Within this process we may catch a glimpse of patterns in the cognitive mechanism. One may postulate that: **Changes in style and associations in the visual arts illustrate changes in the cognitive processes which in turn reflect modifications in the choice of priorities** (*Postulate EA15*). This postulate may well apply to all kinds of art including dance and music, to all continents and to all times (E. Anati 1983). Reversing the words of Postulate EA15 we may state that changes in the cognitive processes cause changes in style and syntactic associations.

From an analysis of thematic, typology of the figures, marks and graphemes, patterns emerge which constitute the 'grammar' of rock art: the images are words in sentences or in composite concepts. Isolated marks are extremely rare as isolated words are rare in a conversation. In rock art there are groups of graphemes which reflect systems of associations that are the syntax. They are sentences composed of groupings or sequences of graphemes just like in the spoken and written languages of today. Usually there is a subject, a verb and a meaning. Their makers, thousands of years ago, were able to reading the rock art.

The decoding of rock art is the key to acquire knowledge on elementary cognitive systems based on universal characteristics of constant associations which go beyond, indeed precede and define the limits of linguistics. Thus, **the existence of logical archetypes may be postulated** (*Postulate EA16*). This is a base for future understanding: **Through rock art we may come to recognize some of the fundamental elements of man's cognitive dynamics** (*Postulate EA17*).

If, on the other hand, one continues to analyze isolated figures without looking at the context and associations, one will end up with a catalogue in which each figure is apart from the rest. It would be like reading each word in a sentence separately without seeing the sentence as having grammatical sense and logical syntax. Defining each assemblage is necessary in order to attempt its decoding. However it should be considered that there are superimpositions, composite associations and cognitive accumulations which have to be taken into consideration.

Sometimes the process is extremely complex. Looking at a panel of Early Hunters painting in a cave of France, we find that there were only three figures to begin with, two animals one in front of the other and an accompanying ideogram; after some generations another figure was added, two thousand years later another four marks had been added. The primary association is singled out, the repetitive elements verified, analogies and comparisons are considered in order to evaluate whether it consists of fortuitous or intentional superimpositions.

In many instances accumulations of marks appear to be intentional even if they are from different periods. Others appear not to be intentional or at least are unrecognizable as such. In both cases, however, we frequently discover that language is expressed by these signs. Sometimes previous graphemes may have been considered as part of the support like the natural shapes of the rock. These may have been used or not in the association of graphemes of the superimposed depictions.

Over and above the specific characteristics found in the Spanish Levantine art, in that of Valcamonica, Tanzania, Gobustan, Madhya Pradesh, the Tassili, or in the decorated Paleolithic caves of France and Spain, a type of language is in the background. This language touches upon prototypes of a universal nature. Provincial characters also exist which we refer to as 'vernacular'. It is of course easy to attribute a dialectal nature to all that we do not understand as language. However, we are increasingly aware of the fact that universal archetypes occupy an extremely relevant place in all art of all times.

The visual art before writing is a 'pre-writing writing' which has the outstanding qualification of being readable in any spoken language. It is composed of pictograms, ideograms and psychograms which are independent from any phonetic bondage. This archetype is present all over the world. The various patterns of grammar and syntax display repetitive patterns according to the category of way of life and economic structure of their makers. For each category specific archetypes are present, which are found all over disregarding the type of dialect or language spoken by their makers.

The system represents universal patterns of visual communication which are potentially readable in any language past or present. In theory it does not seem impossible to adapt the system to contemporary culture and reactivate a graphic system which may be readable in any language of the world.

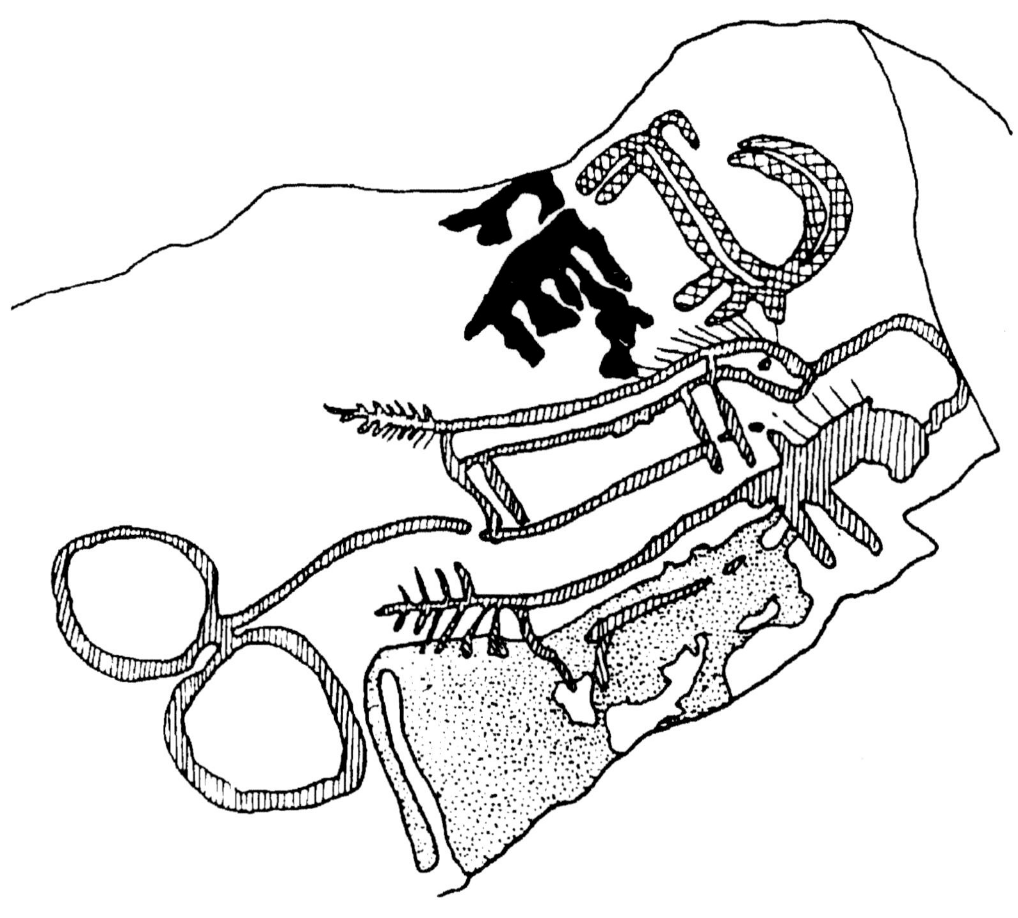

Fig. 14
Evolution and style in rock art. A succession of four phases of rock engravings at Ain Kudeirat, northern Egyptian Sinai. Besides the superimpositions, the difference in age is determined by the shade of patina. The early phase shows the picture of a bovine, then comes a chariot with horses, an antelope follows and, at last, a schematized quadruped (reproduced in black). The sequence is likely to cover no more than 4,000 years, from 3,000 BC to 1,000 AD.
Source: E. Anati, 1979, p. 20. (WARA Archive W00174)
Area Code: B-III. D-II; D-III; E-II.

11
ATTEMPTING A WORLD VISION

The present text intends to identify significant constants in rock art. The main tendency of rock art researchers had been that of describing finds. Usually attempts are made in dating them when possible, according to the means and the capacity of each researcher and, in some cases, relate the rock art makers to specific ethnic groups. Research in rock art had shown more interest in identifying exceptional finds or features than in finding the motivations for constants, paradigms and archetypes.

The query that motivated this study was that of the phenomenology of rock art. This visual expression of the human mind is present in 180 countries, in all continents, and the habit of producing it lasted for 50,000 years. It is ten times longer than the habit of writing and far more widespread than the habit of eating seated on a chair in front of a table, .or that of using writing or toilet paper. Many tribes who do not have those habits are still producing rock art.

What are the common denominators of this immense archive? What are the motivations for producing millions of depictions and signs on tens of thousands of rock surfaces? And what are the contents, the messages of rock art? This volume is an attempt at starting creating some order and a basic conceptual structure that should help us to create a scientific discipline out of a descriptive base of data.

Sequences of rock art with constant features have emerged in the Sahara, Tanzania, the Nile Valley, the Near East, Madhya Pradesh in India, Russian Central Asia, the Arnhem Land in Australia and elsewhere. The five categories already mentioned, Early Hunters, Food Collectors, Evolved Hunters, Animal Breeders and Complex Economy, usually are present in the same chronological order. In Australia, however, no Pastoralist-Animal Breeders rock art has been found. The Australian sequence is mainly composed all over of the Early Hunters, of sporadic cases of Food Collectors and, in some areas in the north of the Evolved Hunters. The Complex Economy category is represented in only a few very recent cases belonging to post-contact times.

In South Africa the main rock art zones show little evidence of Archaic Hunters; rather they appear farther north in Namibia, Zimbabwe and Tanzania. The oldest graphic marks in South Africa are non-figurative signs which may have memorizing roles but are not considered as art. The greatest artistic activity of this zone (probably the richest in figurative rock art thus far known in the world) emerges as the work of the Evolved Hunters, all the way from about 13,000 years ago to recent times. They maintained for millennia the same visual language with only minor modifications. Pastoralists-Animal Breeders and Complex Economy groups are also present. Rock art shows the existence of these Pastoralist and Early Farming populations while in most of the territory the Evolved Hunters' way of life persisted (J.D. Lewis-Williams, 1983).

WORLD ROCK ART: THE PRIMORDIAL LANGUAGE

In Tanzania during the Archaic Hunters' period we come upon a short parenthesis of a different pattern of rock art representing vegetal themes like leaves, plants, fruits, yams and roots, the work of a vegetarian culture whose economy was based on the gathering of fruits and berries. A wealth of vegetal elements are concentrated in this phase while they are practically absent in all other periods. Zoomorphic and anthropomorphic images are depicted as monsters. Humans have zoomorphic features and animals have anthropomorphic features.

Analogous creative episodes of Food Gatherers occur elsewhere. In the Central Sahara a similar type of rock art seems to reflect a population whose lifestyle depended largely on gathering and who made extensive usage of drugs. A similar phenomenon is recognized in Australia, mainly in the Kimberley Peninsula, along the Pecos River and in the Seminole Canyon in Texas, and in a few other areas. Chronologically, in the areas mentioned, this phase is located between the Archaic and the Evolved Hunters, though the absolute dating varies from one area to the other. Later in time, assemblages to be attributed to Food Gatherers are found in Europe, in Latin America, in India and elsewhere.

In Near Eastern deserts the rock art shows sporadic examples related to a Complex Economy, of Food Producers and Agriculturalists. In the Negev desert, Israel, there are even engravings representing ploughs. Rock art reflecting a complex economy represents a brief episode during the Roman period; the stratigraphy of overlappings and superimpositions shows that the artists both before and after this episode were Pastoralists. In itself, the existence of a few drawings which indicate a Complex Economy does not always mean the beginning of a new era. Rock art indeed provides segments of history though we have to admit that history is not always as simple and linear as we would like it to be.

Food, sex and territory for survival appear to have been, in all contexts of all times, the main concerns of the human species and the ones which, directly or indirectly, are most frequently expressed by rock art (E. Anati, 1992). The elementary structure of art follows recurring and widespread paradigms and archetypes. Certain rules of grammar and syntax reflect a primary logic and the presence of universal cognitive principles.

Vernacular characters are accompanying the universally recurring elements. Local styles and features become more common with the development of a Complex Economy and the establishment of sedentary or semi-sedentary settlements. Though the meaning of local variants must be considered, universal paradigms prevail in the art of the hunting populations. The essential patterns are present all over. Clearly it would be unlikely to find representations of llamas in Australia or of kangaroos in Argentina, but within the general framework we come upon animal subjects which are invested with the same kinds of values and similar metaphors for different species in different parts of the world.

The clearest evidence for the presence of universal paradigms lies in the ideograms which are found as constants the world over. Vulvas signs, phallic, cruciform, stick-like, egg-like ideograms, cup marks, cup and ring marks, hand prints, foot prints and animal tracks are to be found in the Paleolithic art of Europe as well as in the context of Early Hunters' art in Africa, Asia and Australia. The same ideograms are found also in other categories and persisted for ages.

The art of the Early Hunters appears to have broad universal characteristics in terms of the subject matter, types of associations and stylistic trends.

That of the Early Gatherers and that of the Evolved Hunters displays many more local features. The real Tower of Babel comes into being when the Hunting and Gathering era approaches its end. As we know, this happened at various dates. In parts of the Near East, complex economies and food production developed before 10,000 years ago while in some corners of the world the same horizon evolved in the last generations.

Art, like most other aspects of culture, becomes then increasingly provincial and more conditioned by surrounding influences. However on the whole many common denominators persist. The most obvious one is the very fact of producing rock art at all and then, as we have seen, there are analogous typologies, choices of subjects, types of associations, constant uses of certain colours, repeated preference for certain kinds of rock surfaces. To be added to these basic elements are details, embellishments and the different stylistic approaches used by the various categories of people. The most essential differences seem to reside in the seasoning rather than in the substance.

In attempting to present the general framework of rock art, it has been necessary to elaborate a methodology requiring a greater use of information which would have been unthinkable only a few years ago. Rock art has been considered as a phenomenon to be treated globally and not simply as a series of local phenomena with no connection to each other.

The present volume is just the introduction to a new discipline, the systematic and scientific study of rock art, which has a broad spectrum of potential developments in various fields of the human and social sciences, from general linguistics to psychology, psychoanalysis and neurology, from art history to the history of religions, from semiotics to elementary logic. A multi-disciplinary subject requires the joint involvement of different specialists and is promising a far-reaching development. In rock art is preserved the conceptual history of mankind for the last 50,000 years. Our roots are marked there by our ancestors. Many chapters of world history are recorded there and await to be decoded.

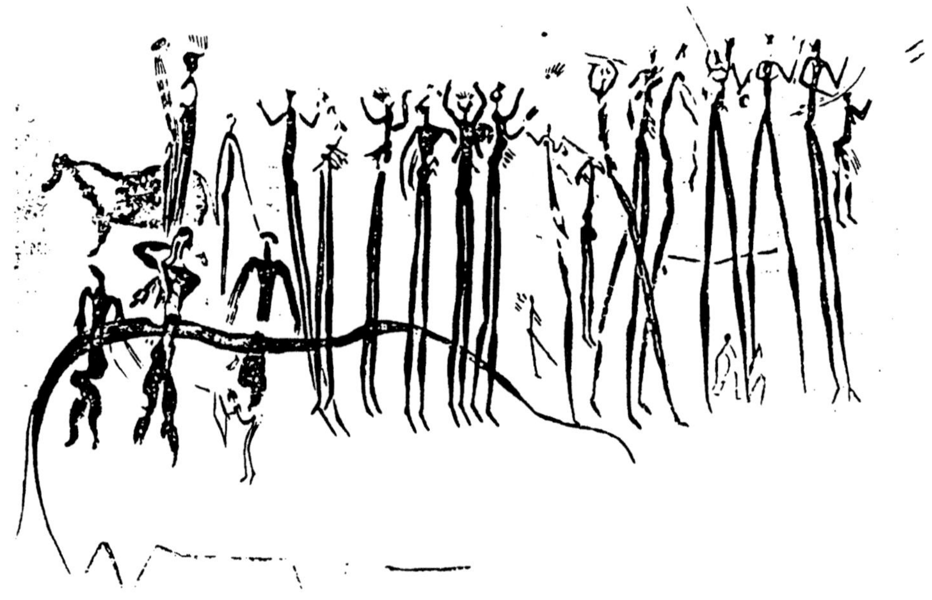

Fig. 15
Superimpositions of ages. Rock paintings of Domboshawa Cave, Zimbabwe. At least three different phases of Evolved Hunters characterized by three different styles of anthropomorphic figures are overlapping paintings of Early Hunters. The clearest image of Early Hunters is the large outline figure of a quadruped on the lower left side of drawing.
Source: E. Goodall et al., 1959, p. 6. (WARA Archive W00175)
Area Code: D-IV. Cat.: A-III; A-IV; C-I.

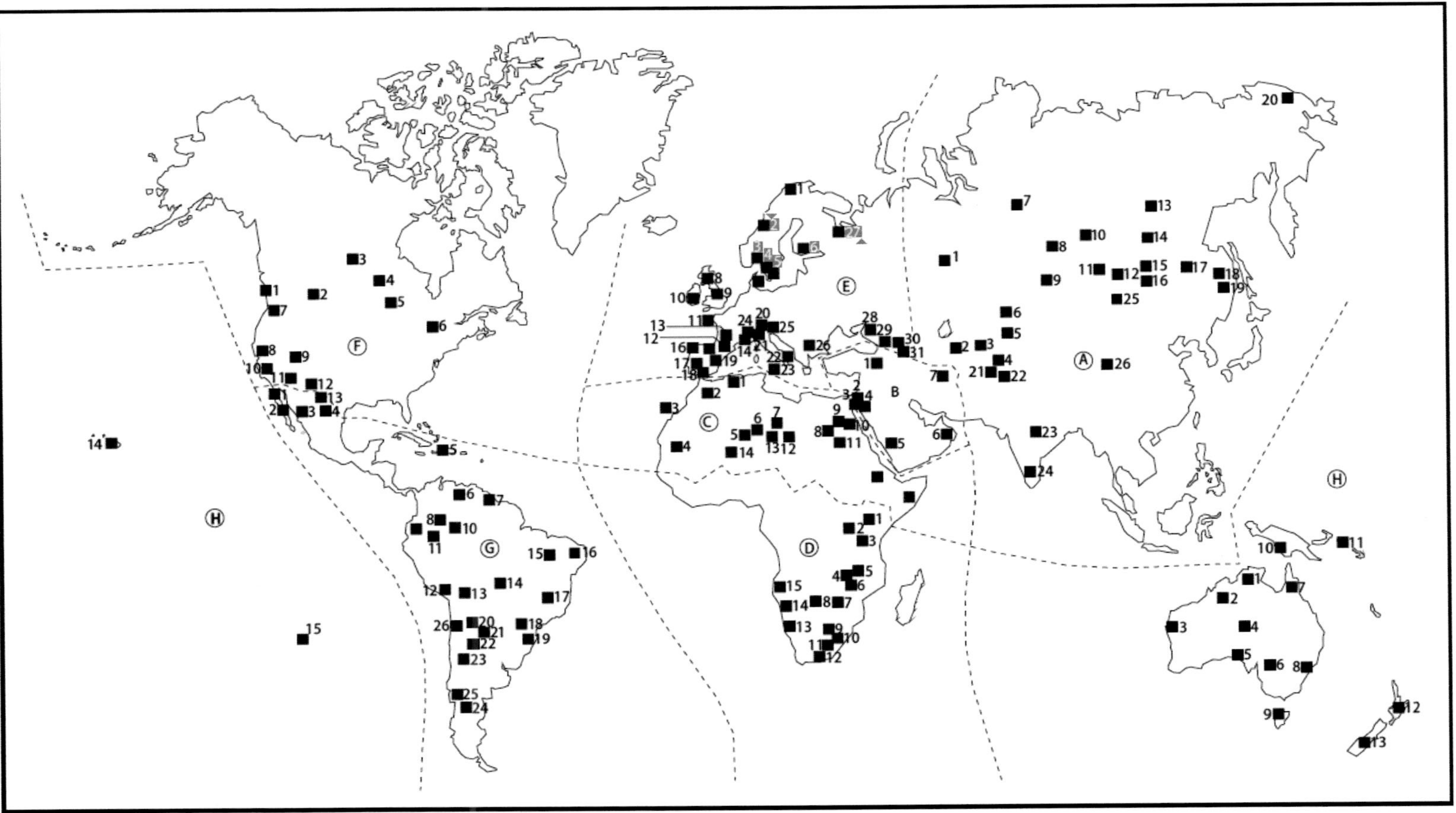

Fig. 16
World distribution major sites of rock art presented in the UNESCO World Report in 1984. Other major sites should be added, especially in China and South East Asia.
Source: E. Anati, 1984, p. 17

12
ANATI'S POSTULATES ON ROCK ART

1. The fundamental human processes of association and 'logic' developed throughout the ages in which the human species acquired its basic behavioral patterns.
2. Universal reflections conditioned by way of life influence behavior, thought, ideology, associative processes, and consequently artistic manifestations.
3. Rock art is a phenomenon of non-urban, non-literate societies.
4. In all the examined zones there are areas of great concentration of rock art which do not reflect an analogous concentration of people.
5. Each of the five categories of rock art (representing respectively the production of Early Hunters, Gatherers, Evolved Hunters, Pastoralists and people with a Complex Economy) displays a limited typological range of subjects which recurs in the rock art of all continents .
6. Three types of signs are to be found grammatically different from each other. They are pictograms, ideograms and psychograms.
7. Repetitiveness and constants of association indicate the presence of conventional concepts in a number of ideograms.
8. In the rock art of non-literate people, pictograms are of four main themes: 1. Anthropomorphic; 2. Zoomorphic; 3. Topographic and Tectiforms; 4. Implements and Weapons.
9. In the cases in which the meanings of the ideogram can be traced back to a single common core a universal pattern is established.
10. Certain rock art techniques are broadly repeated throughout the world which do not reflect processes of acculturation or diffusion.
11. A few basic colours are used in rock paintings all over the world, red being by far the most common in all continents.
12. Even in the absence of direct communication between different populations similar outcomes were reached in places far apart.
13. Repetitive elements, ideograms and pictograms, accompany the dominant figures.
14. In the art of hunters there is the presence of dominant animal species with dialectic relationships between them.
15. Changes in style and associations in the visual arts illustrate changes in the cognitive processes which in turn reflect modifications in the choice of priorities.
16. The existence of logical archetypes is postulated.
17. Fundamental elements of man's cognitive dynamics may be recognized through rock art.

MAIN BIBLIOGRAPHY FOR WORLD ROCK ART

ABRAMOVA Z.A.
  1990   *L'art mobilier paléolithique en Sibérie*, BCSP, vol. XXV-XXIV, p. 81-98.

ANATI E.
  1970   The Rock Engravings of Dahthami Wells in Central Arabia, *BCSP*, vol. 5, pp. 99-158, figs. 60-96.
  1976   *Evolution and Style in Camunian Rock Art*, Capo di Ponte (Edizioni del Centro) .
  1979   *L'art rupestre du Neguev et du Sinai*, Paris (L'Equerre).
  1981   The Origins of Art, *Museum*, vol. 33/4, pp. 200-210.
  1983   *Gli elementi fondamentali della cultura*, Milano (Jaca Book).
  1984   The State of Research in Rock Art, a World Report Presented to UNESCO, *BCSP*, vol. 21, pp. 13-56.
  1986   The Rock Art of Tanzania and the East African Sequence, *BCSP*, vol. 23, pp. 15-68.
  1989   *Origini dell'arte e della concettualità*, Milano (Jaca Book).
  1992   *Radici della Cultura*, Milano (Jaca Book).
  1994   *Archetypes costants and universal paradigms in prehistoric art*, Semiotica, p. 7-17.
  2001   *Gobusta, Azerbaijan*, Capo di Ponte (Edizioni del Centro).

BAHN P.G.
  1991   Pleistocene Images Outside Europe, *PPS*, vol. 57/I, pp. 91-102.

BEDNARIK R.G.
  1992   The Palaeolithic Art of Asia. In S. Goldsmith, S. Garvie, D. Selin and J. Smith (eds), *Ancient Images, Ancient Thought: the Archaeology of Ideology*, pp. 383-390. Proceedings of the 23rd Annual Chacmool Conference, University of Calgary.

BELTRAN A.
  1988 - L'art préhistorique Espagnol: nouveaux horizons et problèmes. Etat de la question, *BCSP*, vol. 24, pp. 13-44.

BREUIL H.
  1952   *Quatre cents siècles d'art parietal*, Montignac (Centre d'etudes et de documentation).

CHALOUPKA G.
  1984   *From Paleoart to Casual Paintings*, Darwin (N.T, Museum of Arts and Sciences).

CHEN Zh.-F.
  1988 - *Arte rupestre preistorica in Cina*, Milano (Jaca Book).

CLEGG J
  1983 - Australian Rock Art and Archaeology, *BCSP*, vol. 20, pp. 55-80.

CLOTTES J. et COURTIN J.
  1994   *La Grotte Cosquer,* Paris (Seuil).

CLOTTES J. Et LEWIS-WILLIAMS J.D.
  1996   *Les Chamanes de la préhistoire,* Paris (Seuil).

ERRICO F.
  1992.   *Technology, motion and the meaning of epipalaeolithic art,* C.A, vol. XXXIII/1, p. 94-109.

ERRICO F. et THÉVENIN A.
  1989.   *La notion du temps au Paléolithique et problem des calendriers lunaires,* in J.-P. Mohen (éd.), *Le Temps de la préhistoire,* Paris (Archeologia), vol. I, p. 46-47.

GIMBUTAS M.
  1989   *The Language of the Goddess,* San Francisco (Harper).

GRANT C.
  1983 -   *The Rock Art of the North American Indians,* Cambridge (CUP).

GRAZIOSI P.
  1987   *L'arte dell'antica età della Pietra,* Florence, (Le Lettere).

HOLM E.
  1984 -   Rock Art of the Matopos, *BCSP,* vol. 21, pp. 57-74.

KECHAGIA H.
  1995   *The row and the circle: semiotic perspective of visual thinking,* Rock Art Research 1995, vol. XII/2, p. 109-116.

KEYSER J.D.
  1991 -   Rock Art of North American Northwestern Plains: An Overview, *BCSP,* vol. 25-26, pp. 101-124.

KUSCH H.
  1986 -   Rock Art Discoveries in Southeast Asia: a Historical Summary, *BCSP,* vol. 23, pp. 99-108.

LAMING A.
  1962 -   *La signification de l'art rupestre paléolithique,* Paris (Picard).

LAYTON R .
  1981   *The Anthropology of Art,* Londres (Granada Publishing).

LEAKEY M.D.
  1983   *Africa's Vanishing Art,* New York e& Melbourne (Cambridge University Press).

LEROI-GOURHAN A.
  1965 -   *Préhistoire de l'art occidentale,* Paris (Citadelle & Mazenod).
  1982 -   *The Dawn of European Art,* Cambridge (CUP).

LEWIS-WILLIAMS J.D.
  1983 -   *The Rock Art of Southern Africa,* Cambridge (CUP).

LOMMEL A.
  1970   Shamanism: The Beginning of Art, *Current Anthropology,* vol. 11/1, pp. 39-48.

LUQUET G.H.
  1926   *L'art et la Religion des Hommes Fossiles,* Paris (Masson).

MARSHACK A.
  1972   *The Roots of Civilization,* New York (McGraw-Hill).

MORI F.
  1970   Proposition d'une chronologie de l'art rupestre du Sahara d'après les fouilles du Tadrart Acacus (Sahara Libyen), in E. Anati (ed.), *Valcamonica Symposium 1968,* pp. 345-356
  1991   La Fonction Sacrale Des Arbis à Peintures Dans le Massifs Centraux du Sahara: L'Acacus, Estratto

da Origini, *Preistoria e Protostoria Della Civilta Antiche*, vol. XV, 1991.

OKLADNIKOV A.P.
 1966   *Petroglyphi Angari*, Moskwa (Akademya Nauk SSSR).

OTTE M. et KOZLOWSKI J.K.
 2000   *Arte paleolitica in Europa centrale e orientale,* in E. Anati (éd), *40000 anni di arte contemporanea,* Capo di Ponte, (Edizioni del Centro), p. 121-138.

PATTERSON-RUDOLPH Carol
 1990   *Petroglyphs & Pueblo Myths of the Rio Grande*, Albuquerque, NM (Avanyu).

SCHOBINGER J. & C.J. GRADIN
 1985   *L'arte rupestre delle Ande e della Patagonia*, Milano (Jaca).

SMITS L.A.
 1988   Recording and Deciphering of Rock Paintings in Lesotho, *BCSP*, vol. 24, pp. 93-99.

WAKANKAR V.S.
 1983   The Oldest Works of Art?, *Science Today*, April 1983, pp. 43-48.

WELLMAN C.
 1979   *A Survey of North American Indian Rock Art*, Graz (Akademische Druck).

WENDT W.E.
 1976 - 'Art Moblier' from the Apollo 11 Cave, Southwest Africa: Africa's Oldest Dated Works of Art, *South African Archaeological Bulletin*, vol. 31, pp. 5-11

Note: This bibliography is primarily meant to allow elaboration of pertinent items mentioned but not dealt with in the present frame because their discussion is provided by the cited texts. A world bibliography of meaningful books, papers and articles in rock art published in the last ten years, includes over 1500 references. It would probably make a volume thicker than this one. Because of the specific purpose of this bibliography, many valuable and important works, relevant to the study of rock art but not pertinent to the aims of this text, could not be mentioned. For the same reason, several of my own previous monographic studies are not cited. My apologies go to all those friends and colleagues who are not mentioned. They will be cited in future reports when pertinent.

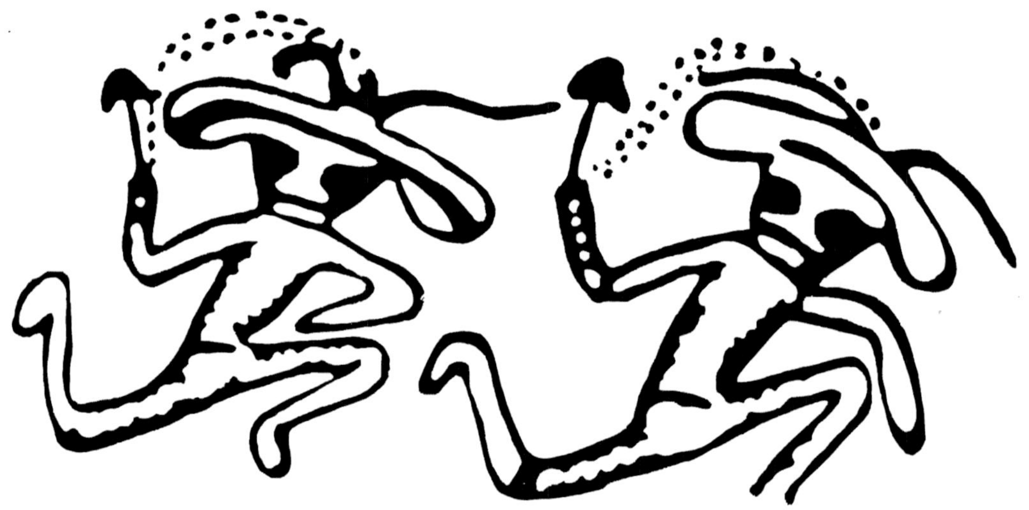

Fig. 17
Rock art produced in a state of hallucination. Tassili, Algeria. Early Gatherers. Detail of a painting illustrating the effect of hallucinogenic mushrooms (cf. fig. 79). Series of dots lead from the mushroom to the head. Horizon of the 'Round Heads style', ca. 5000 BC.
Source: G. Samorini, 1989, Fig. 9. (WARA Archive W00209 – W00138)
Area code: C-II. Cat.: B-I.

PART TWO

A PRELIMINARY TYPOLOGICAL REPERTORY OF WORLD ROCK ART

The following typological repertory of rock art is conceived with the purpose of providing general guidelines on the characters and the range of possibilities of visual expressions in the various categories of rock art. It does not intend to be an exhaustive repertory of the typologies but mainly a selection of elementary significant examples.

In some of the captions, interpretations are proposed. They are working hypotheses intended to stimulate thinking. Several of the interpretations derive from the repetitiveness of the themes and their comparative analysis; others derive from ethnographic parallels. These were taken into consideration when the same meaning is given to the same sign in more than two geographical areas. The main ethnographic sources have been the Pueblo American Natives, the Bedouins of the Negev and Sinai, the Nyau from Malawi, the Sandawe and Hadza from Tanzania, the San from South Africa and several groups of the Australian Aborigines from the Northern territory.

Most of such interpretations derive from comparative analyzes of different groups of rock art from different geographical areas. This study is in progress with the intent of producing a 'World Data Base' on rock art and its meaning. Such interpretations should be taken as 'tentative'. It was however considered useful to present them at an interim stage for an open and constructive debate. The reading of rock art is going to be one of the main goals of forthcoming research in this field, and progress may be obtained in the way of 'trial and error'. Comments and alternative interpretations would be welcome and, if pertinent, will be cited in the forthcoming data base.

In consideration of the comparative character of this repertory, unless relevant for the understanding of the specific depiction, measures have been omitted. They are available in the bibliography cited and in the WARA archives. Also dates and absolute chronologies have been omitted, but again, they are usually available in the bibliography, and can be provided upon request. Chronology in connection to categories of rock art may have local values.

The relative chronological succession of the five categories, when more than a category is present in the same area, has a frequent progression from A to E (A. Archaic Hunters; B. Food gatherers C. Evolved Hunters; D. Pastoralists; E. Groups with Complex Economy). The absolute chronology may vary considerably from area to area. While Archaic Hunters art was still being produced in Central Australia in this century, in the Near East, in parts of China, Europe and North

Africa, it stopped being produced 10,000 years ago. The art of Complex Economy and the pastoral art started, in a few areas, 10,000 years ago but never reached some parts of the world.

The main references considered are the '*Area Code*', the typological '*Category*' and the '*Kind*' of art. The present repertory is referring entirely to rock art, that means to just two of the kinds of immobiliary art: Rock Engravings (A-1) and Rock Paintings (A-2); the *Kind* is mentioned in the caption. The other two classifications appear at the bottom of each caption. Most of the present repertory is composed of drawings. For those interested in confronting the drawings with photographs, or with other tracings, bibliographic references are provided.

CATEGORIES OF PREHISTORIC AND TRIBAL ART (CAT)

Code	Category	Sub-code	Type
A	Early Hunters (no bow and arrow)	I	Pre-figurative
		II	Archaic Syntax
		III	Classical Syntax
		IV	Final Early Hunters (Epi-Palaeolithic Syntax)
B	Food Gatherers	I	Early Gatherers (Vegetarians)
		II	Synthesis Collectors (Mesolithic Syntax)
		III	Late Gatherers ('Late vegetarians')
C	Evolved Hunters (with bow and arrow)	I	Hunters without Domesticated Animals
		II	Hunters with Domesticated Dog
		III	Hunters with Incipient Animal Breeding and/or Incipient Agriculture
		IV	Fishermen and Seafarers
D	Pastoralists and Animal Breeders	I	Hunting-and-Pastoral Groups
		II	Nomadic and Transhumant Pastoralists
		III	Sedentary Animal Breeders (with or without Garden Agriculture)
E	Complex Economy	I	Incipient Agriculturalists Without Metallurgy (Neolithic Syntax)
		II	Agriculturalists and/or Traders with Metallurgy (Metal Ages Syntaxes)
		III	Agriculture and Fishing
		IV	Urban or literate peoples

KINDS OF PREHISTORIC AND TRIBAL ART (KIND)

Code	Kind	Sub-code	Type	Criteria
Code A	Immobiliary art (Not removable)	I	Rock Engravings	Visual art which affects the surface structure
		II	Rock Paintings	Visual art which does not modify the structure of the surface
		III	High and Low Reliefs	Three dimensional operations on the surface
		IV	Monumental	Statues, poles, stele, statuary which cannot be removed by less than 5 people (more than 250 kg.)
		V	Geoglyphs	Geoglyphs Pebble drawings, sand drawings and other designs on soil surface
Code B	Mobiliary Art (Removable Less than 250 kg)	I	Movable monuments (statues, pillars, standards, other three dimensional items)	Monuments which cannot easily be carried by a single person (10 to 250 kg)
		II	Statuettes	Three-dimensional objects which can be carried by a single person (less than 10 kg.)
		III	Plaquettes A. Paintings B. Engravings C. High and Low reliefs (typological subdivisions)	Two-dimensional paintings and engravings on 'non-functional' objects
		IV	Decorations on tools (same use of A-B-C)	'Functional' items & other objects of daily use
		V	Parure, masks and talismans (typological subdivisions)	Objects used for body decoration
		VI	Musical instruments (typological subdivisions)	Objects used to produce sound
		VII	Furniture and others (typological subdivisions)	Other movable art items not included in previous subdivisions

GEOGRAPHIC CLASSIFICATION OF AREAS (AREA CODE)

Code	World area	Sub-Region	
A	Asia (except the Near East)	I	Russian territories and former USSR territories in Asia
		II	China, Korea and Mongolia
		III	India, Pakistan, Afghanistan, Nepal
		IV	Southeast Asia
		V	Japan
B	Near East	I	Anatolia, Turkey
		II	Syria-Lebanon-Iraq
		III	Israel-Sinai-Jordan
		IV	Arabia
		V	Iran
C	Northern Africa Atlantic Coastal Areas	I	Mediterranean and Northern African
		II	Sahara
		III	Sahel
		IV	Egypt and Sudan
		V	Horn of Africa
D	Southern Africa	I	West-Central Africa and Congo Basin
		II	Kenya, Tanzania, Uganda
		III	Mozambique, Malawi, Zambia, Angola
		IV	Namibia, Botswana, Zimbabwe and South Africa
E	Europe	I	Western Europe
		II	Scandinavia
		III	Eastern Europe
		IV	The Balkans
F	Northern America	I	Canada, Alaska and Greenland
		II	The United States
G	Latin America	I	Meso-America including Mexico to Panama
		II	Colombia, Venezuela, Guyana, Ecuador
		III	Brazil, Peru, Bolivia, Paraguay
		IV	Uruguay, Argentina, Chile
H	Oceania	I	Australia
		II	Melanesia: New Guinea, Bismarck and Solomon Islands
		III	Polynesia North: North Pacific (north of the Equator)
		IV	Polynesia South: South Pacific (south of the Equator)
		V	Micronesia

AREA CODE OF COUNTRIES

Country	Code	Sub-code	Country	Code	Sub-code
Afghanistan	A	III	Bosnia-Herzegovina	E	IV
Albania	E	IV	Botswana	D	IV
Algeria, Mediterranean	C	I	Brazil	G	III
Algeria, Sahara Region	C	II	Brunei	G	I
Andorra	E	I	Bulgaria	E	IV
Angola	D	III	Burkina Faso	D	I
Antigua & Barbuda	G	I	Burma	A	IV
Argentina	G	IV	Burundi	D	II
Armenia	E	III	Cameroon	D	I
Australia	H	I	Canada	F	I
Other Australian territories:			Cape Verde	D	I
Australian Antarctic Territories	H	IV	Central African Rep.	D	I
Ashmore & Cartier Islands	H	IV	Chad	C	III
Christmas Islands	H	IV	Chile	G	IV
Cocos Islands	H	IV	Chine, P.R.	A	II
Heard island and Mcdonald Island	H	IV	China, Taiwan	A	II
Nortfolk Islands	H	IV	Colombia	G	II
Austria	E	I	Comoros	D	III
Azerbaijan	E	III	Congo, D.R.	D	I
Bahamas	G	I	Congo, R.	D	I
Bahrain	B	IV	Costa Rica	G	I
Bangladesh	A	III	Côte d'Ivoire	D	I
Barbados	G	II	Croatia	E	IV
Belarus	E	III	Cuba	G	I
Belgium	E	I	Cyprus	B	I
Belize	G	I	Czech Republic	E	III
Benin	D	I	Denmark	E	II
Bhutan	A	III	*Other Danish territories:*		
Bolivia	G	III	*Faeroe Islands*	E	I

Country	Code	Sub-code	Country	Code	Sub-code
Greenalnd	F	I	Georgia	E	III
Djibuti	C	V	Germany	E	I
Dominica	G	I	Ghana	D	I
East Timor	A	IV	Greece	E	IV
Ecuador	G	I	Grenada	G	II
Egypt, Nile Valley and East	C	IV	Guatemala	G	I
Egypt, Saharean	C	II	Guinea	D	I
El Salvador	G	I	Guinea-Bissau	D	I
Equatorial Guinea	D	I	Guyana	G	II
Eritrea	C	V	Haiti	G	II
Estonia	E	III	Honduras	G	I
Ethiopia	C	V	Hungary	E	III
Fiji	H	IV	Iceland	E	I
Finland	E	II	India	A	III
Other Fin territories:			Indonesia	A	IV
Åland Islands	E	II	*Other Indonesian territories*		
France	E	I	*Irian*	H	II
Other French territories:			Iran	B	V
French Guiana	G	II	Iraq	B	II
French Polynesia	H	IV	Ireland	E	I
French Southern & Antarctic Territories	H	IV	Israel	B	III
Guadaloupe	G	II	Italy	E	I
Martinique	G	II	Jamaica	G	I
Mayotte	D	II	Japan	A	V
New Caledonia	H	IV	Jordan	B	III
Réunion	D	III	Kampuchea	A	IV
Saint Barthélemy	G	I	Kenya	D	II
Saint Martin	G	I	Kirghizistan	A	I
Saint Pierre & Miquelon	F	I	Kiribati	H	IV
Wallis & Fortuna islands	H	IV	Korea, D.P.R.	A	II
Gabon	D	I	Korea, R.	A	II
Gambia	C	III	Kuwait	B	IV

Country	Code	Sub-code	Country	Code	Sub-code
Laos	A	IV	*Other Netherlands territories:*		
Latvia	E	III	*Aruba*	G	I
Lebanon	B	II	*Netherlands Antilles*	G	II
Lesotho	D	IV	New Zealand	H	IV
Liberia	D	I	*Other New Zealand territories:*		
Lybia, Mediterranean	C	I	*Cook islands*	H	IV
Lybia, Saharean	C	II	*Niue*	H	IV
Liechtenstein	E	I	*Ross Dependency*	H	IV
Lithuania	E	III	*Tokelau*	H	IV
Luxembourg	E	I	Nicaragua	G	I
Macedonia	E	IV	Niger	C	III
Madagascar	D	III	Nigeria	D	I
Malawi	D	III	Norway	E	II
Malaysia	A	IV	*Other Norwegian territories:*		
Maldives	A	III	*Bouvet Island*	D	IV
Mali	C	III	*Jan Magen*	F	I
Malta	E	I	*Svalbard*	E	II
Marshall Islands	H	V	Oman	B	IV
Mauritania	C	III	Pakistan	A	III
Mauritius	D	III	Palau	A	V
Mexico	G	I	Panama	G	I
Micronesia	H	V	Papua New Guinea	H	II
Moldavia	E	III	Paraguay	G	III
Monaco	E	I	Peru	G	III
Mongolia, P.R.	A	II	Philippines	A	IV
Montenegro	E	IV	Poland	E	III
Morocco	C	I	Portugal	E	I
Mosquat	B	IV	*Other Portuguese territories:*		
Mozambique	D	III	*Azores*	G	I
Namibia	DH	IV	*Madera*	C	I
Nauru	A	IV	Qatar	B	IV
Nepal	E	III	Romania	E	III
Netherlands	G	I	Russia, Asian	A	I
Russia, European	E	III	Sweden	E	II

Country	Code	Sub-code	Country	Code	Sub-code
Rwanda	D	II	Switzerland	E	I
Saint Kitts & Nevis	G	I	Syria	B	II
Saint Lucia	G	II	Tadjikistan	A	I
Saint Vincet & the Grenadines	G	I	Tanzania	D	II
San Marino	E	I	Thailand	A	IV
São Tomè e Princìpe	D	I	Togo	D	I
Saudi Arabia	B	IV	Tonga	H	IV
Senegal	C	III	Trinidad and Tobago	G	II
Serbia	E	IV	Tunisia	C	I
Seychelles	D	III	Turkey, Asian	B	I
Sierra Leone	D	I	Turkey, European	E	IV
Singapore	A	IV	Turkmenistan	A	I
Slovakia	E	III	Tuvalu	H	IV
Slovenia	E	IV	Uganda	D	II
Solomn Islands	H	II	United Arab Emirates	B	IV
somalia	C	V	United Kingdom	E	I
South Africa	D	IV	*Other UK territories:*		
Spain	E	I	*Akrotiri & Dhekelia*	B	I
Other Spanish territories:			*Anguilla*	G	I
Canary islands	C	I	*Bermuda*	F	II
Ceuta	C	I	*British Antarctic Territories*	H	IV
Isla de Alboran	E	I	*British Indian Ocean Territories*	H	IV
Isla de Chafarinas	E	I	*British Virgin Islands*	H	IV
Isla Perejil	E	I	*Cayman Islands*	G	I
Melilla	C	I	*Falkland Islands*	G	IV
Peñòn de Alhucemas	E	I	*Gibraltar*	E	I
Sri-Lanka	A	III	*Montserrat*	E	I
Sudan	C	IV	*Pitcairn Islands*	A	II
Suriname	F	II	*South Georgia & the South Sandwich Islands*	G	IV
Swaziland	D	IV	*St. Helena and Depend.*	D	III
Turks & Calcos Islands	G	I	*Navassa Island*	G	II

Country	Code	Sub-code	Country	Code	Sub-code
Ukraine	E	III	*Northern Mariana Islands*	H	III
United States of America	F	II	*Palmyra Atoll*	H	III
Other USA territories:			*Trust Terr. Pacific Isl.*	H	II
Alaska	F	I	*Virgin Islands*	G	II
Hawaii	H	III	*Wake Island*	H	III
Puerto Rico	G	I	Uruguay	G	IV
American Samoa	H	IV	Uzbekistan	A	I
Baker Island	H	III	Vanuatu	H	IV
Guam	H	III	Vatican City State	E	I
Howland Island	H	III	Venezuela	G	II
Jarvis Island	H	III	Viet-Nam	A	IV
Johnston Atoll	H	III	Yemen	B	IV
Kingman Reef	H	III	Zambia	D	III
Midway Atoll	H	III	Zimbabwe	D	III

STANDARD TYPOLOGICAL REPERTORY OF WORLD ROCK ART

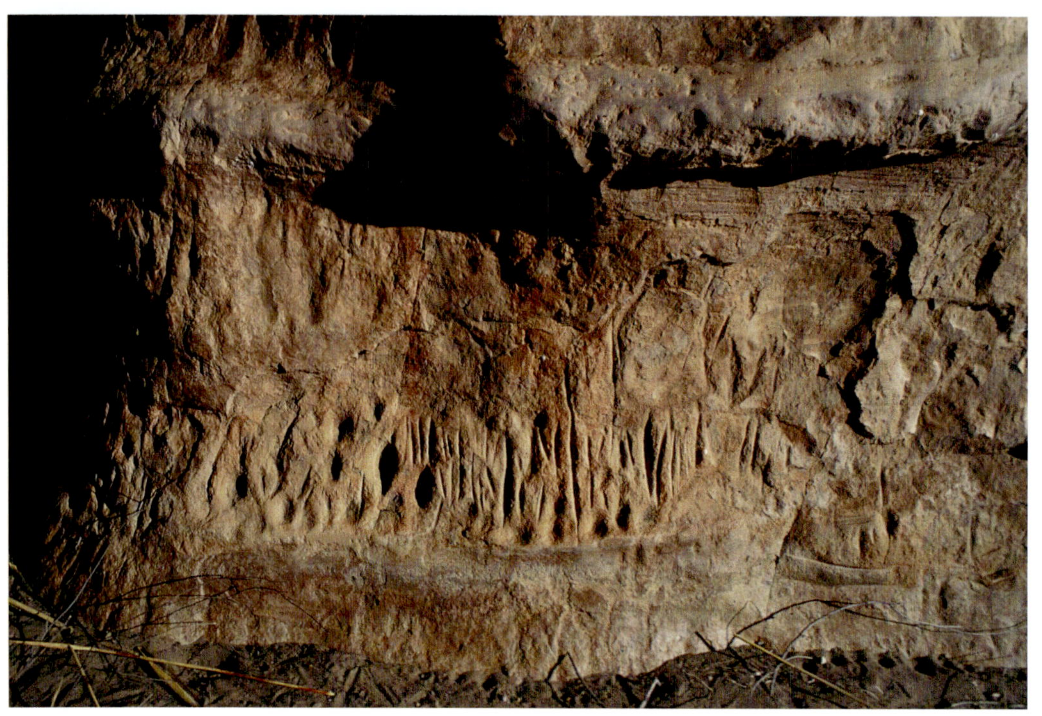

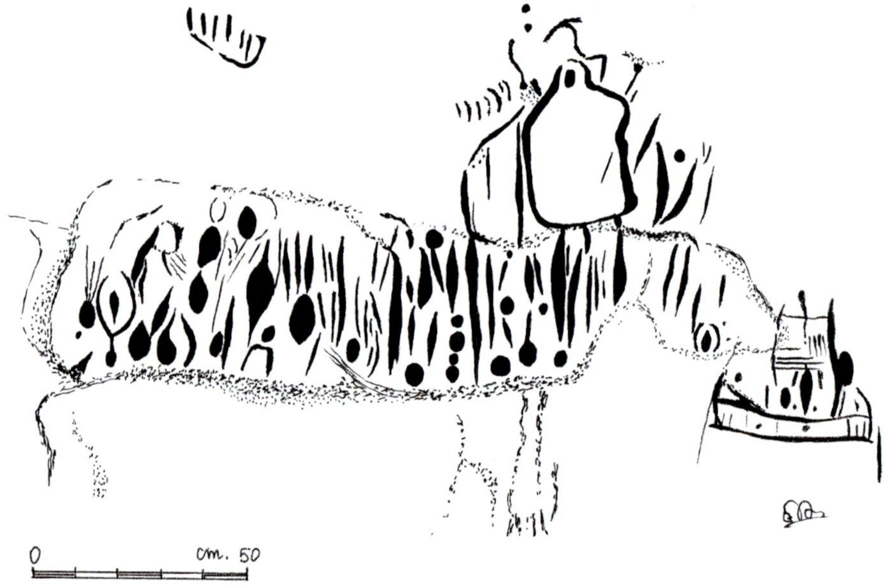

A. Early Hunters

Fig. 18
Turtle Place, Kununarra, Kimberley, Australia. Rock engravings by Early Hunters. Composition of cup marks and bâtonnet marks. This kind of association spreads all over the world in the most ancient phases of graphic manifestations. The whole area where the engravings concentrate has shape of the body of an animal or of some fantastic being. Source: photo E. Anati EA2000:CXXVI-36, (cf. Flood 1997, pp. 120-132). (WARA Archive W07028)
Area Code: H-I. Cat: A-I.

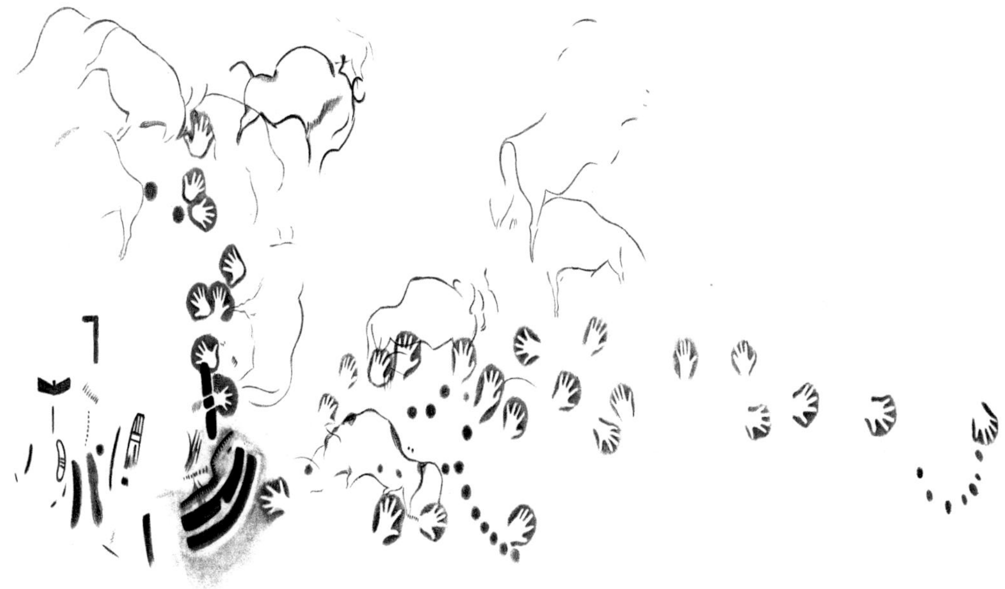

Fig. 19
Rock painting of Early Hunters. Castillo cave, Spain. Two phases of paintings are present. The later represents associations of quadrupeds, mainly bisons and horses. This kind of association is defined as 'Classic Syntax'. The earlier phase is an accumulation of hand stencils and of signs some of which represent tools. This kind of association is defined as 'Archaic Syntax'.
Source:Tracing by H. Breuil, in H. Alcalde del Rio, H. Breuil & L. Sierra, 1912, pl. 46. (WARA Archive W00176)
Area code: E-I. Cat.: A-II, A-III.

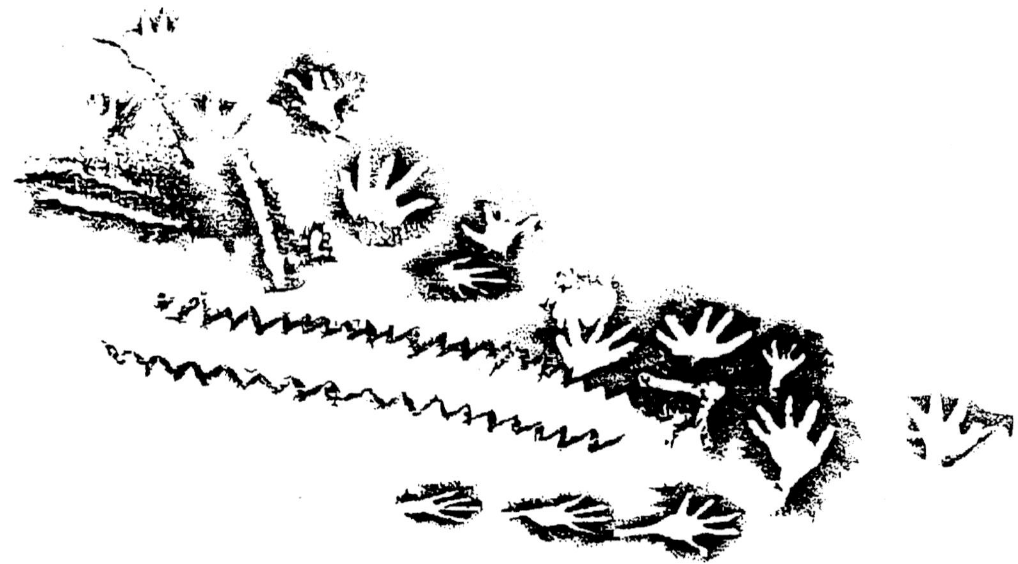

Fig. 20
Association of ideograms of Early Hunters. Rock paintings in Queensland, Australia, where there are also engravings (omitted in the drawing). Stencils of human hands are associated with stencils of animal limbs, zig-zags and tools ('Archaic syntax').Length of traced part 1.50 meters. Source: Drawn from a photograph of J. Clegg, 1983, p. 69. (WARA Archive W00178)
Area code: H-I. Cat.: A-II

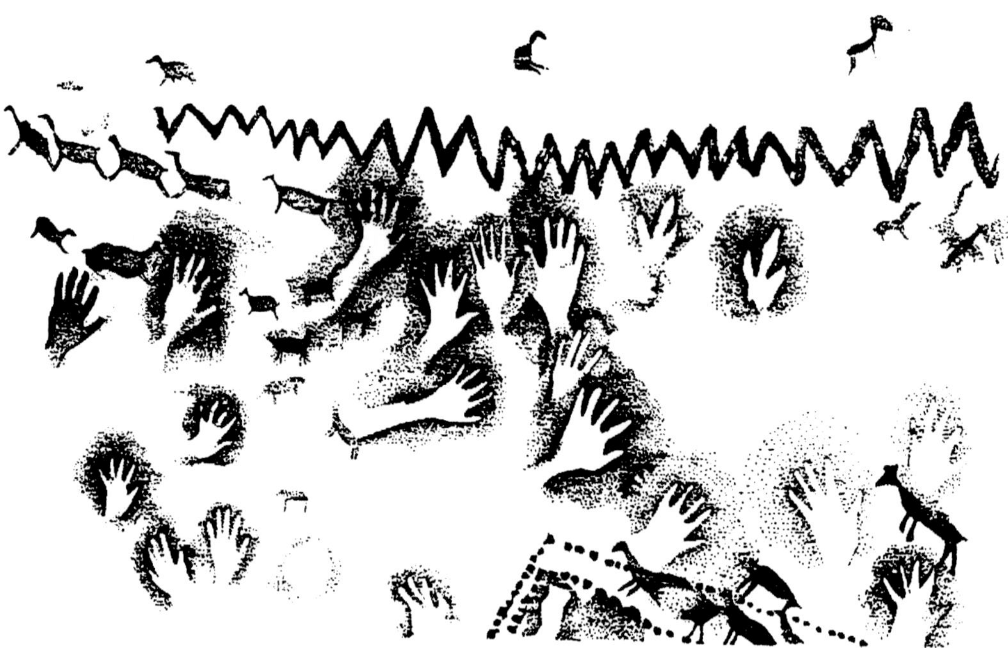

Fig. 21
Hand stencils and other symbols of Early Hunters. Rock paintings of Rio Pinturas, Santa Cruz, Patagonia, Argentina. Human hands and stencils of animal feet are accompanied by a long zig-zag ('Archaic syntax'). The animal figures and the rows of dots are later additions. Length of traced part 2.60 meters.
Source:Drawn from a photograph of G.C. Ligabue; cf. E. Anati, 1989, pl. 4. (WARA Archive W00179)
Area code: G-III. Cat.: A-II

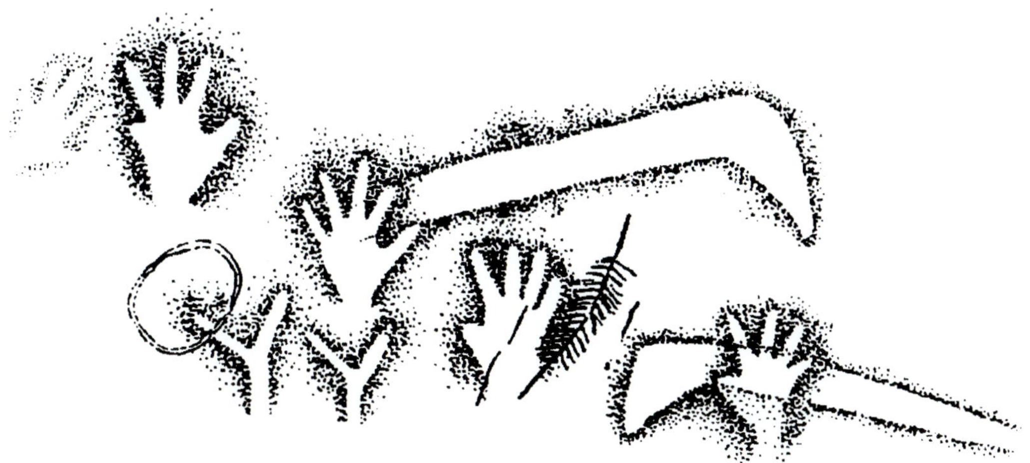

Fig. 22
Association of ideograms of Early Hunters. Rock paintings of Nabarlek, Arnhem Land, Australia. Stencils of three elements: hand-prints, animal footprints and tools. Three of the four hands are mutilated. In a later moment two more ideograms were added: disk (female) and arbolet (male). It is not unlikely that the later addition tends to explain the significance of the tool being hold or superimposed by the hand
Source: D. Lewis, 1988, p. 199. (WARA Archive W00177)
Area code: H-I. Cat.: A-II.

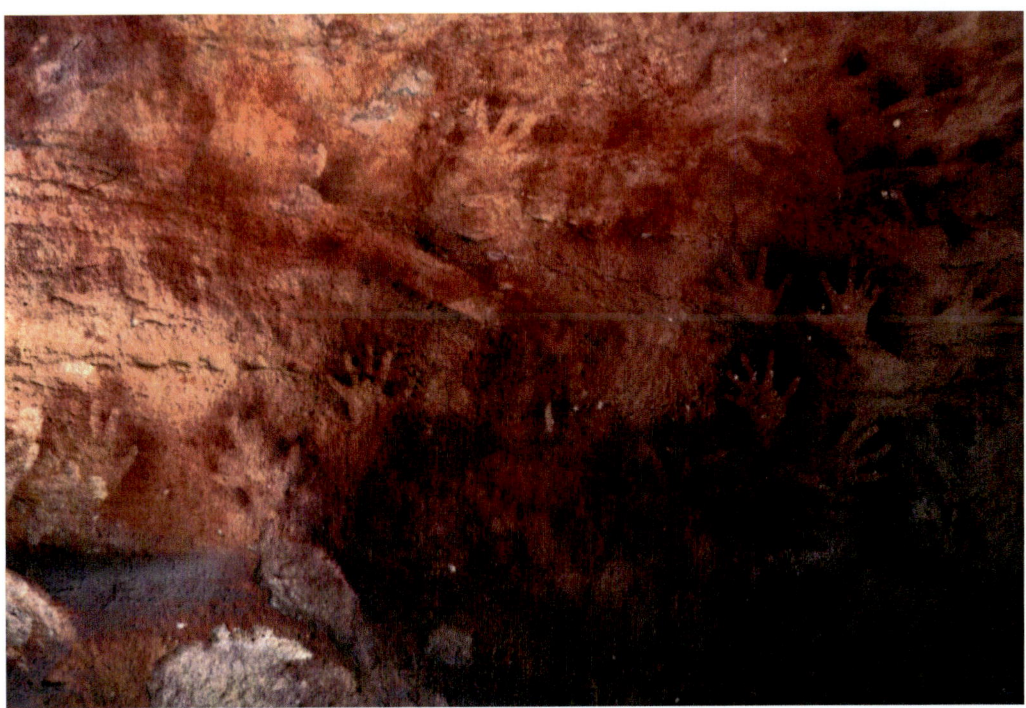

Fig. 23
Hand stencils from Dingo Ridge, York peninsula, Australia.
Source: WARA-88: MH XXI-2. (WARA Archive W00180)
Area code: H-I . Cat.: A-II.

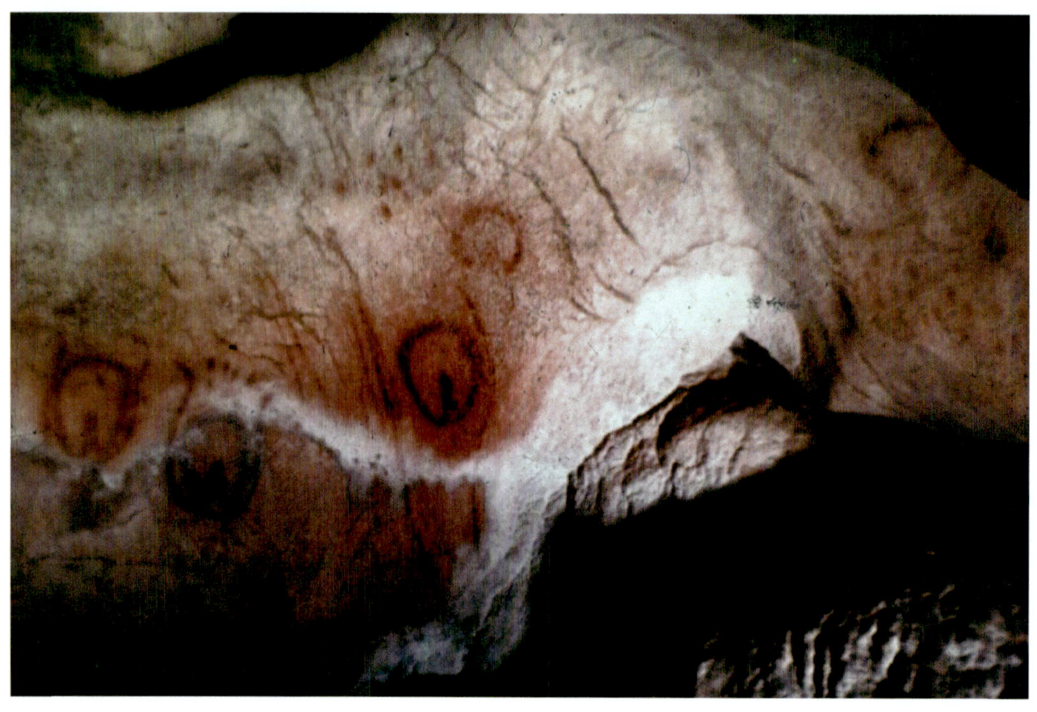

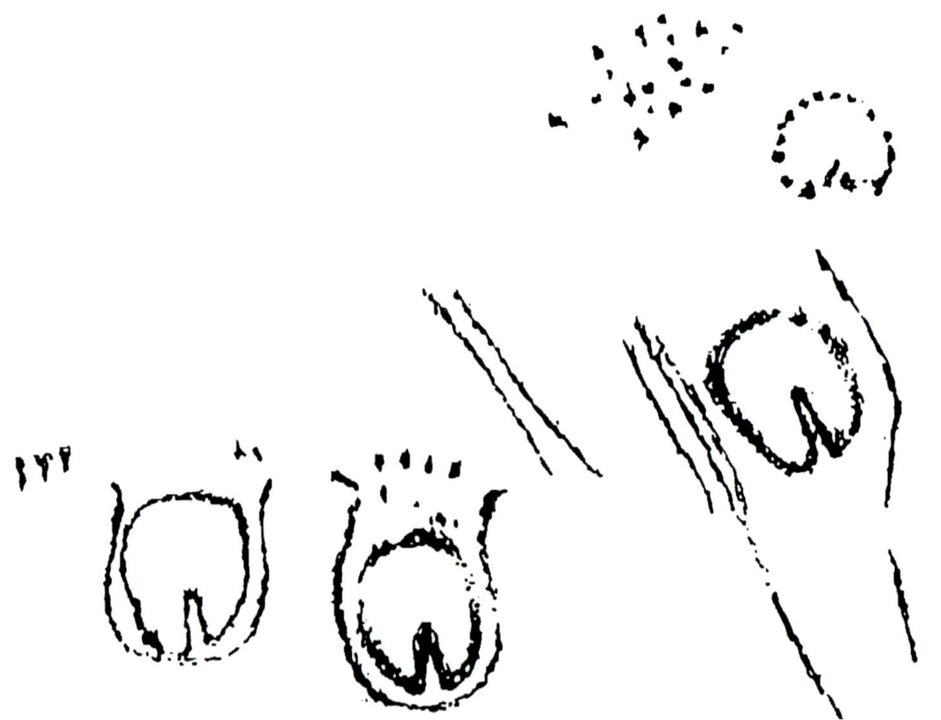

Fig. 24 a – b
Rock paintings in the cave of Tito Bustillo, Spain, showing the natural context of the above painting. The shape and colours of the surface have determinated the location of the paintings and interplay with them.
Source: WARA-87:EA-XXII. (WARA Archive W00187)
Area code: E-I. Cat. A-II.

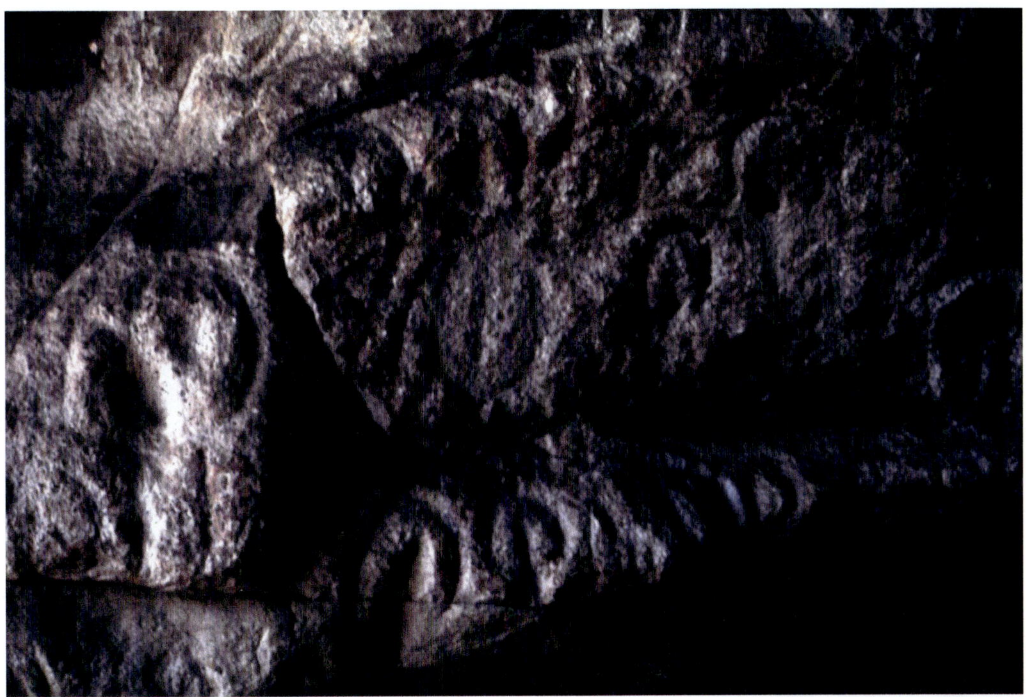

Fig. 25
Deeply engraved 'vagina' patterns from the Mulegé, San Borjita, Baja California, Mexico. Proto-figurative or Archaic syntax.
Source: WARA-81: AA-XXII-12 (WARA Archive W00183)
Area Code: G-I. Cat.: A-II.

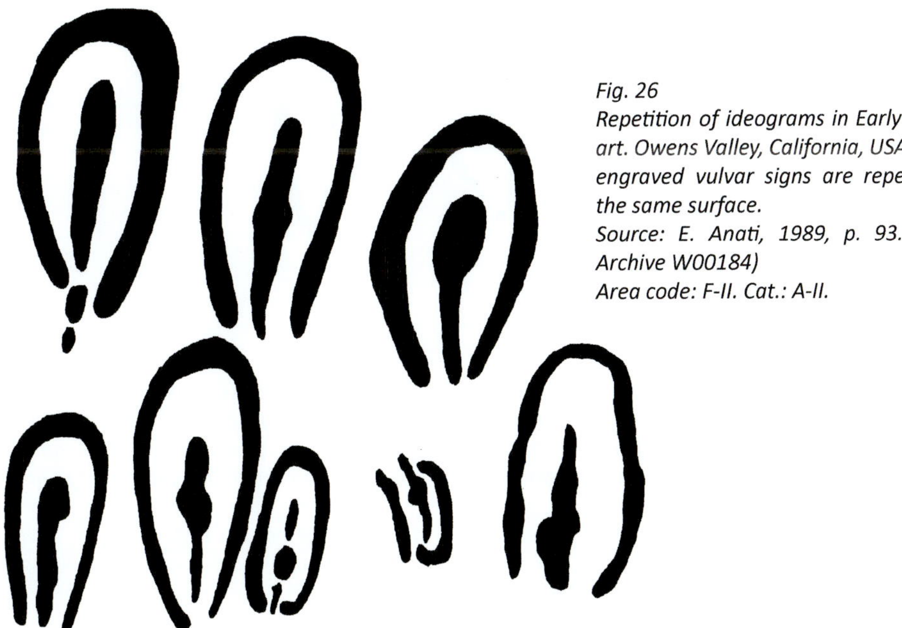

Fig. 26
Repetition of ideograms in Early Hunters art. Owens Valley, California, USA. Deeply engraved vulvar signs are repeated on the same surface.
Source: E. Anati, 1989, p. 93. (WARA Archive W00184)
Area code: F-II. Cat.: A-II.

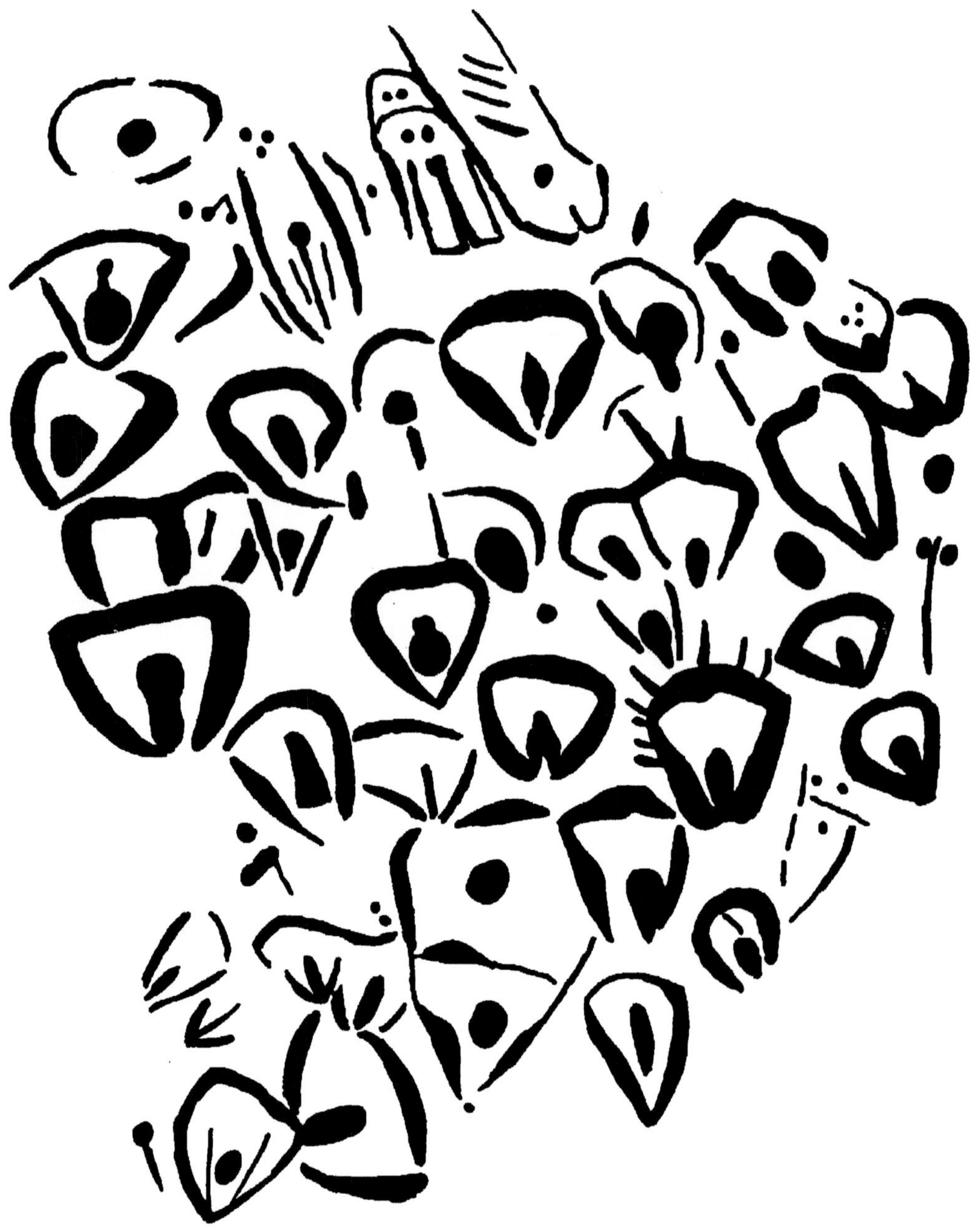

Fig. 27
Proliferation of 'vaginas'. Deeply engraved rock surface at Pachene, Chimanes, Bolivia. Over 30 vagina-ideograms show a variety of shapes on the same surface. On the upper part of the surface there is a cup-and-ring ideogram, a phallic depiction and other marks with obvious sexual significance. This composition is an accumulation of signs with an 'Archaic syntax' which is likely to be over 20,000 years later than similar compositions from the Old World.
Source: Drawn from a photograph of the Froebius Institute in A.A. Fernandez Distel,1990, p. 79. (WARA Archive W00181)
Area Code: G-III. Cat. A-II.

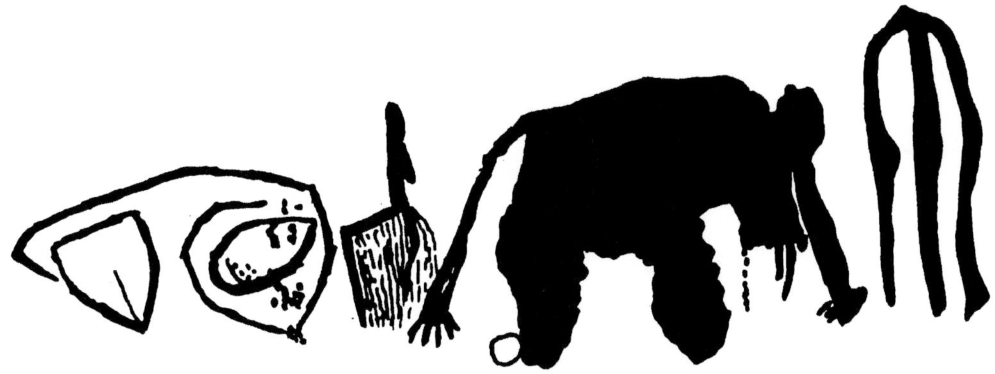

Fig. 28
Early Hunters in Northern Africa. Dakhla, Upper Egypt. Deeply engraved sequence of pictograms and ideograms typical of Early Hunters. The female figure near the tail of the elephant is executed by a different hand in a different style. It is likely to have been added when the previous sequence was not fully understood any more and required more explicit details (it may be an attempt to read the message). From left to right: two ideograms are related by a line, one of them is a vulvar sign, the other is an oval or disk which is likely to stand for 'female'. Then comes the later feminine figure and the elephant. At the right end another ideogram, which is widespread in Early Hunters art and may indicate 'union' or 'intercourse'. The elephant has a disk near its hind legs which indicates 'female'. The elephant is likely to be the totemic symbol or the name of a woman concerned by this message.
Source: E. Anati, 1989, p. 67. (WARA Archive W00192)
Area code: C-IV. Cat.: A-II; E-I.

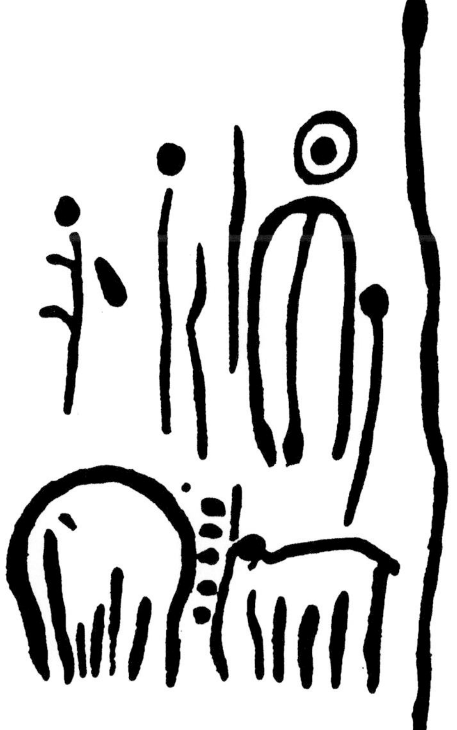

Fig. 29
Proto-figurative style of Early Hunters. Chifubwe Stream, Solwezi, Zambia. This group of deep engravings is nearly 2 meters in height. In the lower part there are two schematic figures representing (totemic?) quadrupeds (elephants?). Between them there is a vertical row of five dots. Above, there are several vertical lines of various types, dots, the 'arbolet' (male) ideogram, the ideogram dot-and-line and what is considered to be an 'intercourse' sign with a cup-and-ring (female) sign above it. Source: Drawn after a photograph of B. Woodhouse, in E. Anati, 1989, p. 94. (WARA Archive W00193)
Area code: D-III. Cat.: A-I.

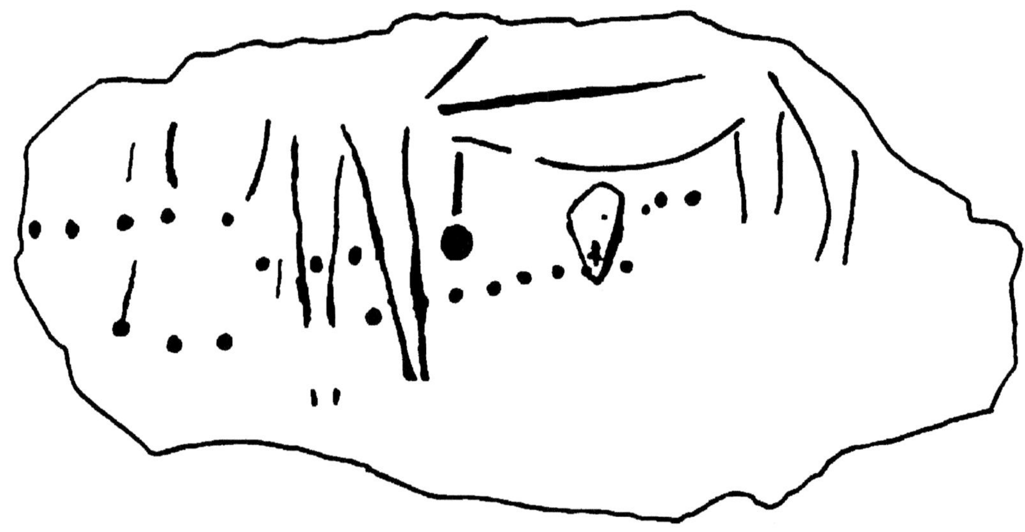

Fig. 30
A stone block with engravings displaying the 'Archaic Syntax'. La Ferrassie, Dordogne,France. A schematic quadruped outline is surrounded by ideograms. A vulvar sign occupies a central position. Rows of dots, lines and groups of lines and the ideogram dot-and line are present.
Source: E. Anati, 1989, p. 96. (WARA Archive W00188)
Area code: E-I. Cat.: A-II.

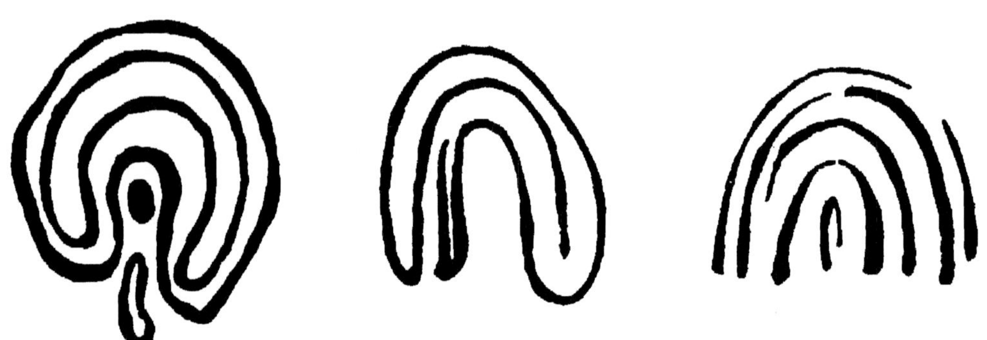

Fig. 31
Stylization in Early Hunters' art. Province of Santa Cruz, Argentina. Deep engravings of what is being defined as stylized vulvar signs. The first one shows some anatomic details. The two others are just schemes.
Source: J. Schobinger & C. Gradin, 1985 p. 36
Area: Code: G-III. Cat.€A-II

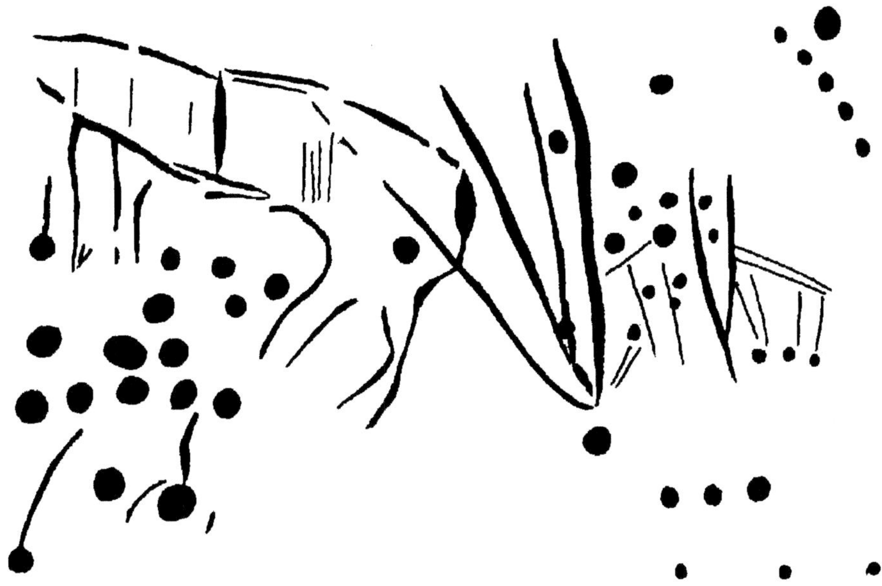

Fig. 32
A rock-shelter surface with engravings displaying the 'Archaic Syntax', Murray river, Australia. A schematic quadruped outline is surrounded by ideograms. What appears to be a vulvar sign (and probably another one) occupies a central position. Rows of dots, lines and groups of lines and the ideogram dot-and-line are present. Source: Drawn from a photograph in E. Anati, 1989, p. 96. (WARA Archive W00189) Area code: H-I. Cat.: A-II

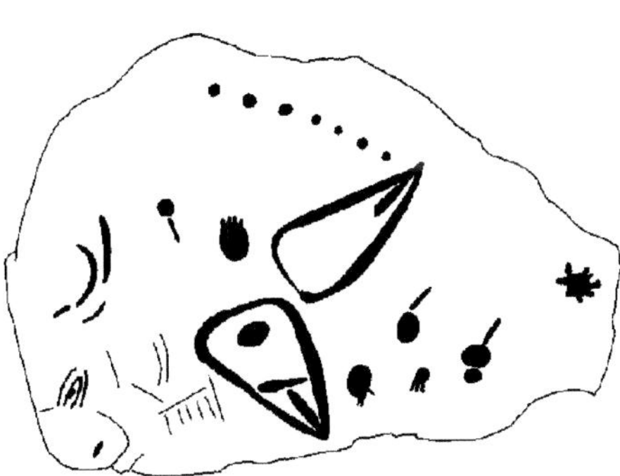

Fig. 33
Choice of natural shapes by Early Hunters. La Ferrassie, Dordogne, France. A stone block having a natural shape reminiscent of a bison's body has been completed by engravings of the horns and the eye (see left). On its surface two vulvar ideograms and cup marks have been added ('Archaic syntax'). Female (vulvar) signs associated to animal figures are widespread in the archaic syntax. The animal image indicates the totemic identity of the female signs. Source: drawn by E. Anati, 1989, p. 93. (WARA Archive W00182) Area code: E-I. Cat.: A-II.

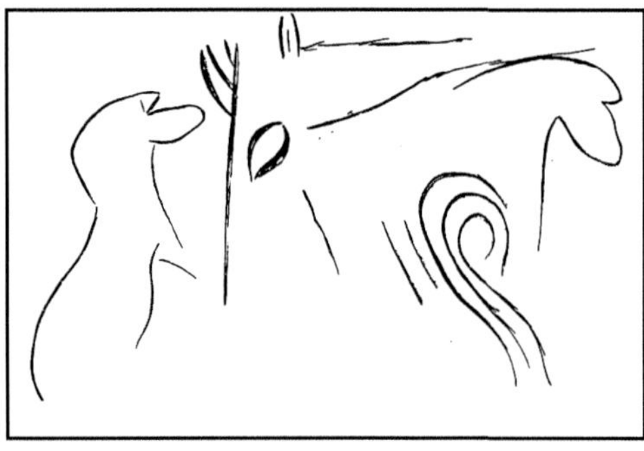

Fig. 34
Altamira cave, Santander, Spain. Wall engraving of the Archaic type Archaic Hunters. Two animal figures, one vertical and the other horizontal, are associated to two repetitive type ideograms with the value of a male, the branch, and a female, the eyeshaped sign. Under one of the animals there is a group of sinuous lines. Over the two pictures the union of two ideograms can be found, one a male (the arrow), the other a female (the lips). Source: relief by H. Breuil, 1912. (WARA Archive W00194).
Area Code: E-I. Cat: A-II.

Grammar Analysis	Syntax Analysis
Pictograms: two animal figures (horses). one vertical, the other horizontal.	Vertical animal with male ideogram.
Ideograms: two male signs (branch and arrow)	Horizontal animal with female ideogram.
Ideograms: two female signs (lips and eye)	Union of a female ideogram (lips) and a male one (arrow).
Psychogram: sinuous lines bundle.	Psychogram made of sinuous lines, exclamation or omen.

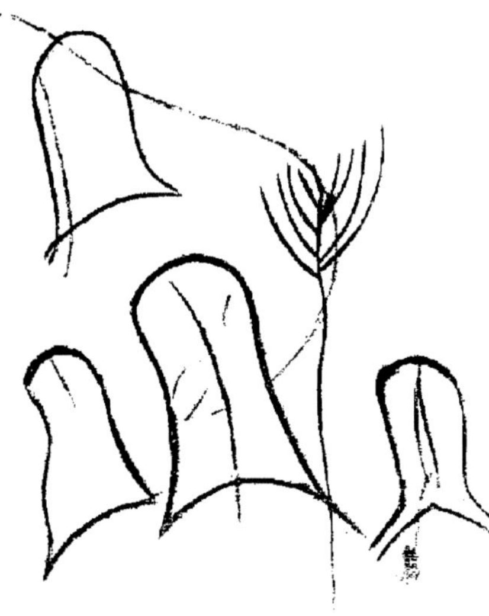

Fig. 35
Castillo Cave, Spain. The painting is an accumulation of three phases maintaining an Archaic Syntax. Four shapes that have originally been defined as 'scutiforms' are likely to be vulvar symbols. They have been painted in red. In their middle, in black, a male symbol named 'bâtonnet' has been added. Upon these figures the schematic silhouette of a quadruped has been added, with a pink line. Each phase has added content. This painting is located on a protrusion of the rock surface which has the natural shape of a mammoth. Stalagmitic formations resemble the trunk and the front legs of the mammoth. The story of this painting starts from the natural shape that have stimulated the human mind. The vulvar signs are related to the mammoth which is likely to be a reference to the totemic animal related to the four female symbols. The male signs is adding an explicit message to the previous depictions. Finally, the addition of the quadruped may be the signature of a newcomer diverting the message to another totem. Tracing by H. Breuil in E. Anati, 1989, p. 198 (WARA Archive W07148) Area Code: E-I

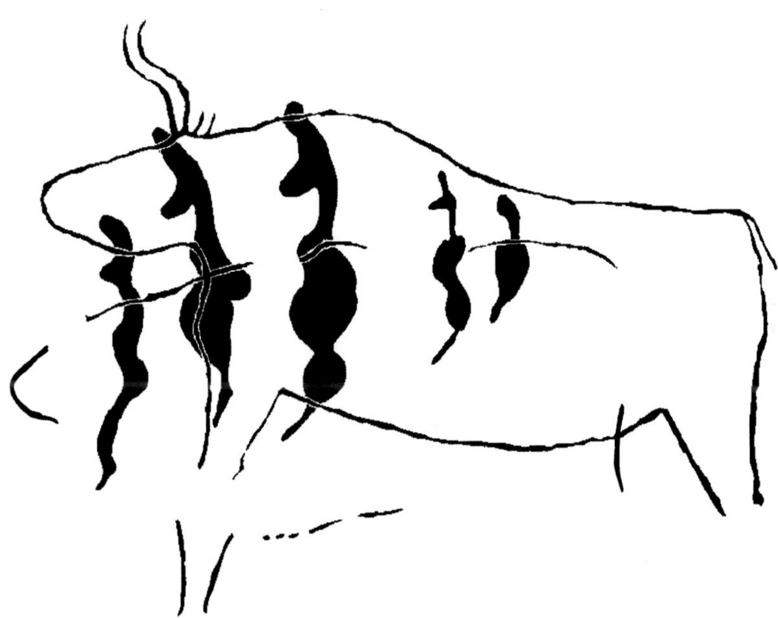

Fig. 36
Ovelapping of two different styles of 'hunters-gatherers' in Gobustan, Azerbaijan. Subject matter concerns anthropomorphic images in the early phase and zoomorphic images in the later.
Source: E. Anati 2001, p. 43. (WARA Archive W05814)
Area Code: E–III. Cat: A-III; B-I.

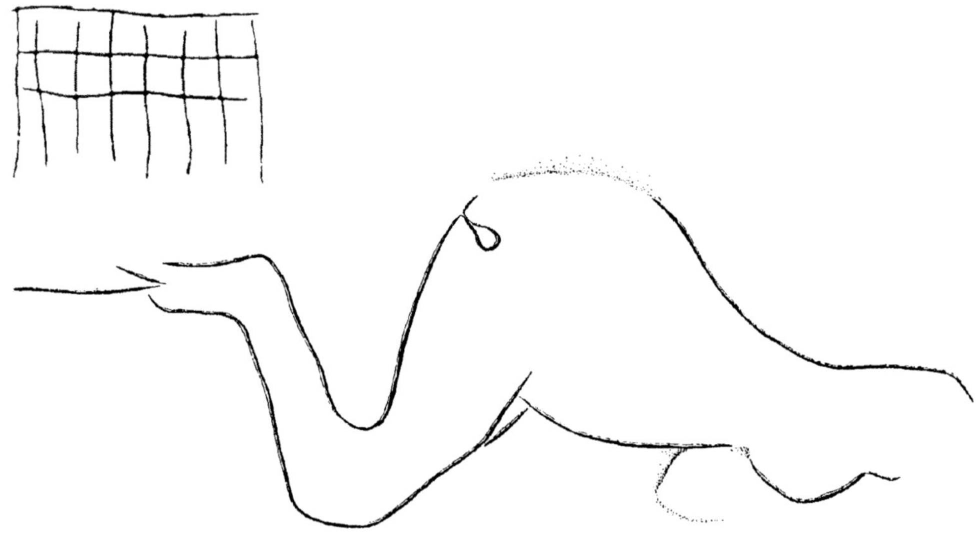

Fig. 37
Gabillou, Sourzac, Dordogne, France. Female figure with the indication of the vulva opening. An arrow shaped ideogram reaches her foot. Over there is a psychogram made of a rectangle and vertical signs.
Source: J, Gaussen, 1964 relief, in E. Anati, 1995, p. 104. (WARA Archive W06797)
Area Code: E-I. Cat: A-III.

Pictograms	Ideograms	Psychogram

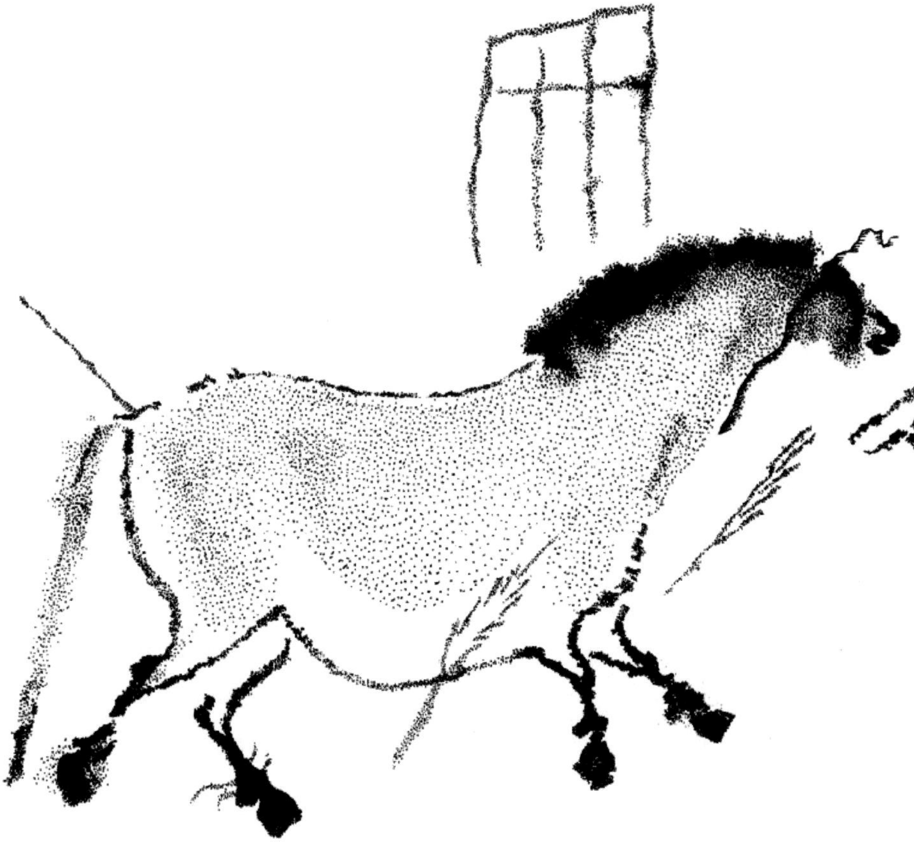

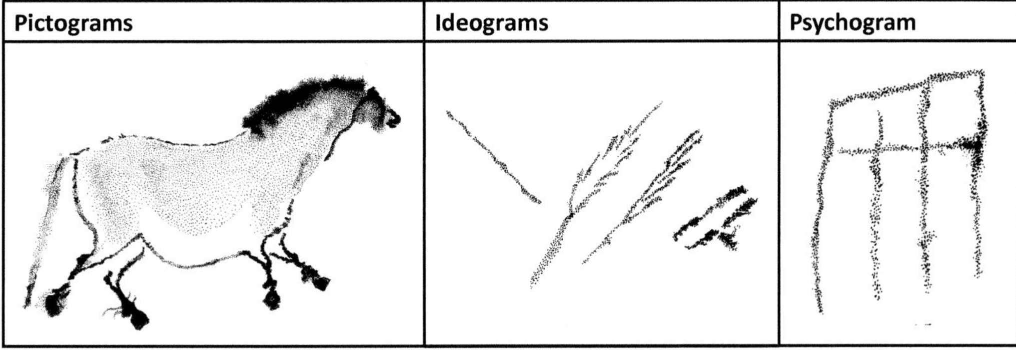

Fig. 38
Lascaux Cave, France. Horse painted with black outline and ochre-coloured base painting. This pictogram comes with yellow 'bâtonnet' ideograms and black 'lips'. Over the pictogram there is a brown-red psychogram made of a rectangle and vertical signs.
Source: CCSP relief, in E. Anati, 2000. (WARA Archive W01115).
Area Code: E-I. Cat: A-III.

Pictograms	Ideograms	Psychogram

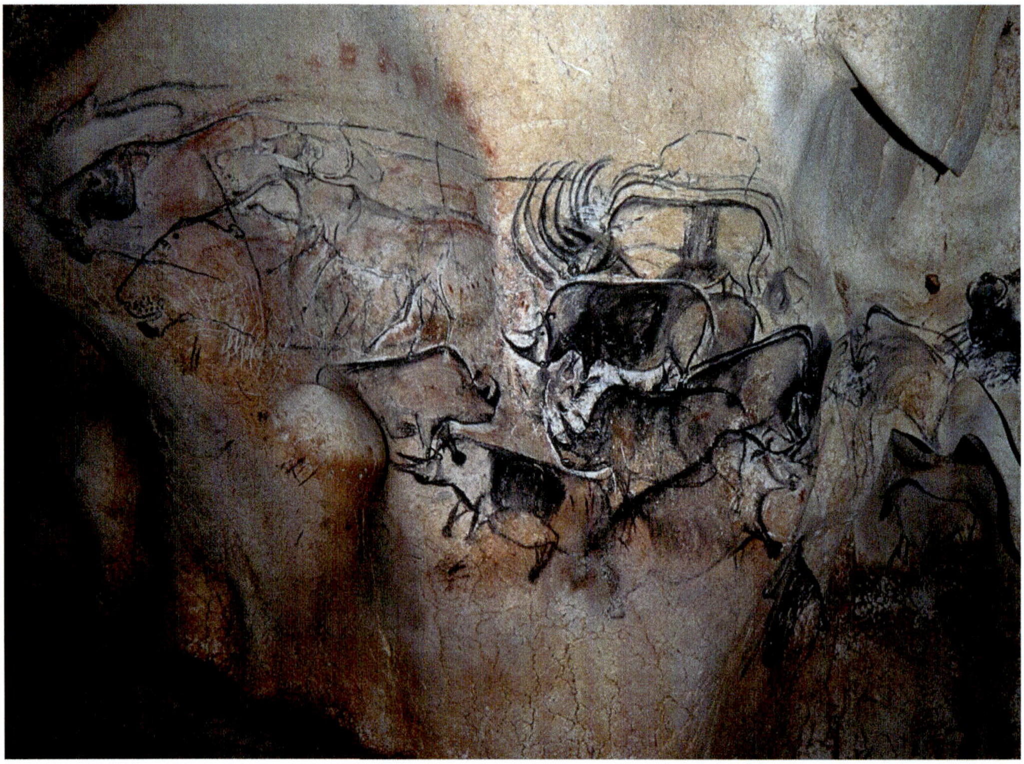

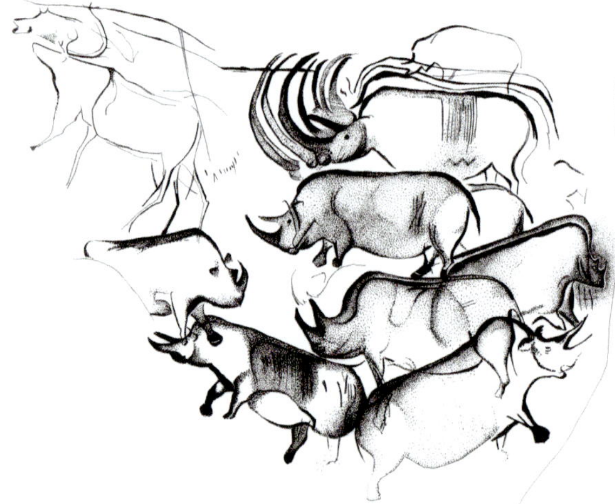

Fig. 39 a - b
Chauvet Cave, Ardèche, France. The 'Classical' style in its early phases displays an 'Archaic Syntax' of repetition and accumulation of images. Tracing by CCSP (WARA Archive W02466) from a photo of the French Ministry of Culture and communication, in E. Anati (ed) 2000. (WARA Archive W05293)
Area Code: E-I. Cat: A II-III.

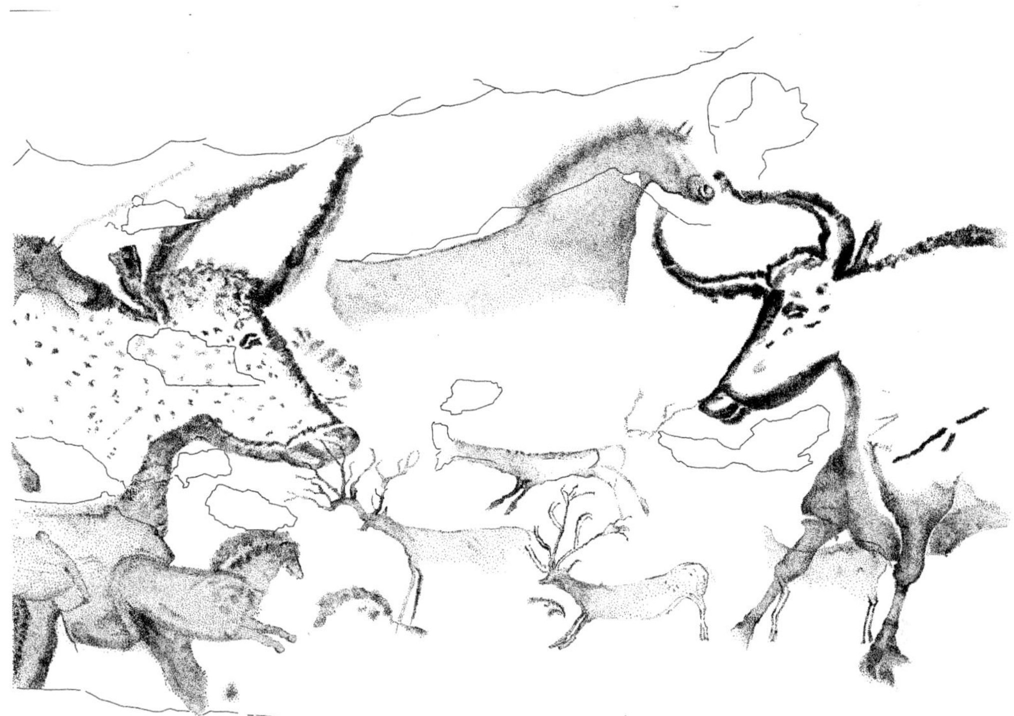

Fig. 40
Lascaux Cave, Dordogne, France. The classical syntax displays a conceptual dialogue between the figures.
Tracing by CCSP (WARA Archive W07419)
Area Code: E-I. Cat: A-III.

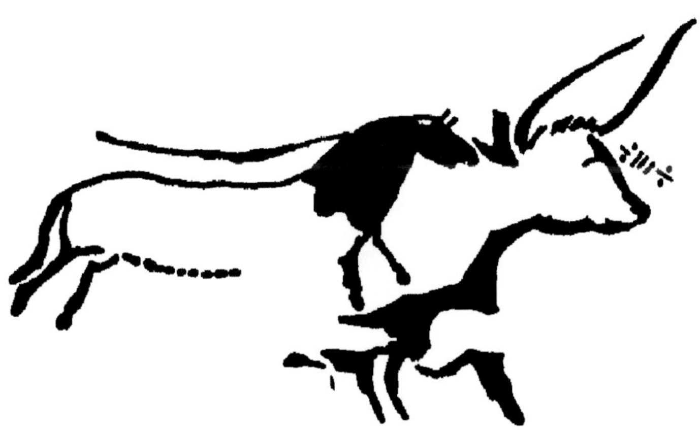

Fig. 41
Lower. Lascaux Cave, Dordogne, France. Classical Syntax, association of ox and horse accompanied by a
sequence of ideograms. The dominant figure is that of the ox and its size is much bigger than that of the
horse. Source: Tracing by A. Leroi-Gourhan, 1965. (WARA Archive W07171)
Area Code: E-I

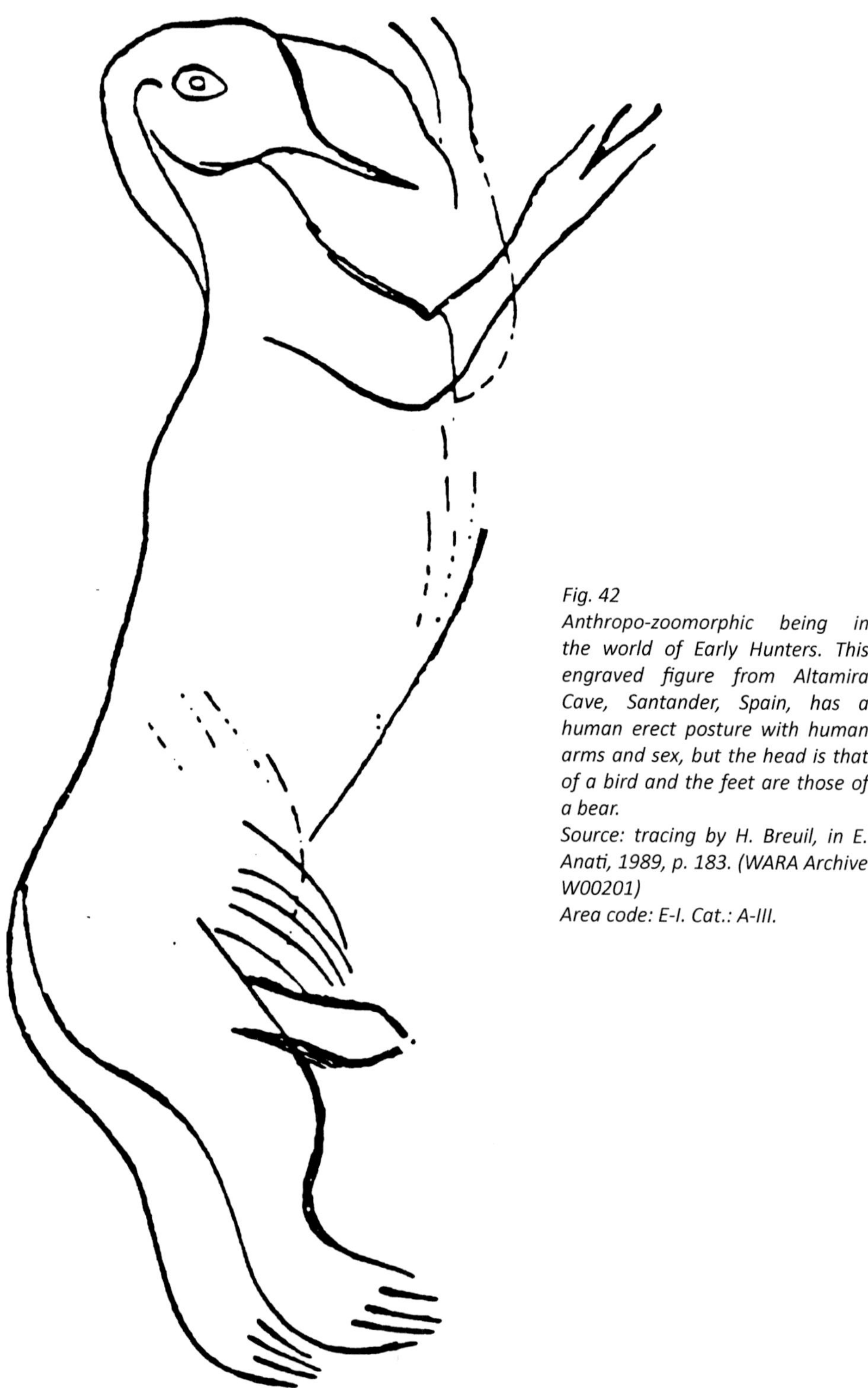

Fig. 42
Anthropo-zoomorphic being in the world of Early Hunters. This engraved figure from Altamira Cave, Santander, Spain, has a human erect posture with human arms and sex, but the head is that of a bird and the feet are those of a bear.
Source: tracing by H. Breuil, in E. Anati, 1989, p. 183. (WARA Archive W00201)
Area code: E-I. Cat.: A-III.

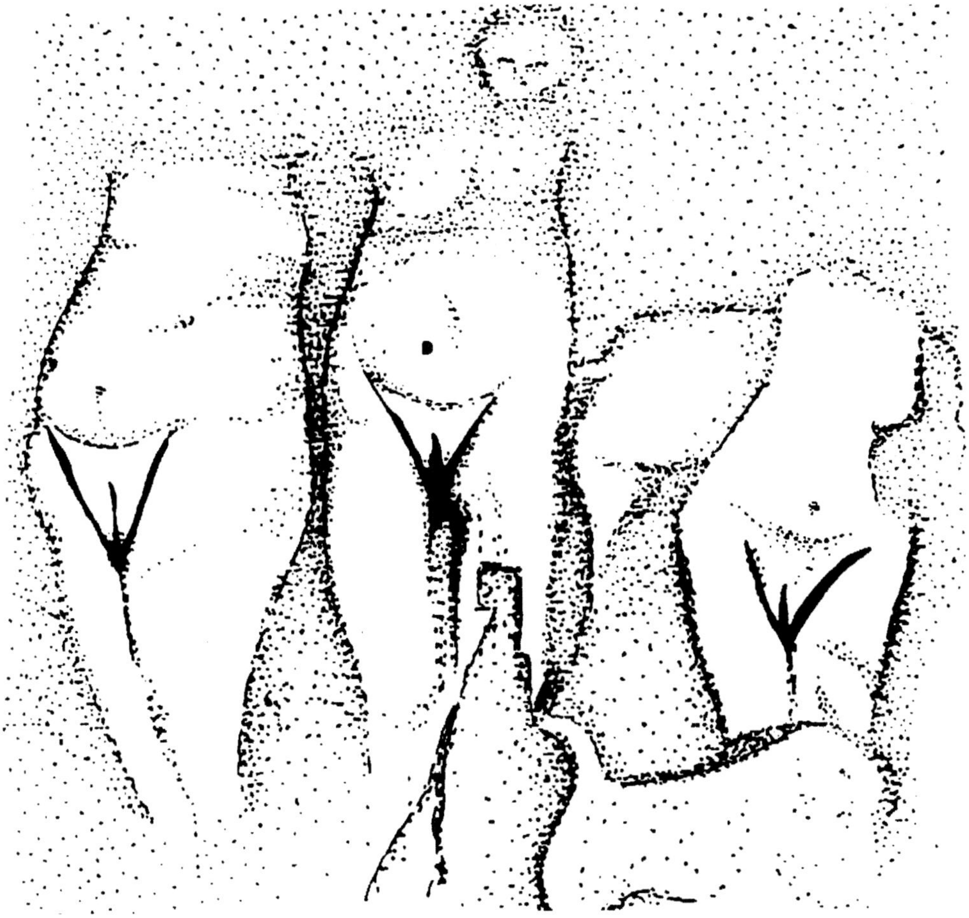

Fig. 43
Animal metaphors. Early Hunters high-reliefs. Angles-sur-Anglin, Vienne, France. The feminine body to the right is connected with two bisons, one below and one on top. The overlapping appears to be intentional and is likely to have a metaphoric meaning. (An evolved example of 'Archaic Syntax').
Source: E. Anati, 1989, p. 51. (WARA Archive W00190)
Area code: E-I. Cat.: A-II.

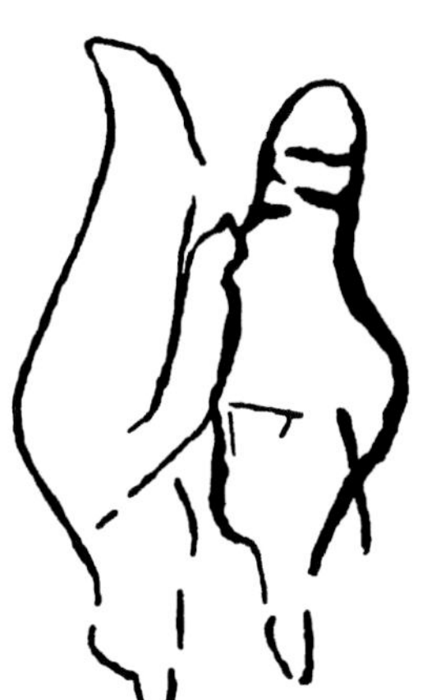

Fig. 44
The figurative syntax of Early Hunters. Rock engravings of Totes Gebirge, Austria. A couple of anthropomorphic figures is reduced to schemes, where the ideograms are indicative: the exaggerated penis for the male and the pubic triangle for the female. Heads and limbs are disregarded. The 'bâtonnet' on the back of the female is likely to express the action or the relationship the artist intended to express. It appears as a sort of verb in a visual sentence, like 'to do' or 'to penetrate'.
Source: E. Anati, 1982, p. 148.
Area Code: E-I. Cat.: A-II.

Fig. 45
Metaphoric associations of Early Hunters. El Pindal cave, Spain. This red painted panel shows the association of elephant and horse. The dominant animal is the elephant. On the body of the elephant there is a large red spot. By the left side two rows of five lines, one is straight, the other is undulated.
Source: Tracing by H. Breuil, in H. Alcalde del Rio, et al., 1912, p. 61. (WARA Archive W00195)
Area code: E-I. Cat.: A-III.

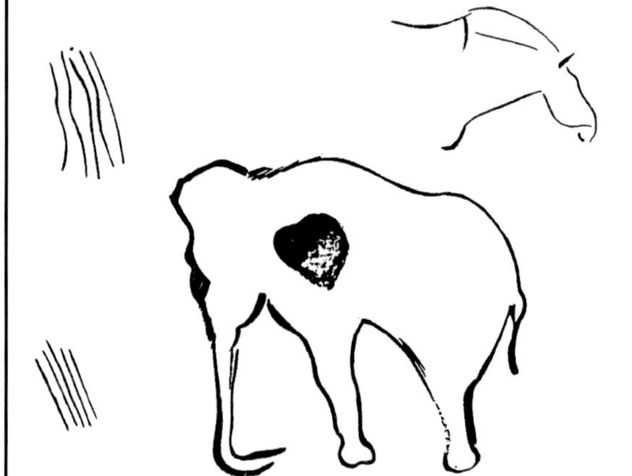

Fig. 46
Metaphoric associations of Early Hunters (schematic tracing). Mongoni Wa Kolo, Tanzania. A giraffe and an elephant, in outlined red paint, are facing each other. A paddle-like ideogram is below the face of the elephant and two rows of dots are on its body. Between the giraffe and the elephant there is a snake-like ideogram.
Source: E. Anati, 1989, p. 192. (WARA Archive W00196)
Area code: D-II. Cat.: A-III.

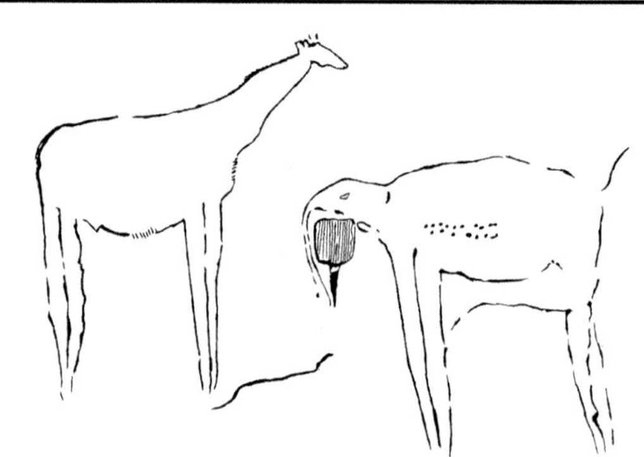

Fig. 47
Rock paintings of Early Hunters. Kiesese, Tanzania (schematic tracing). A large elephant (3.50 meters long) and three giraffes. The elephant is the dominant figure and has been repainted at least twice, both before and after the giraffes.
Source: E. Anati, 1989, p. 194. (WARA Archive W00197)
Area code: D-II. Cat.: A-III.

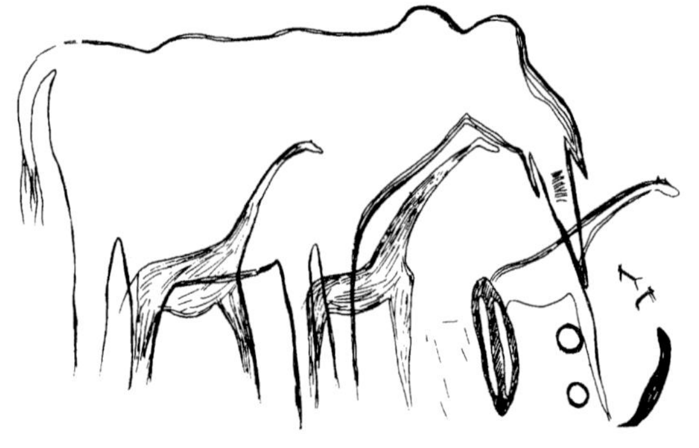

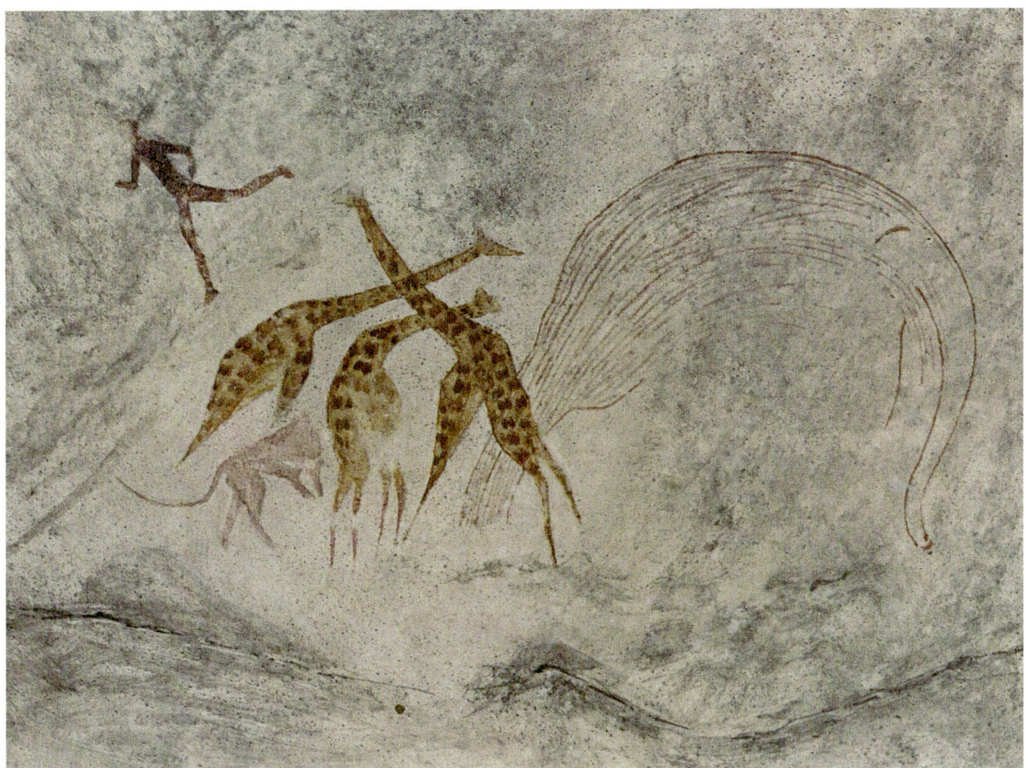

Fig. 48
Accumulation of rock paintings from different periods. Tassili, Algeria. Three phases are recognized. A stylized elephant drawn with thin lines appears to be the oldest detectable depiction. Three giraffes have been added later and re-painted at least twice. The feline has been painted between the giraffes and an anthropomorphic being above them. Between the second and third phase the concept of the composition and the significance have been changed. The association of the elephant-giraffe reflects a metaphoric mentality of Early Hunters while the two figures added later by an Evolved Hunter makes it a realistic scene in which the feline is attacking the giraffes.
Source:Drawn by J. Tchudi; in E. Anati 1989, p. 195. (WARA Archive W00198)
Area Code: C-II. Cat.: A-III; C-I.

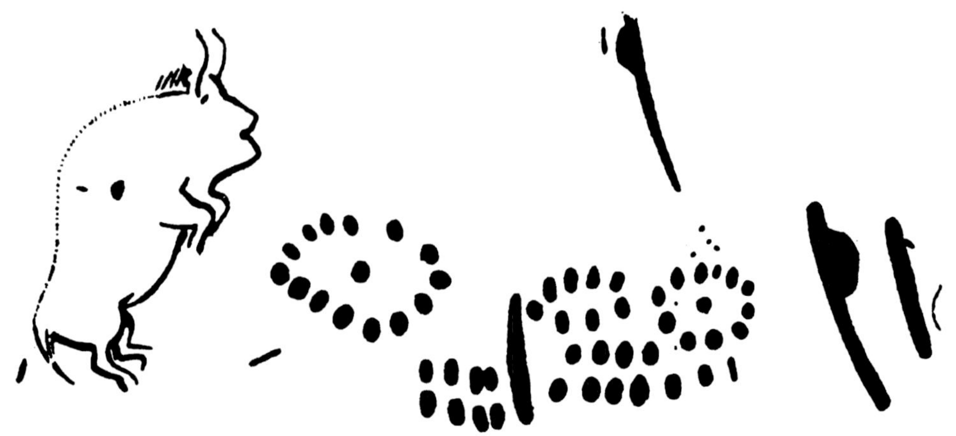

Fig. 49
A Bison and its ideograms. Niaux, Ariège, France. Dots, lines and tools painted in brown and red follow an intentional sequence.
Source:M. Raphael, 1945, p. 88. (WARA Archive W00202)
Area Code: E-I. CAT.: A-III.

Pictogram	Ideograms		
vertical bison with a dot on his body	intentional sequence of point	vertical line between two assemblage of points	tools having a handle and a blade

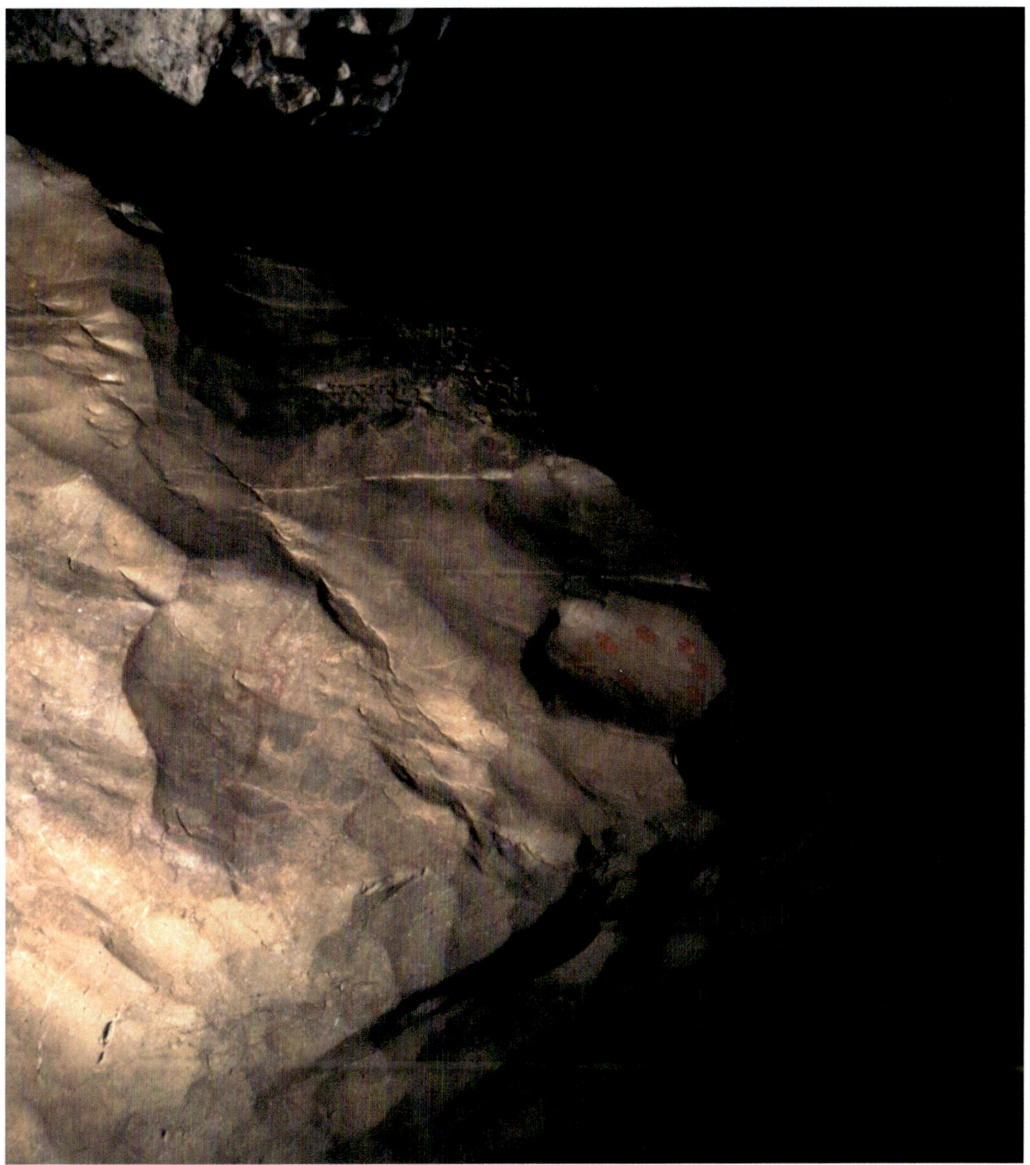

Fig. 50
Niaux Cave, France. The natural shapes of the rock are completed by red paint to form a standing bison. See previous tracing.
Source: EA98LXXVIII01; Photo by E. Anati (WARA Archive W00203).
Area Code: E-I. Cat.: A II-III.

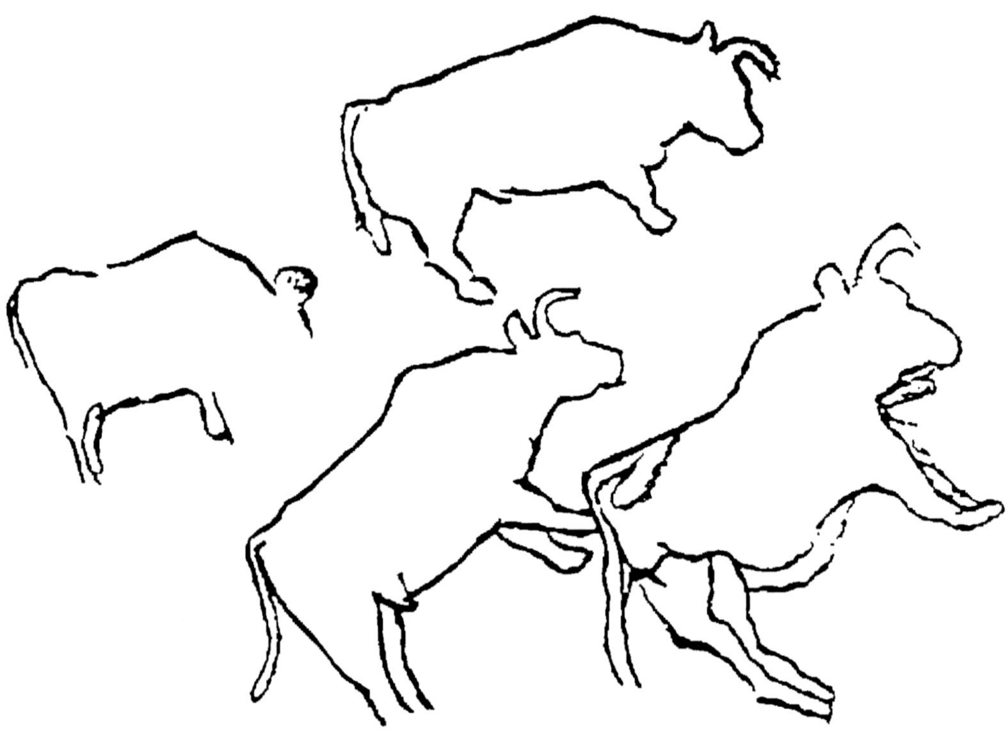

Fig. 51
Open air rock engravings of Early Hunters. Kom Ombo, Egypt. The four bovines are engraved in a levitating posture, apparently without concern for a 'ground level'.
Source: Tracing by P.E.L. Smith in E. Anati, 1989, p. 178 (WARA Archive W00225)
Area Code: C-IV. Cat.: A-V

Fig. 52
Deeply engraved bovines from Gobustan. Two of the animals have a line separating the head from the rest of the body. This has been interpreted as lasso-catching which may imply some sort of early attempt at domestication. The figures are between m. 1 and 0.80 in length. The style is that of final Archaic Hunters. The anthropomorphic figure centered on one of the bovines is a later engraving, but may be an international addition.
Source: I.M. Diafrarsade, 1973, rock 30. (WARA Archive W00226)
Area Code: E-III. Cat.: A-V

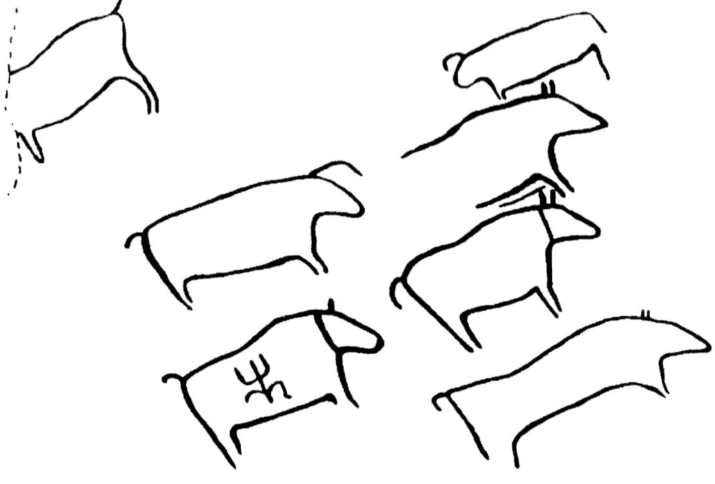

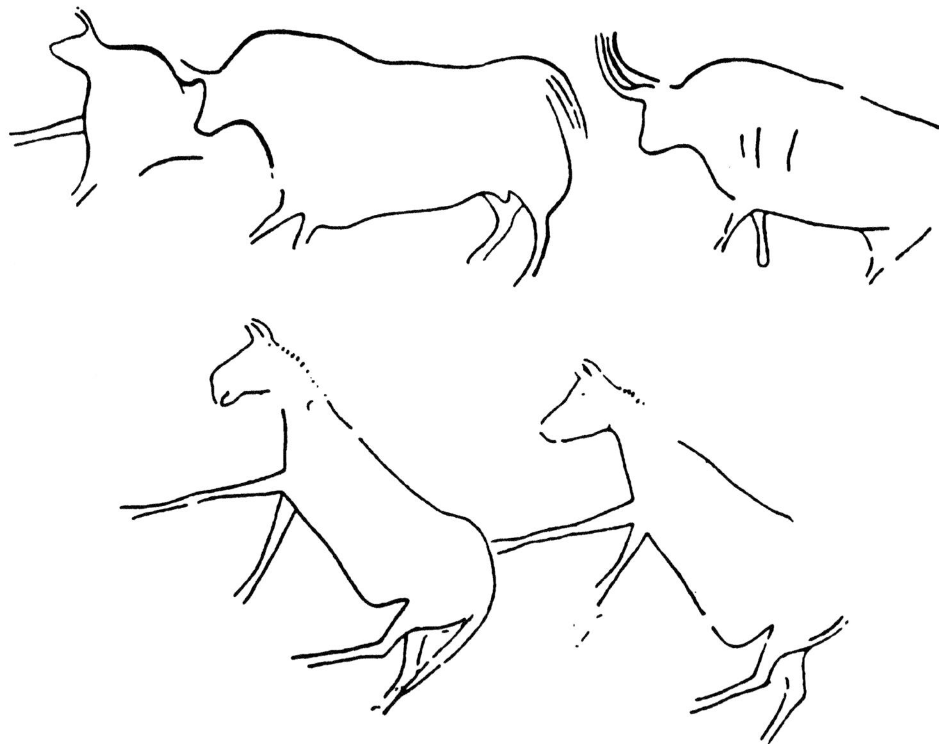

Fig. 53
Association of animal species in the art of Early Hunters. Monte Pellegrino, Sicily, Italy. Bovines and horses.
Source: Tracing by J. Bovio Marconi, 1955, p. 60. (WARA Archive W00199)
Area code: E-I. Cat.: A-III.

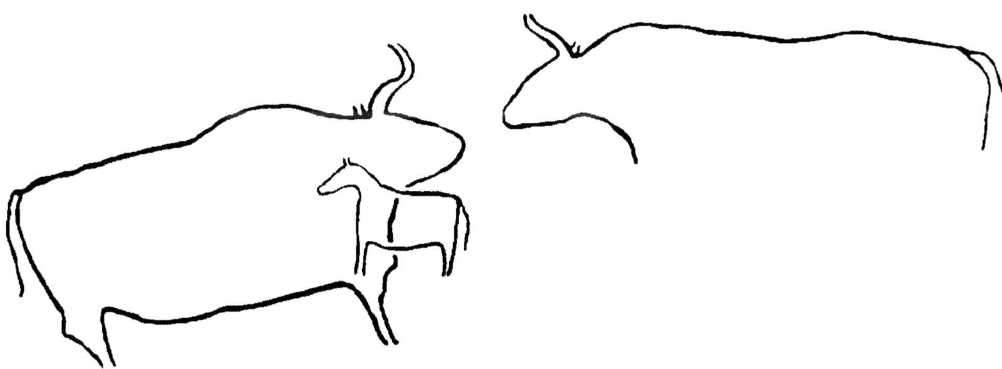

Fig. 54
Buyukdash, Gobustan. Azerbaijan Rock n 39. Early Hunters accumulation of figures. Two large bovines, deeply engraved, are facing each other. A small equine is superimposed above one of the animals. The bovine on the right measures more than 2m in length.
Source: Redrawn after I.M. Djafarsade, (WARA Archive W00223)
Area Code: E-III. Cat: A-III.

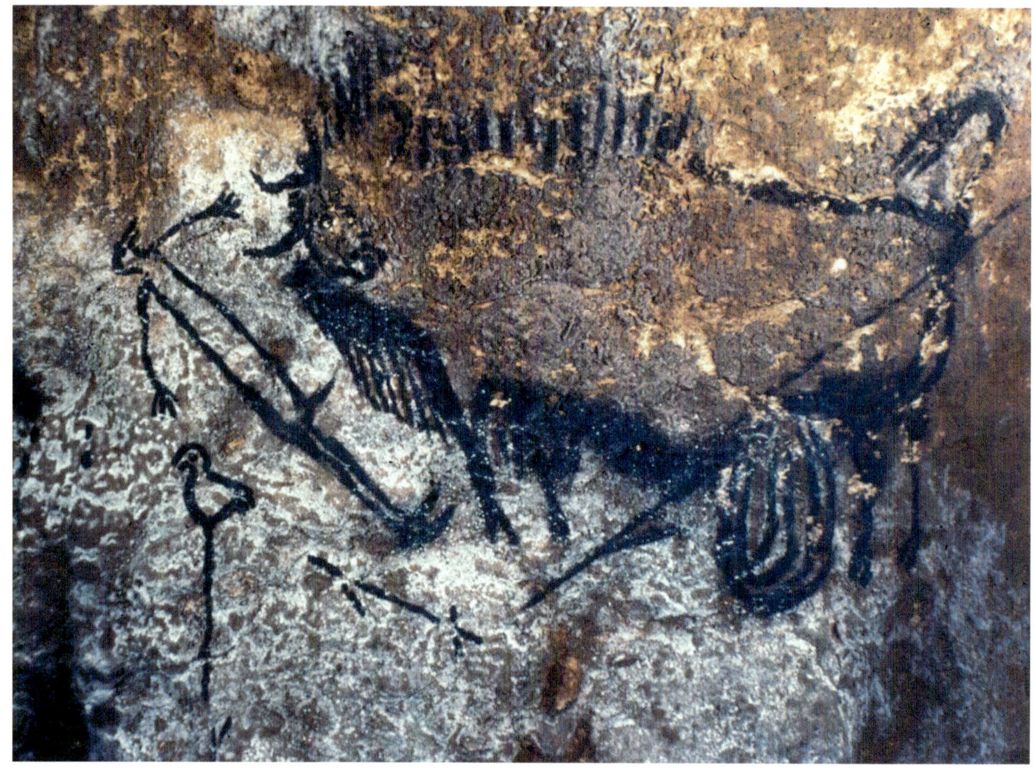

Fig. 55
The composite conception of an evolved phase of Early Hunters. Detail of a 'Classic' composition from Lascaux, Dordogne, France. A bison is charging an ithiphallic bird-man. Both pictograms are accompanied by ideograms: Near the bird-man there is a bird-standard and on top of the bison there is a spear. Below both pictograms there is another ideogram, a 'bâtonnet' which is likely to indicate the type of relationship between the two pictograms or the type of action which is taking place. This association of five graphemes illustrates the syntactic system used and the metaphoric concepts of its maker. A provocative hypothesis considers that it represents a story, an event or a myth, in which an aggressive ms. 'Bison-Spear' is facing mr. Birdman.
Source: A. Leroi-Gourhan, 1981, pl. 93. (WARA Archive W01910)
Area code: E-I. Cat.: A-III.

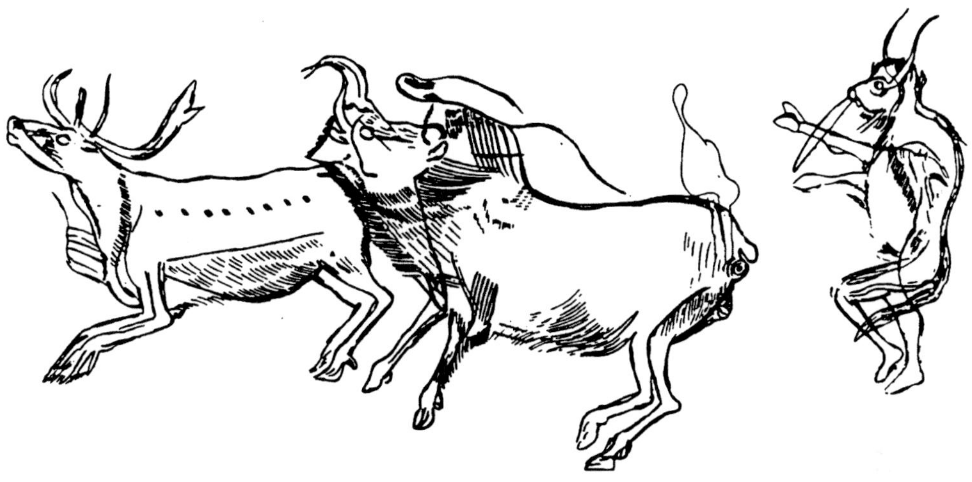

Fig. 56
Metaphors in a sequence of Classic Early Hunters. Caverne du Volp, Ariège, France. A masked, or anthropo-
zoomorphic figure is playing the musical bow. At the center of the tracing, a zoomorphic figure appears to be
a combination of deer and bison. Like the first figure, this one appears to have a double or mixed identity. A
raindeer is drawn to the left with a series of dots on its body. There are ideograms in various spots and the
thin outline of a female on the back of the central zoomorphic figure. The Classic syntax has a deep conceptual
content. Myths and stories await to be decoded.
Source: H. Breuil & H. Begouen, 1958, Fig. 63 (WARA Archive W00200)
Area code: E-I. Cat.: A-III.

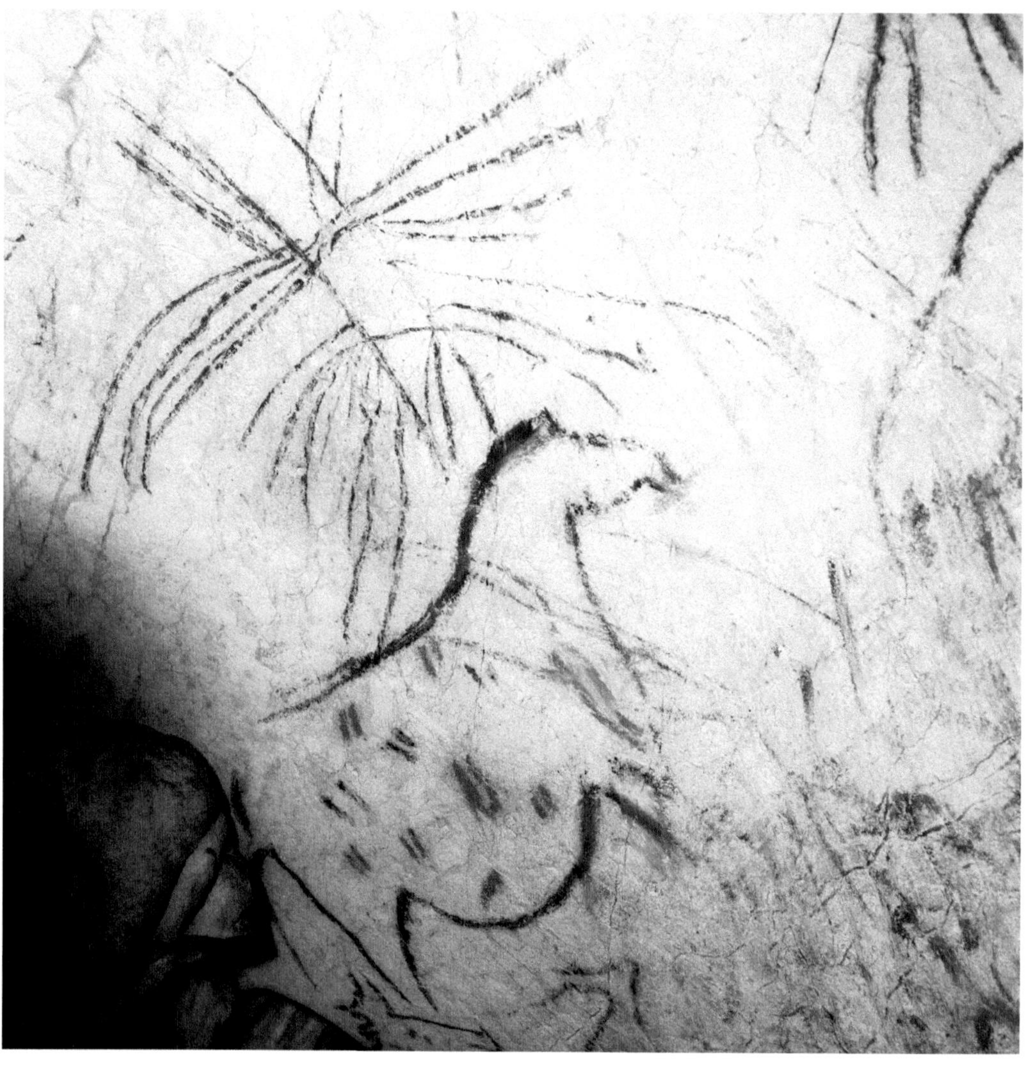

Fig. 57
Pictograms, ideograms and psychogram. La Pilena, Spain. This dark brown painting shows a horse (pictogram).
On its body an ideogram is repeated ten times. Made of two parallel lines, it is defined as 'lips' and has
the significance of 'female'. These ideograms have been made at different times with different shades of
the colour red, brown and black. Nevertheless, the ideogram is always the same. Above the horse there is a
psychogram: a rectangle emanating lines. It may have been added by a different hand. A relatively simple
painting seems to hide a long and complex story.
Source: E. Anati, 1989, p.167
Area code: E-I. Cat.: A-III

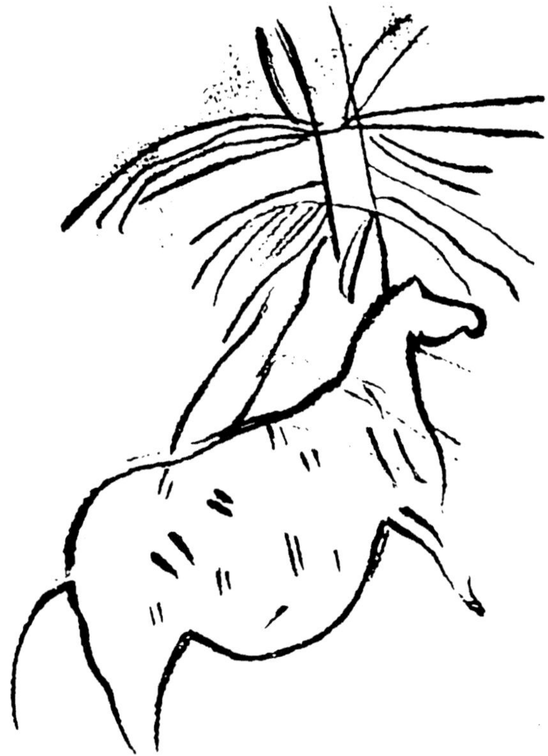

Fig. 58
Prehistoric art elementary grammar. Pictograms, ideograms and a psychogram from La Pileta, Spain. Painting referred to the art of Archaic Hunters, classic syntax. The pictogram is a brown horse, on his body an ideogram made of two parallel lines is repeated ten times. Over the horse a black psychogram appears: it is a rectangle radiating outward. What is the message behind this composition? An elementary reading would suggest: 'Pleasure or satisfaction (the psychogram) for the horse clan or totemic moity, who has provided 10 females'. Source: Tracing H. Breuil, 1915. (WARA Archive W00206)
Area Code: E-I. Cat: A-I.

Pictograms	Ideograms	Psychogram
Horse	Two parallel lines definited 'lips' are repeat 10 times	Rectangle that emanates energy rays

Fig. 59
Addaura cave, Sicily, Italy. Transition phase from archaic hunters to evolved hunters. In the upper part of the panel, a group of masked people in dancing posture surround two exhibiting, or in any case getting attention, figures. It is considered the most ancient 'scene' of European rock art. The main characters are men. It overlaps three previous phases with animal figures and signs, but where no scene is recognized.
Source: Anati, E. 1993, p. 103 (WARA Archive W00232)
Area Code: E-I. Cat: A.III; A-IV; C-I.

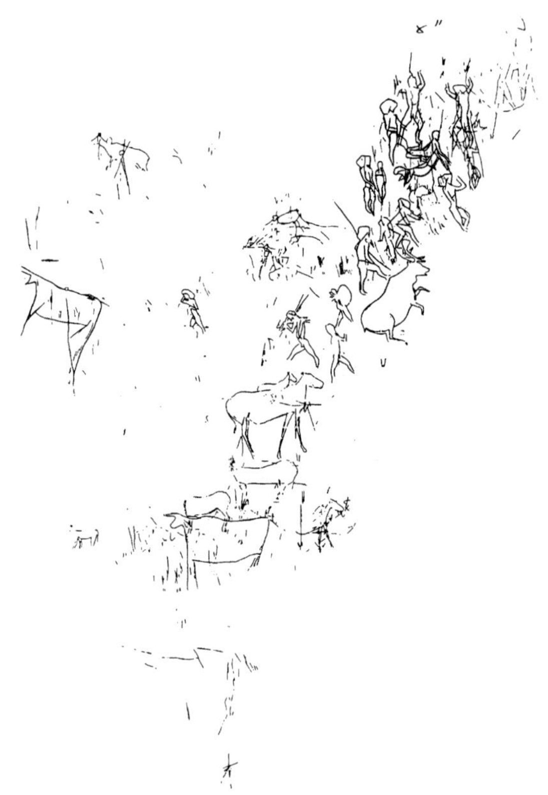

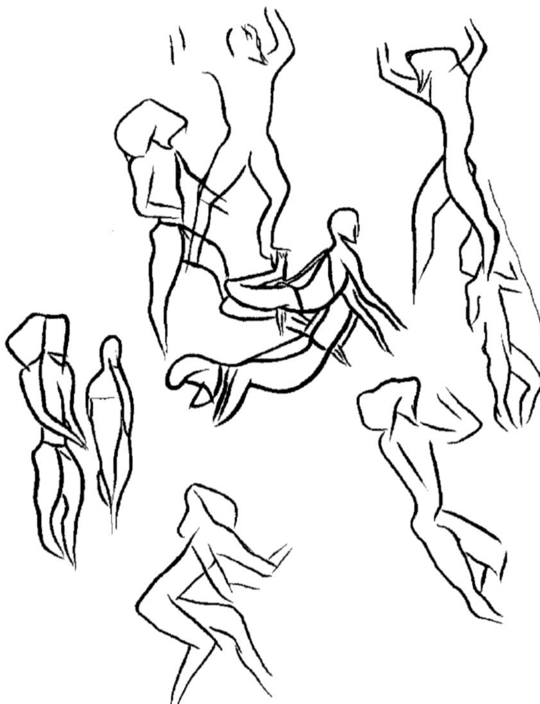

Fig. 60
Addaura cave, Sicily, Italy. Detail of the scene of masked people in dancing postures. Detail of picture 59. They make a circle around two people exhibiting or exhibited. This scene does not show the usual Early Hunters' syntax. Several hypothesis have been proposed about its dating and some researchers consider it Palaeolithic. Its syntax relates to Evolved Hunters and it is likely to be Early Neolithic.
Source: Anati, E. 1993, p. 102 (WARA Archive W00231)
Area Code: E-I. Cat: C-I.

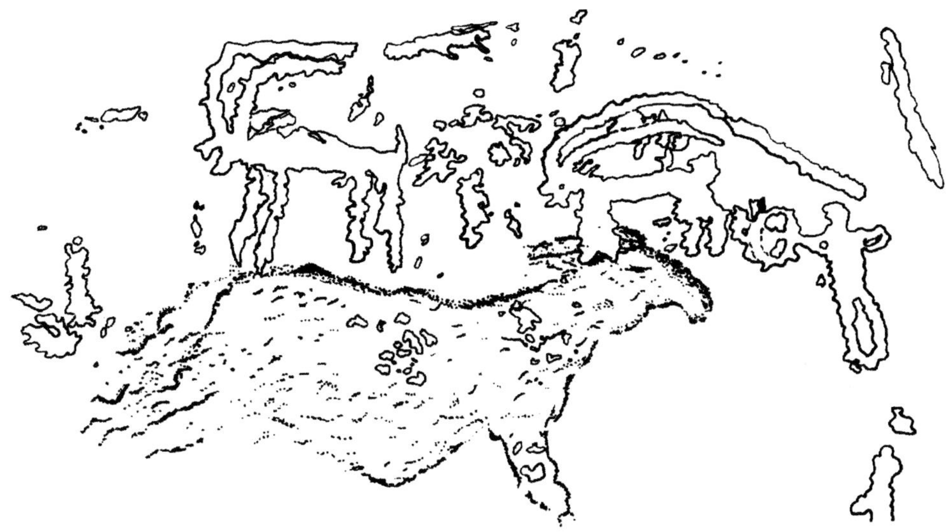

B. Final Early Hunters

Fig. 61
Rock engravings at Har Karkom, Negev desert, Israel. The tracing shows the figure of an animal typical of Early Hunters, on which hunting scene of Evolved Hunters is overlapped.
Source: E. Anati, 1993, p. 62 (WARA Archive W05984)
Area Code: B-III. Cat: A-IV; C-III.

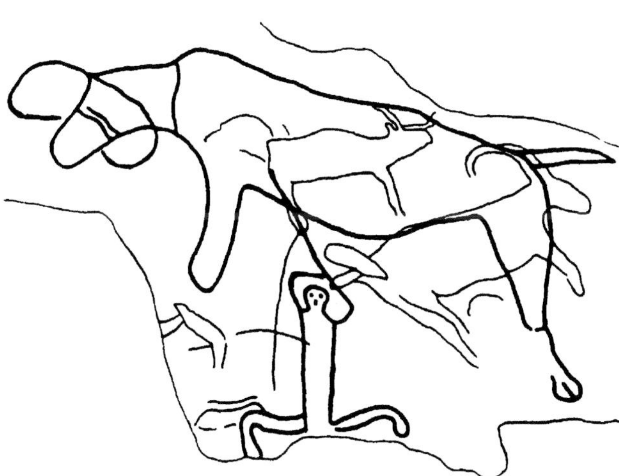

Fig. 62
From association to scene; Kilwa, Saudi Arabia. Two phases of engravings are recognized on this surface. The earlier phase represents the association of animals and signs engraved with fine incision. One of the animals appears to be caught by a leg trap. The later phase, thicker engravings, represents a scene (of hunting?). An anthropomorphic figure and a large bovine, over 2m long. Final phase of the Early Hunters period.
Source: E. Anati, 1979, p. 30. (WARA Archive W00229)
Area code: B-III. Cat.: A-III, A-IV.

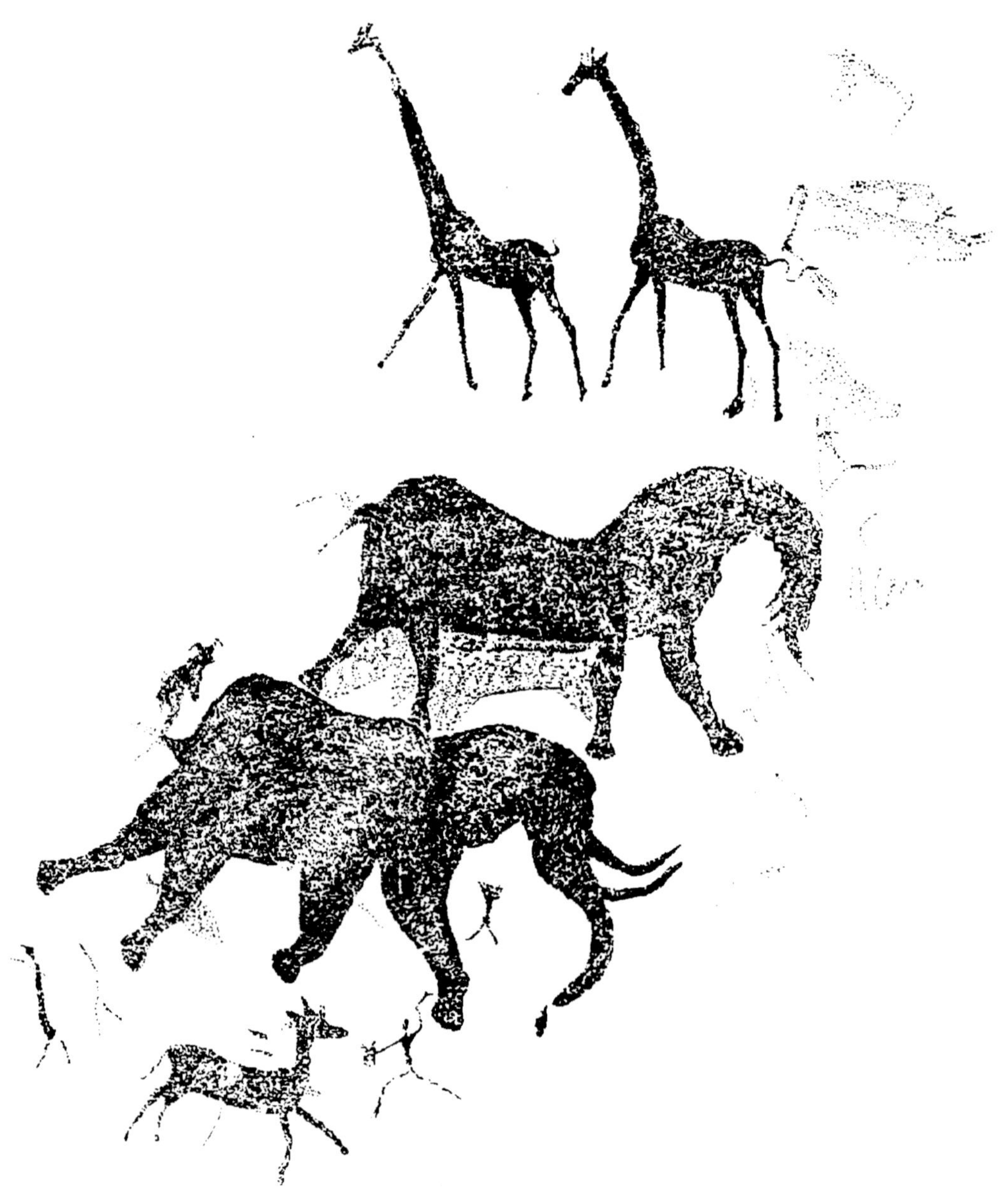

Fig. 63
Elephants go to the right and giraffes go to the left so they must meet. Final 'Early Hunters', Marandellas, Zimbabwe.
Source: Drawn from a photograph of L. Frobenius, 1962, pl. 67.(WARA Archive W00222)
Area Code: D-IV. Cat.: A-V

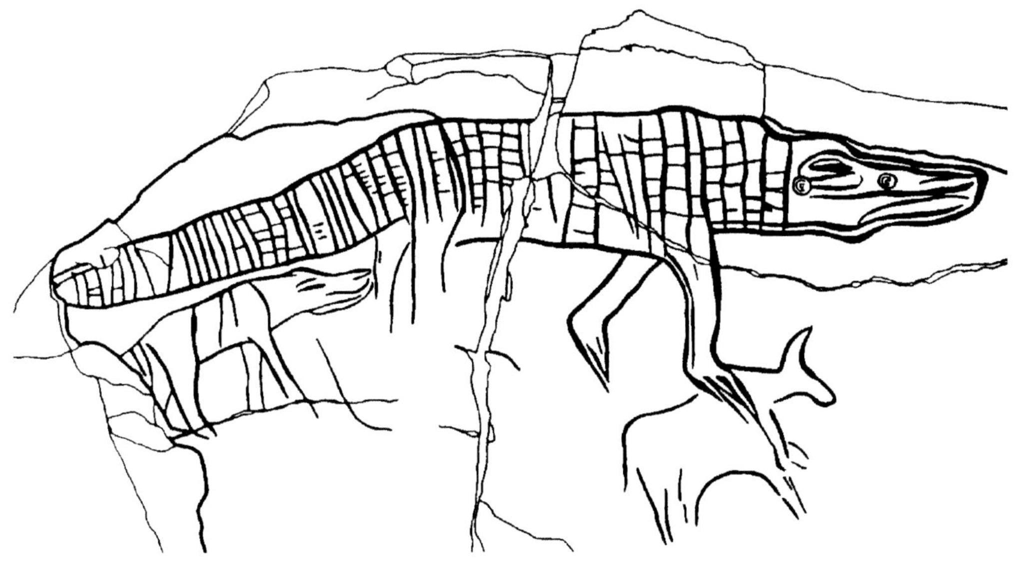

Fig. 64
Crocodiles in the middle of the desert? Rock engravings from Wadi Mathendush, Fezzan, Libya. Climate must have been quite different in the Sahara when these figures were engraved. The main crocodile is 2.50 meters long.
Source: Drawn from a photograph in K. Striedter, 1984, p. 72. (WARA Archive W00220)
Area code: C-II. Cat.: A-IV.

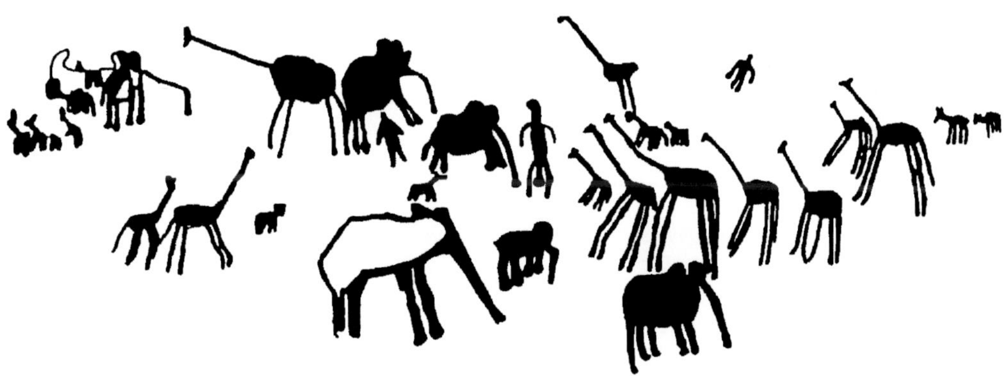

Fig. 65
Elephants go to right and giraffes go to left, so they must meet. Humans are observing but not hunting. Final 'Early Hunters'. Wadi el Arab, Nubia, Egypt.
Source: Drawn from W.F.E. Resch, 1967, p. 61/a. (WARA Archive W00221)
Area code: C-IV. Cat.: A-IV.

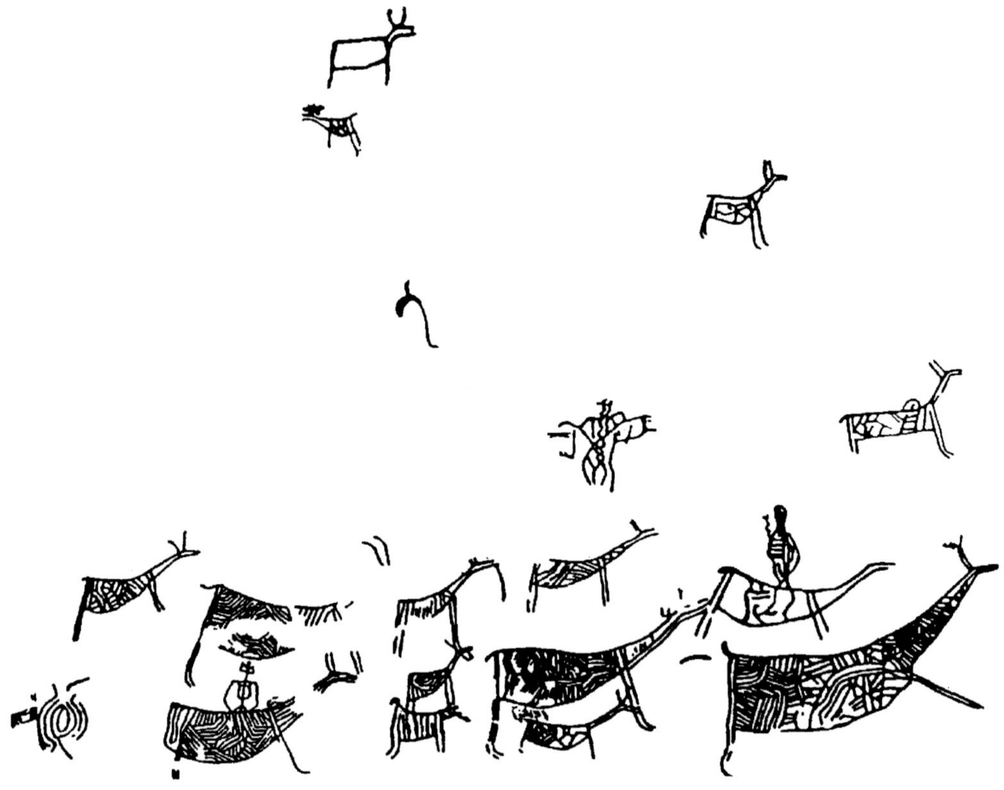

Fig. 66
Final 'Early Hunters' art may describe not just external shapes but also the content of the internal structure. Some of the animals and humans of this large-size rock engraving, nearly 5 meters long, from Vingen, Norway, display what was believed to be a structural or schematic representation of their anatomy, in a style which is referred to as 'X-ray style'.
Source: Tracing by E. Bakka, 1973. (WARA Archive W00230)
Area code: E-II. Cat.: A-IV

Fig. 67
The animal metaphor. Rock engravings of Luine, Valcamonica, Italy. The association of animals, in 'Final Early Hunters' groups often appear to have a metaphoric significance. The animal figure, in many cases, seems to represent the item, person or power that responds to the name or qualifications of the animal. In this panel two animals are associated, one is an elk, the smaller one is a wild caprine.
Source: E. Anati, 1976, p. 59. (WARA Archive W00224)
Area Code: E-I. Cat.: A-IV.

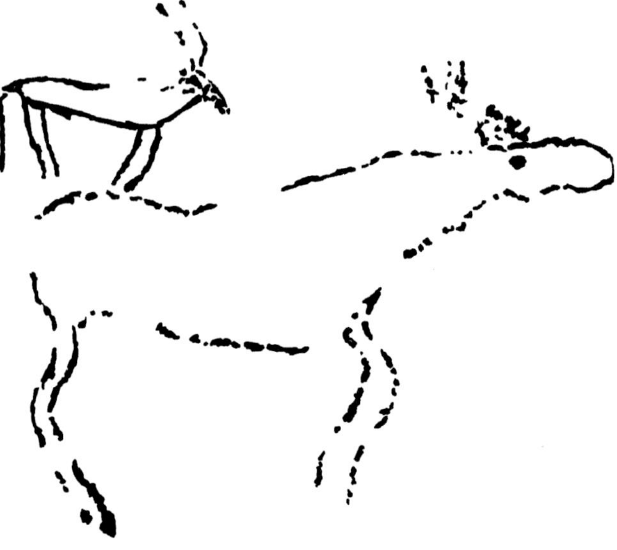

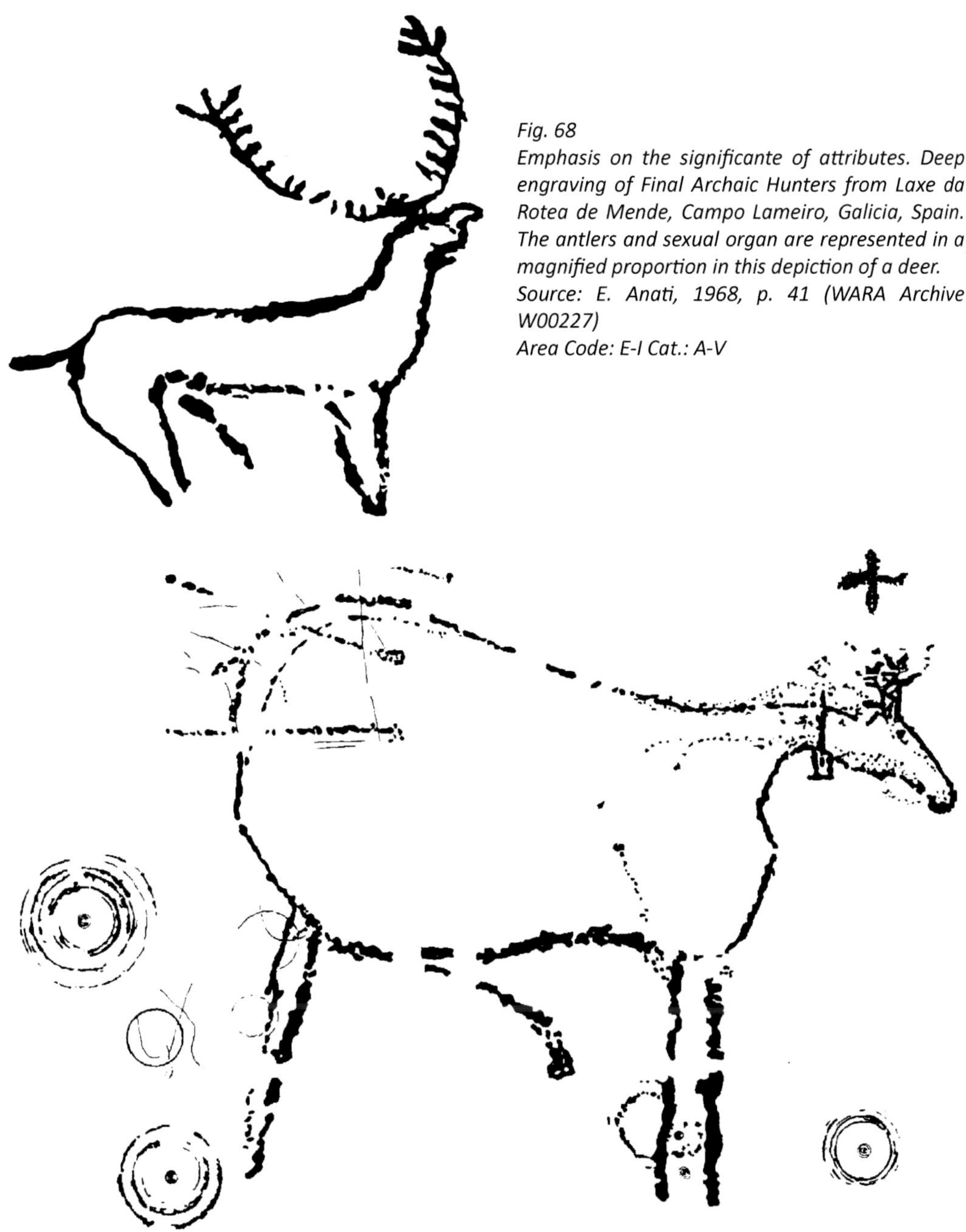

Fig. 68
Emphasis on the significante of attributes. Deep engraving of Final Archaic Hunters from Laxe da Rotea de Mende, Campo Lameiro, Galicia, Spain. The antlers and sexual organ are represented in a magnified proportion in this depiction of a deer.
Source: E. Anati, 1968, p. 41 (WARA Archive W00227)
Area Code: E-I Cat.: A-V

Fig. 69
Accumulation of ideograms. Rock engravings, Luine, Valcamonica, Italy. A large cervide with a magnified sexual organ, is wounded by several arrows. In the Epi-Paleolithic period the animal had been re-engraved twice, changing the shape of the muzzle and the back. The collar is made by a different pecking and is a later addition. It is likely to indicate a wish to posses the animal. Also, the concentric circles appear to be later additions. Their conceptual relation to the main figure is not clear. The cross above the head of the animal is made with a metal point and is likely to be a sign of 'Christinisation' of the panel.
Source: E. Anati, 1976, p.56 (WARA Archive W00228) Area code: E-I Cat.: A-V

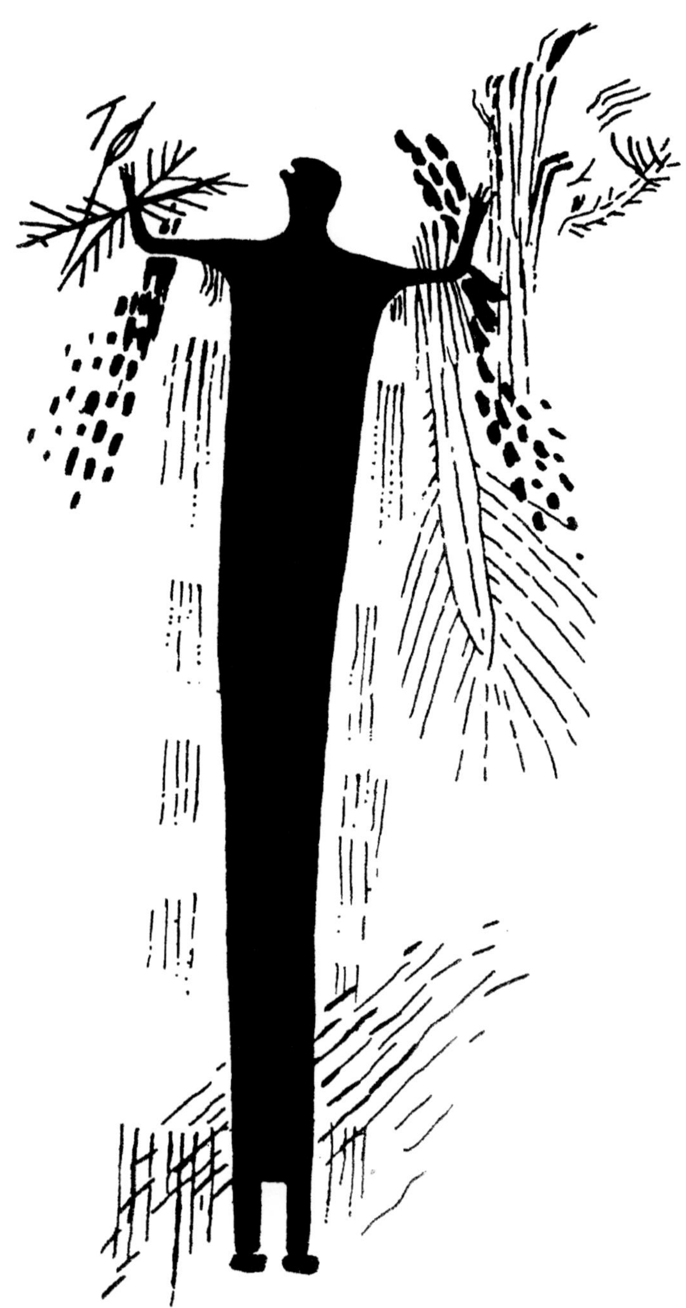

C. Gatherers

Fig. 70
Panther Cave, Seminole Cayon, Texas, USA. Rock painting of Food Gatherers. Anthropomorphic figure over 2 m high, having a mask or a zoomorphic face indicating his totem. The arms are branches which produce fruits and emanate energy rays. In the art of Gatherers, ideograms, pictograms and psychograms often appear in a syncretic composition.
Source: tracing by Wellman, in E. Anati, 1995. (WARA Archive W07173)
Area Code: F-II. Cat: B-I.

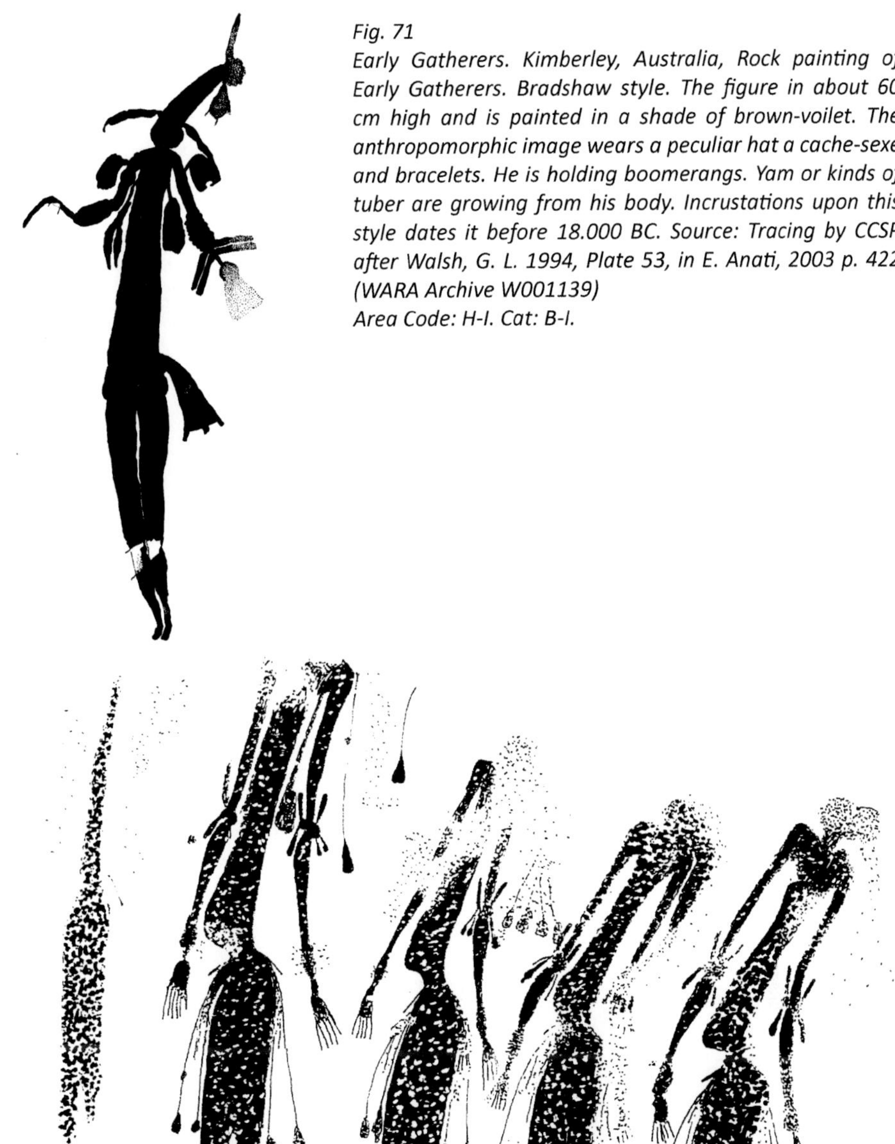

Fig. 71
Early Gatherers. Kimberley, Australia, Rock painting of Early Gatherers. Bradshaw style. The figure in about 60 cm high and is painted in a shade of brown-voilet. The anthropomorphic image wears a peculiar hat a cache-sexe and bracelets. He is holding boomerangs. Yam or kinds of tuber are growing from his body. Incrustations upon this style dates it before 18.000 BC. Source: Tracing by CCSP after Walsh, G. L. 1994, Plate 53, in E. Anati, 2003 p. 422 (WARA Archive W001139)
Area Code: H-I. Cat: B-I.

Fig. 72
Early Gatherers. Kimberly Australia. Group of elegantly dressed people from the Bradshaw style. The figure to the left is about 1 m high.
Source: Welch, D. 1993, in E. Anati, 2003 (Archivio WARA W06812)
Area Code: H-I. Cat: B-I.

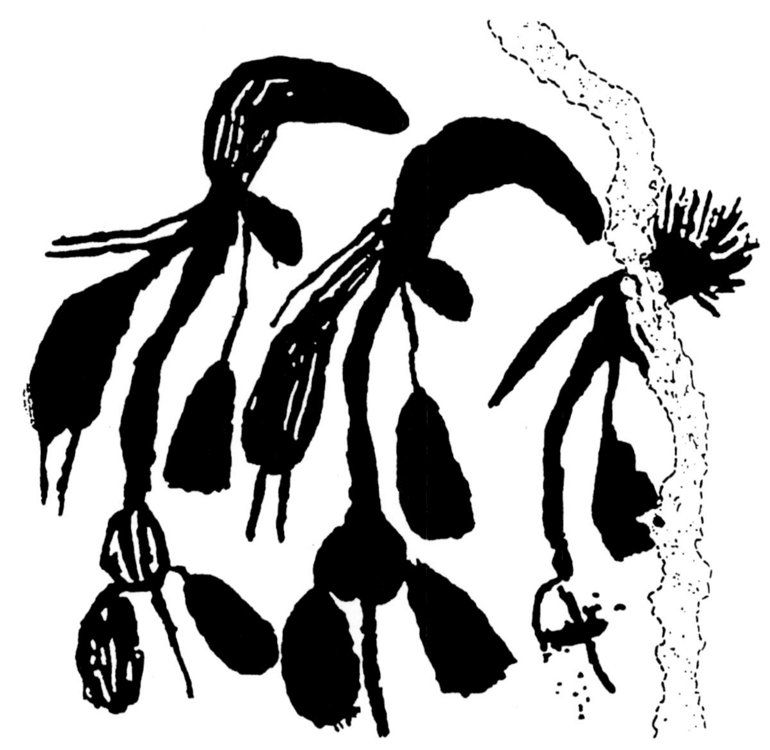

Fig. 73
Depiction of vegetalia by Food Gatherers. Rock paintings of Nabarlek, Arnhem Land, Australia. Anthropomorphized yams, with limbs and heads composed of yam tubers. The painting is in dark red while the natural colour of the yam is yellowish-brown. The colour is used for its symbolic meaning, not for reproducing 'naturalistically' the anthropomorphic yam.
Source: D. Lewis, 1988, p. 290. (WARA Archive W00215)
Area code: H-I. Cat.: B-I.

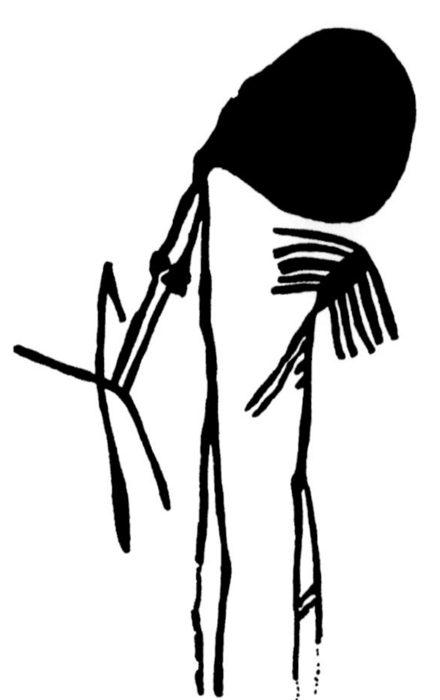

Fig. 74
Rock painting of Gatherers from Koongarra Saddle, Kakadu, Northern Territories, Australia. A couple of unlucky Mimi spirits. The male, with a big pear-shaped head, has a bad spear that cannot be used with the spear thrower (the spear thrower is not in his hands). The female with long hair has 'tied legs' (two lines between the legs), likely to mean that she is not copulating. Both of them are unable to perform their task.
Source: David Welch, 1990, p. 122, Fig. 35. (WARA Archive W00216)
Area Code: H-I. Cat.: B-I.

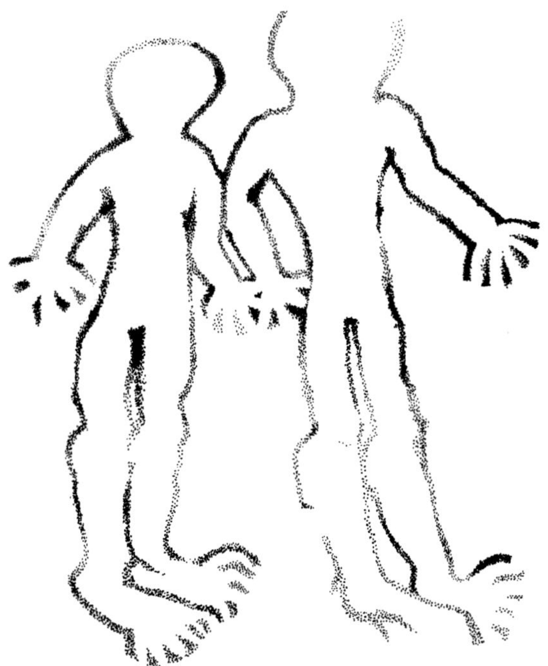

Fig. 75
Rock paintings from Tadrart Acacus, Libya.
Early Gatherers red painted outline of
anthropomorphic beings with round heads
and emphasized hands and legs.
Source: tracing by CCSP (WARA Archive
W01087)
Area Code: C-II. Cat.: B-I.

Fig. 76
Mammamet, Libya. Rock engravings of 'Flower
people'.
Source: tracing by CCSP from photo of K. Striedter.
(WARA Archive W01104)
Area Code: C-II. Cat: B-I.

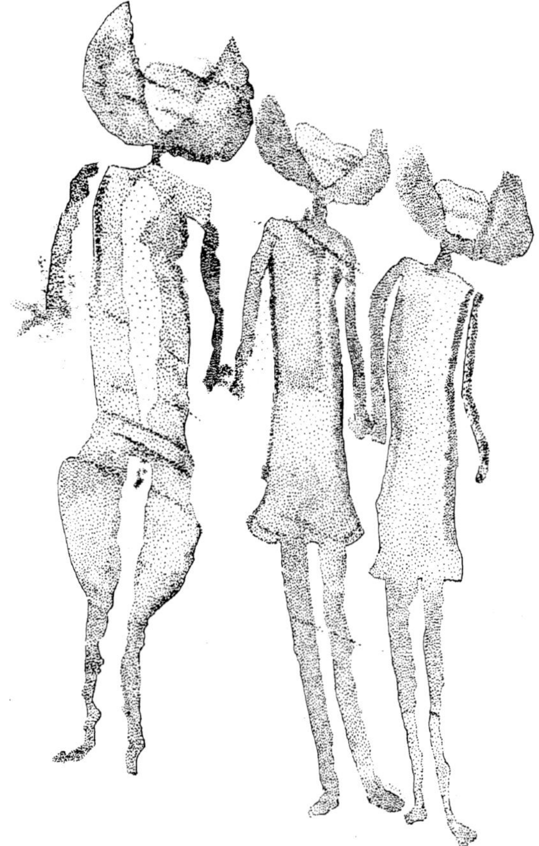

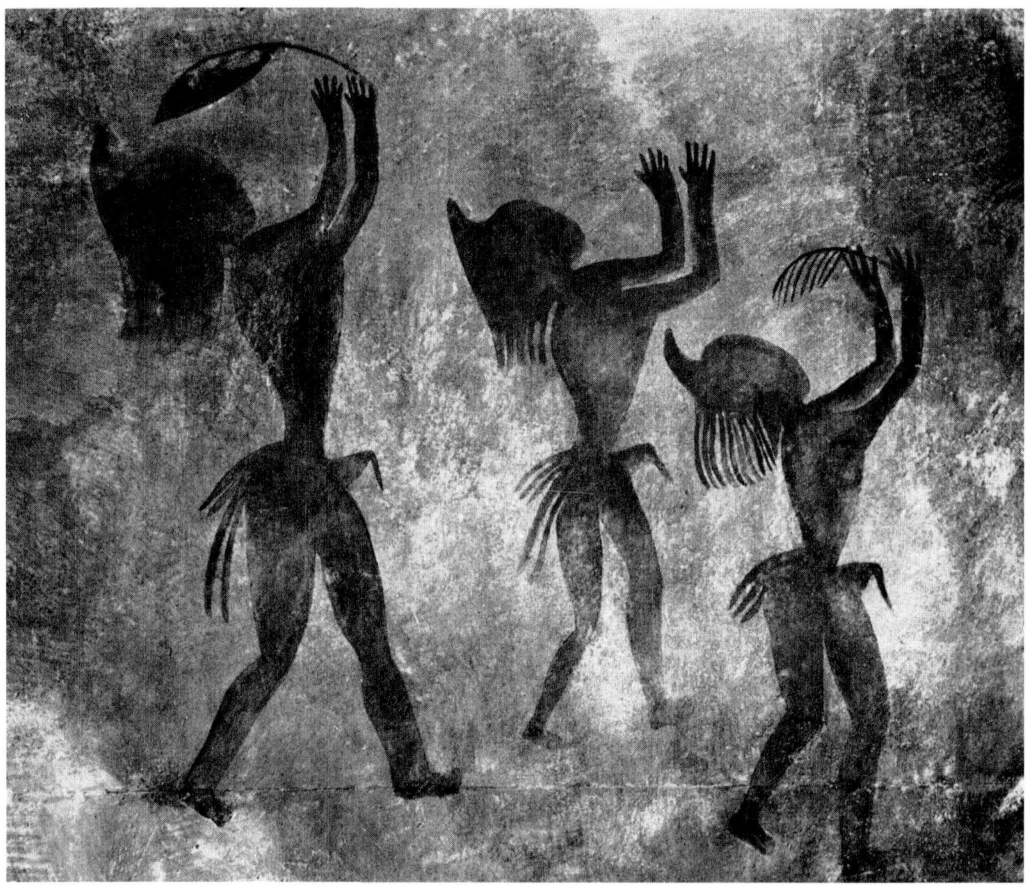

Fig. 77
Brown rock paintings from Tadrart Acacus, Libya. Later phase of Early Gatherers. A dance or worship scene.
Vegetalia are held in the hands of two of the beings.
Source: Painted reproduction supervised by F. Mori, WARA 88: XX-3. (WARA Archive W00212)
Area Code: C-II. Cat.: B-I.

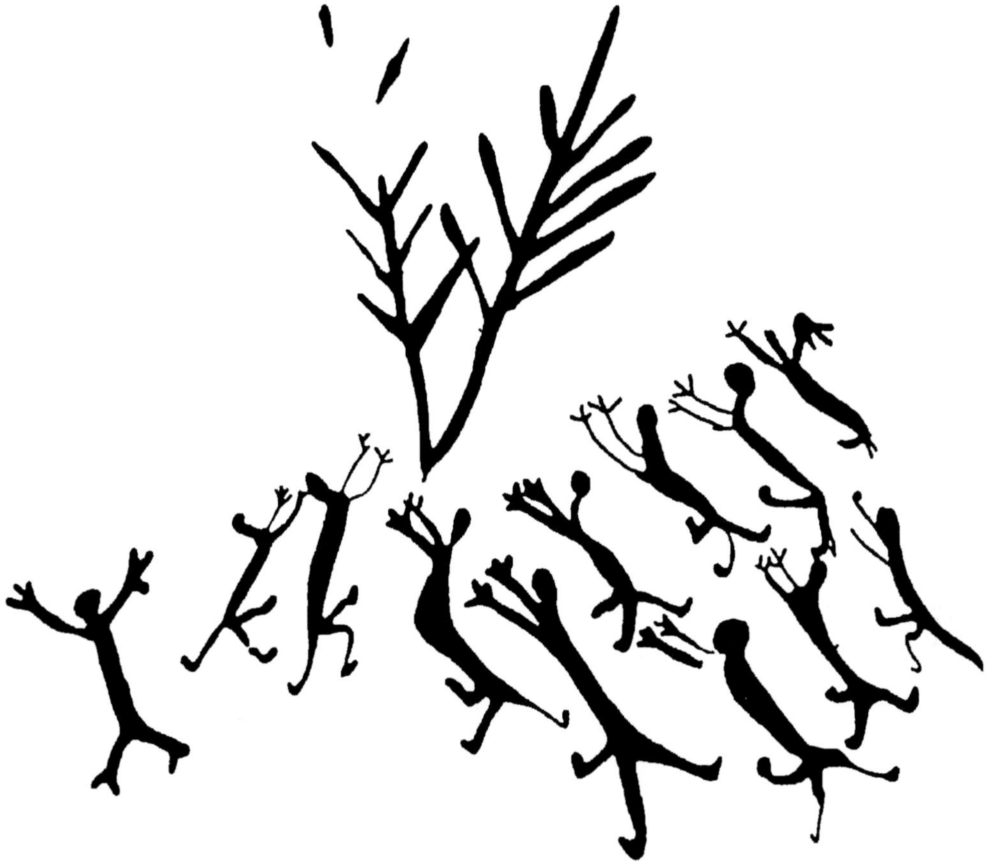

Fig. 78
Worshipping vegetation. Rock paintings of a late phase of Early Gatherers, Toca da Extrema II, Piaui, Brazil. Twelve people are addressing a plant. One of them is depicted in front view, the other eleven are shown in profile. They are ithyphallic and have their arms uplifted toward the plant as if they were in thanksgiving. The plant is likely to have aphrodisiac qualities.
Source: N. Guidon, 1984, pl. 63 (WARA Archive W00265)
Area Code: G-III. Cat.: B-I.

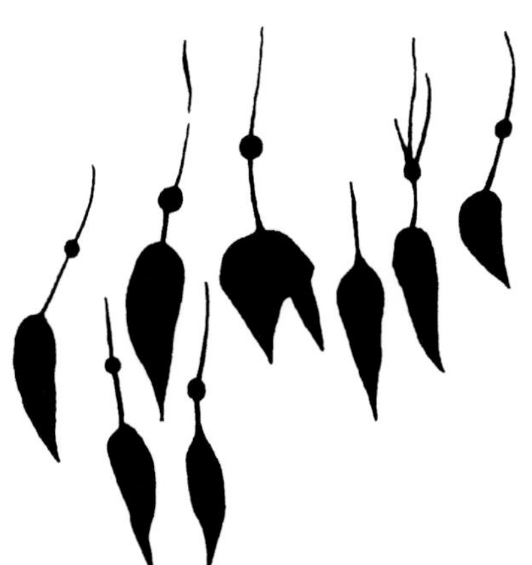

Fig. 79
Anthropomorphic roots in the art of a late phase of Early Gatherers. Runanza, Domboshawa, Zimbabwe.Source: Drawn after a photograph by E. Goodall, 1959, p. 79. (WARA Archive W00266)
Area code: D-IV. Cat.: B-I.

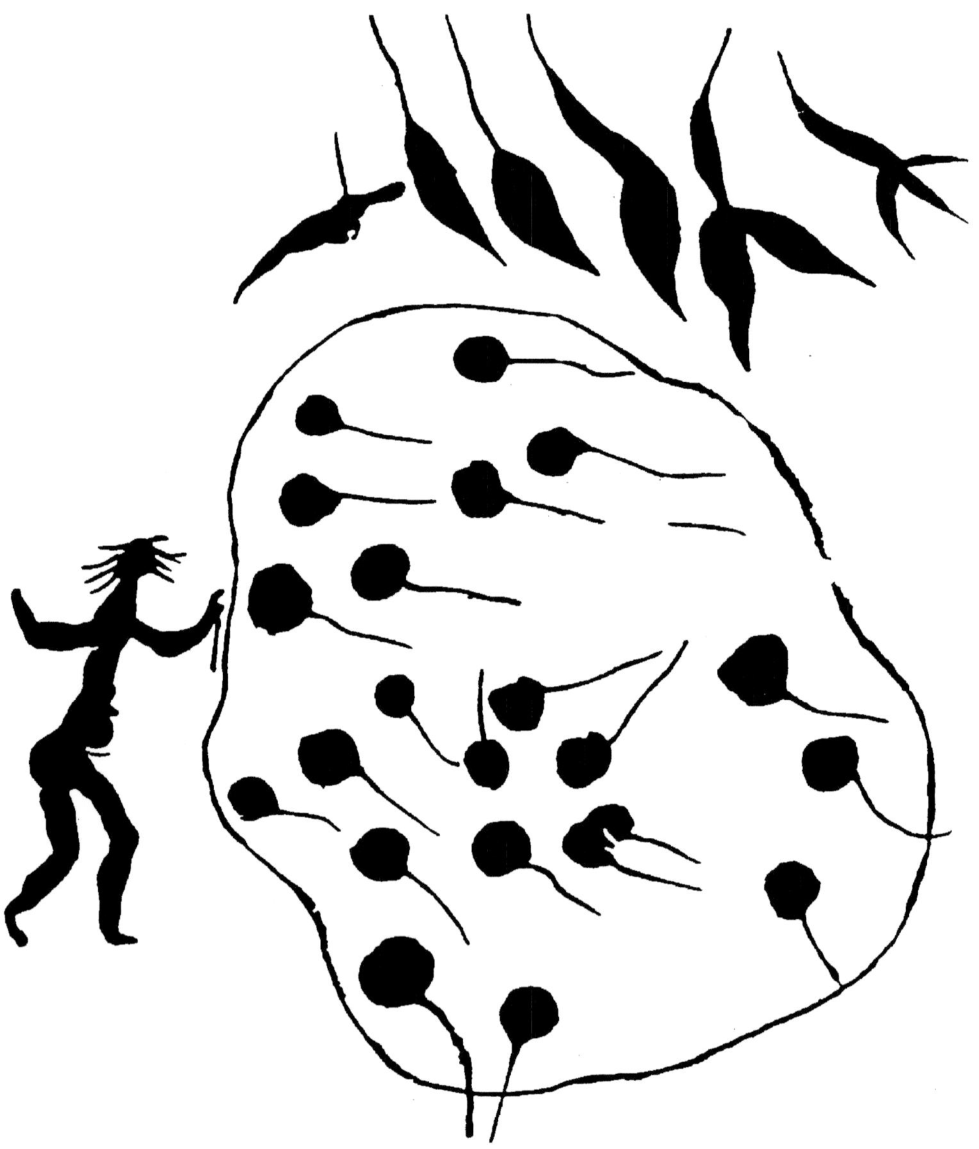

Fig. 80
The shaman communicates with roots. Rock paintings of Late Gatherers from Madzangara, Mtoko, Zimbabwe. The shaman is addressing a kind of edible tubers, 22 of which (rounded with a tail) are surrounded by a line, while longer tubers are left out. Food gatherers may represent plants or roots to refer to their qualities or powers. Similar metaphors are common with animals in hunters' rock art.
Source: E. Goodall, 1959, p. 83. (WARA Archive W00267)
Area code: D-IV. Cat.: B-I.

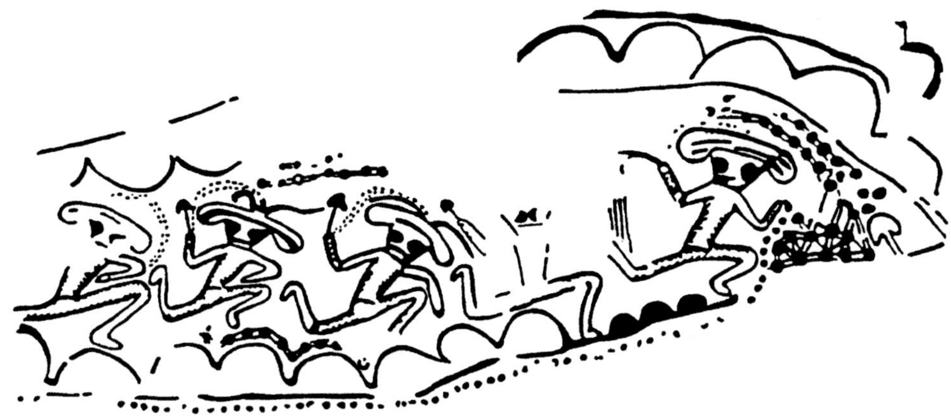

Fig. 81
Rock art produced in a state of hallucination. Tassili, Algeria. Early Gatherers, General tracing (cf. Fig. 17 detail) of a painting illustrating the effect of hallucinogenic mushrooms. Series of dots lead from the mushroom to the head. Horizon of the 'Round Heads style', ca. 5000 BC. Source: G. Samorini, 1989, Fig. 9. (WARA Archive W00209 – W00138)
Area code: C-II. Cat.: B-I.

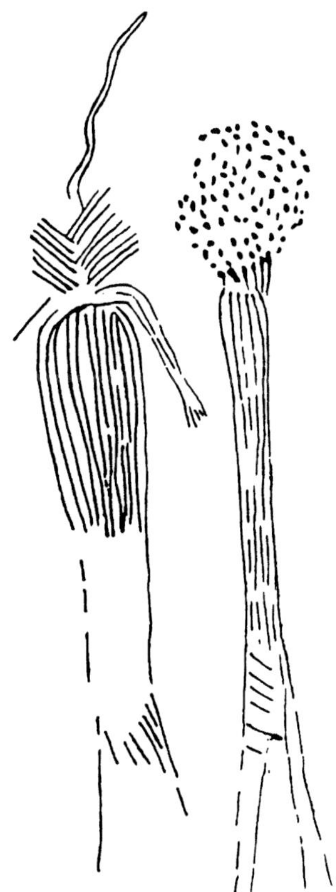

Fig. 82
Rock paintings of Early Gatherers. Kundusi, near Kondoa, Tanzania. Two anthropomorphic beings have, as heads, ideograms which define their identity. One of the heads is a combination of outgoing lines with a wavy emanation. The other is an assemblage of dots Source: M. Leakey, 1983, p. 73. (WARA Archive W00210)
Area code: D-II. Cat.: B-I.

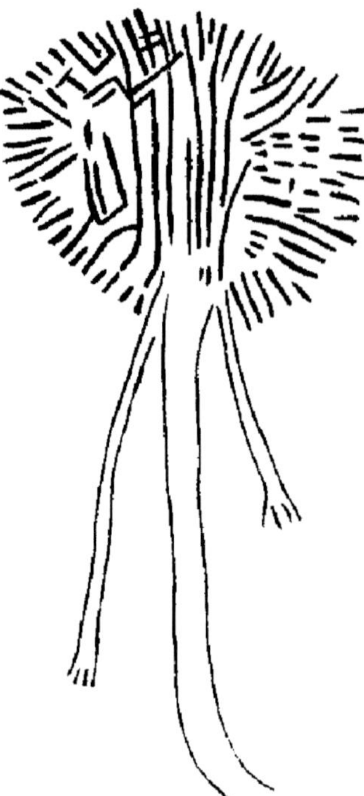

Fig. 83
Rock painting of Food Gatherers. Pahi, Tanzania. Image of an anthropomorphized tree.
Source: tracing by M. Leakey 1983, in E. Anati, 1995. (WARA Archive W07175)
Area code: D-II

Fig. 84
Kisesse, Tanzania. Painting of Early Gatherers. A small anthropomorphic figure with animal head takes care of a large being covered by dots. His head is faceless.
Source: Tracing of CCSP from a photography by Leakey, M. (WARA Archive W01829)
Area Code: D-II. Cat: B-I.

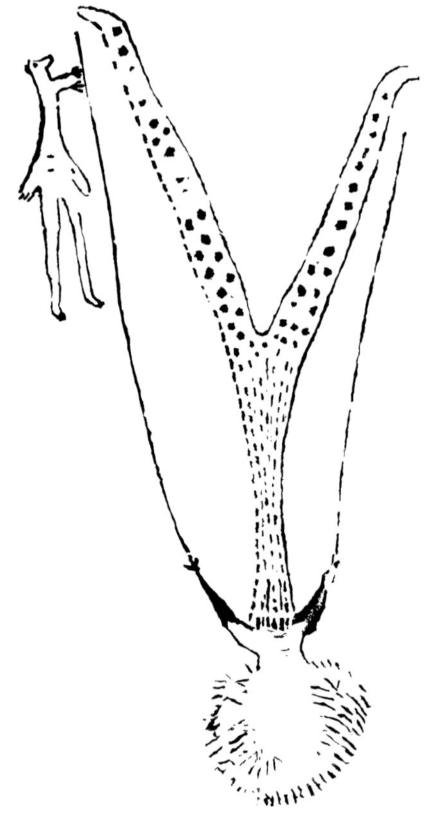

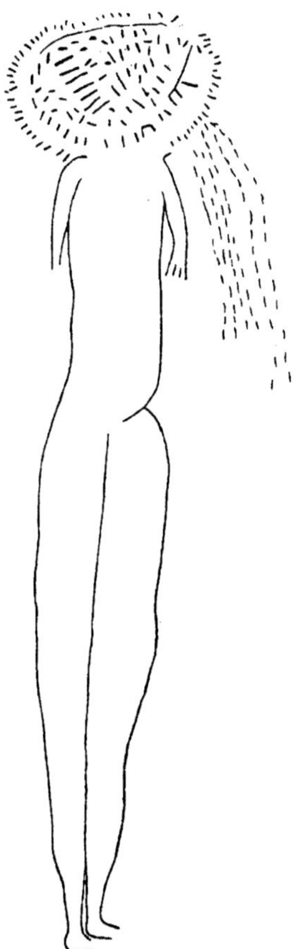

Fig. 85
Rock painting of Early Gatherers from Pahi, Tanzania. An anthropomorphic being with a round head made of dots is producing words or sounds.
Source: M. Leakey, 1983, Fig. 44. (WARA Archive W00213)
Area Code: D-II. Cat.: B-I.

Fig. 86
Rock paintings of Early Gatherers from Kundusi near Kondoa, Tanzania. Four beings with hidden faces, all have a distinctive oblique line on their heads. They seem to make a team for dance or some other performance.
Source: M. Leakey, 1983, p. 76. (WARA Archive W00214)
Area Code: D-II. Cat.: B-I.

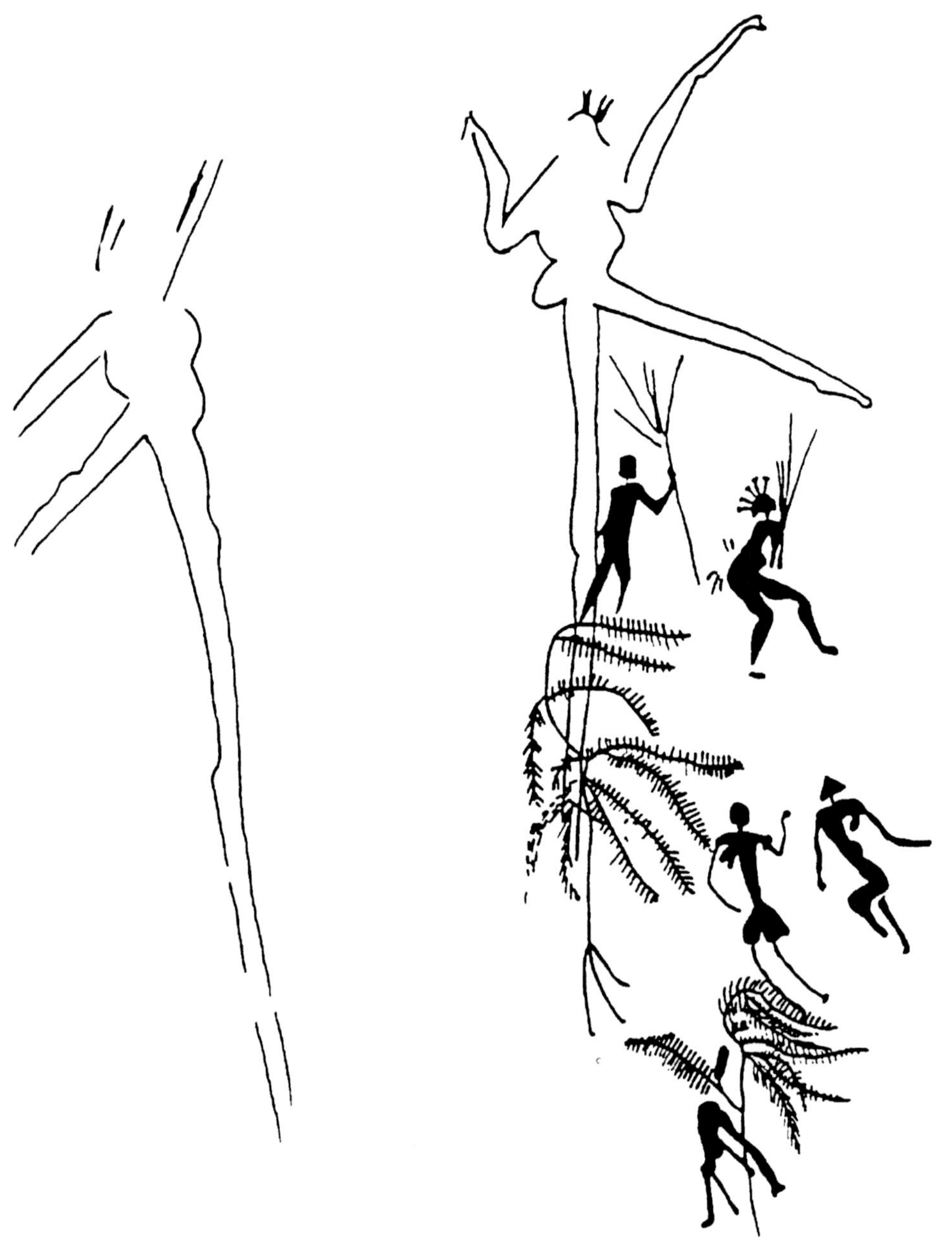

Fig. 87
Dreams of the Gatherers. Red rock paintings at Epworth, Zimbabwe. Three phases are detected on this surface. The early phase shows two beings in thin outline. Both of them have a very long leg and a short one. They seem to be dancing. A second phase is characterized by small human figures. Twice a man is following a woman. In the upper scene the woman, with a strange head-dress holding sticks in the hands, is going away from the man. In the middle scene the woman seems to be calling the man, who is running toward her. The lower man is alone and seems to be going away. The whole assemblage seems to evocate some sort of a love story. In the third phase, bushes are represented.
Source: Drawn from a tracing of E. Goodall, 1959, p. 70. (WARA Archive W00208)
Area code: D-IV. Cat.: B-I; B-III.

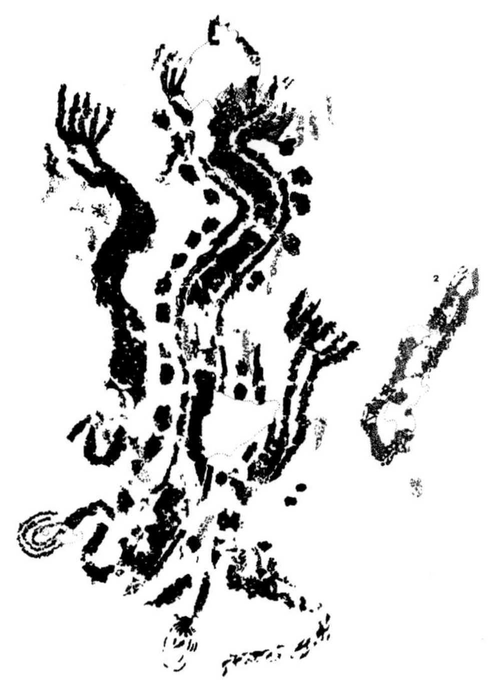

Fig. 88 a - b
Pla de Petracos, Castell de Castells, Valence, Spain and Barranc de l'Infern, Vall de Laguart, Valance, Spain.
Rock paintings defined as 'macroschematic' reflect a state of hallucinogen alteration. They are attributed to
an evolved phase of food collectors making use of doping substance.
Source: Murset in E. Anati 2000. (WARA Archive W01893 – W01894)
Area Code: E-I. Cat: B-III.

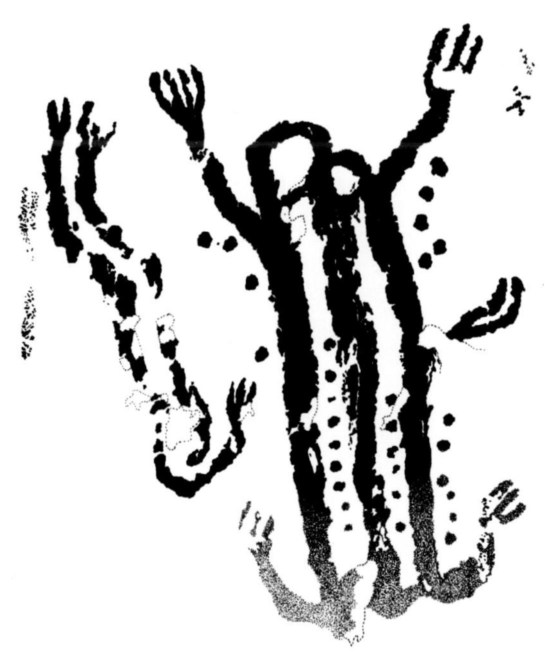

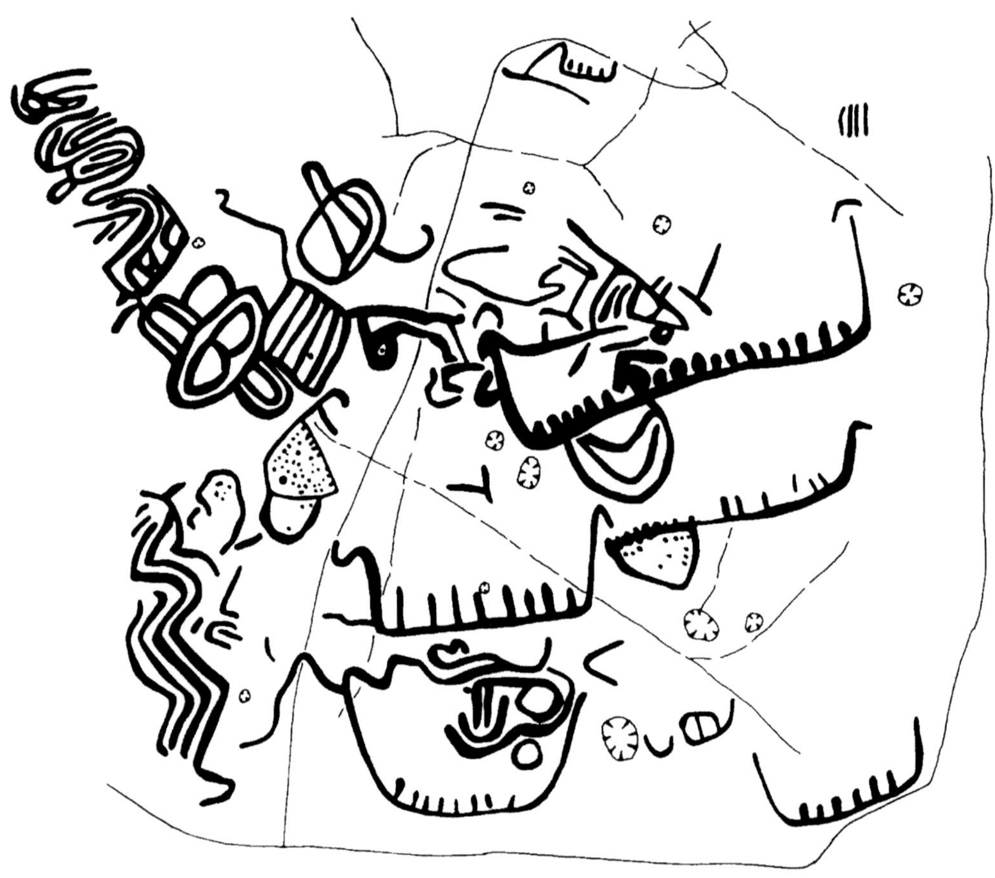

Fig. 89
Rock engravings of Gatherers – fisherman from the Solomon islands, Melanesia. Figure of boats are accompanied by ideograms and zig-zag lines.
Source: D. Roe, 1990. (WARA Archive W06805)
Area Code: H-2; Cat: B-II.

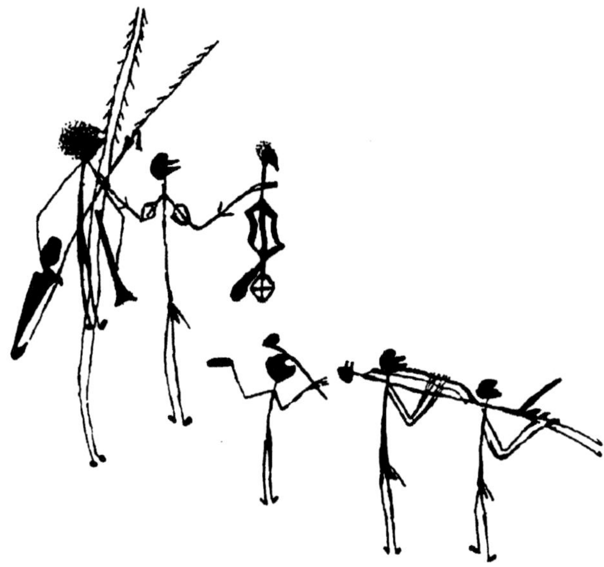

D. Late Hunters-Gatherers

Fig. 90
Narrative mortuary scene. Evolved Hunters syntax. Cannon Hill, Arnhem Land, Australia. This scene is composed of two parts. To the right, two people are carrying the dead and are followed by a smaller human figure holding an axe. To the left two people are equipped for hunting. Both display spears of remarkable size and elaborate spear-throwers. One of the human figures is larger in size than the other. The arm's muscles are emphasized. This figure is likely to be the evocation of the high qualities of the dead man. Scenes like this one reflecting a moment of daily life in a rather naturalistic way are rare in early Australian rock art.
Source: D. Lewis, 1988, p. 370. (WARA Archive W00253)
Area code: H-I. Cat.: C-I.

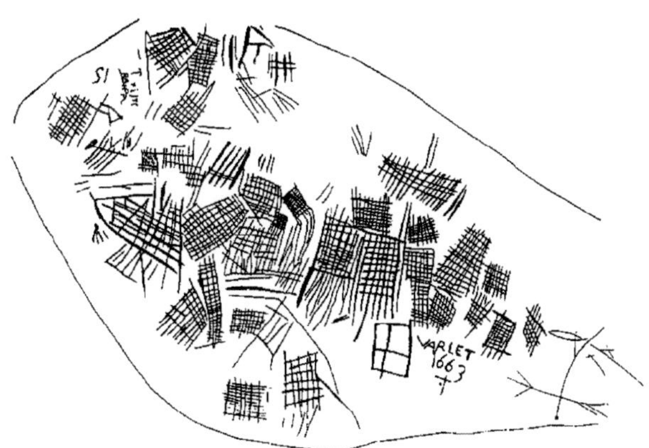

Fig. 91
Rock engravings from the Fontainbleau Forest near Paris, France, illustrating the art of food gatherers of Mesolithic tradition which persisted till rather late following a way of life of forest food collecting which included mollusks in their diet.
Source: J. Hinout, 1998. (WARA Archive W07178)
Area Code: E-I; Cat: B-II

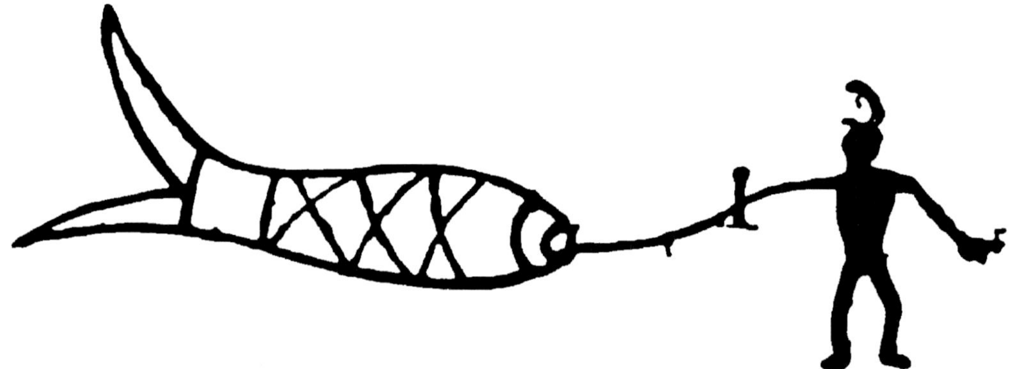

E. Late Fishers-Hunters-Gatherers

Fig. 92
A fisherman scene. Rock paintings of Gongxian, Sichuan, China. The 3 'X's painted on the body of the fish are likely to have a meaning which is still in use today: 'very large!' The feather on the head of the man indicates his high status or his fame (as a fisherman?).
Source: Chen Zhao Fu, 1988, p. 212. (WARA Archive W00272)
Area code: A-II. Cat.: C-V.

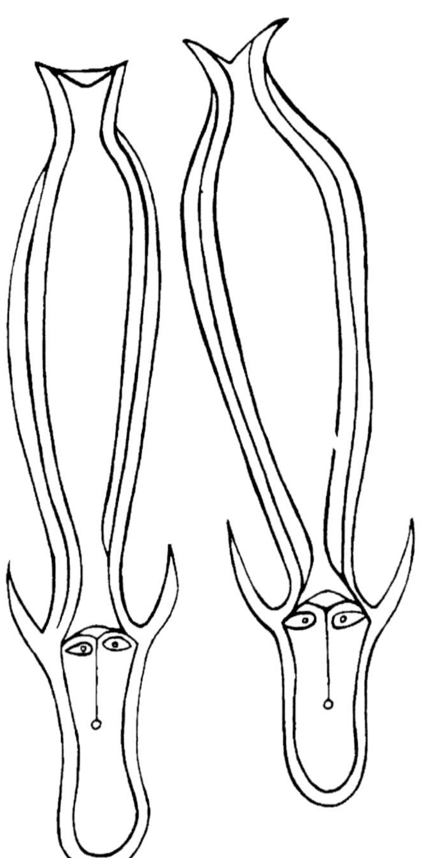

Fig. 93
Imaginary sea creatures, anthropomorphic seals. Rock engravings of Anakena, Easter Island.
Source: Georgia Lee, 1986, p. 80. (WARA Archive W00273)
Area Code: H-I V. Cat.: C-V.

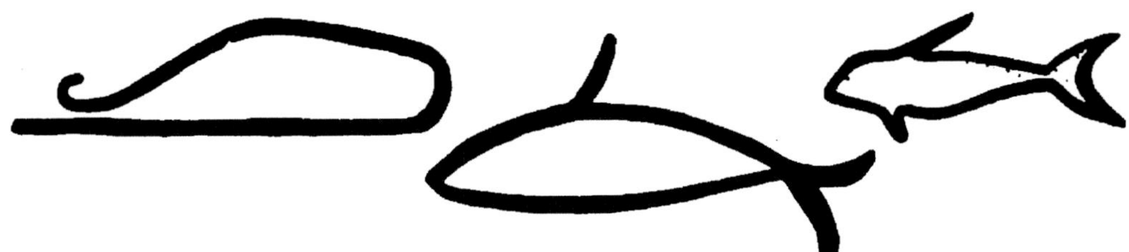

Fig. 94
'Fishing for compliments'. Deep Rock engravings of islanders from Cape Alitak, Kodiac Island, Alaska, USA.
Idealization of fish shapes reflects a tendency to exalt the source of food.
Source: B. & R. Hill. 1974, p. 231. (WARA Archive W00271)
Area code: F-I. Cat.: C-V.

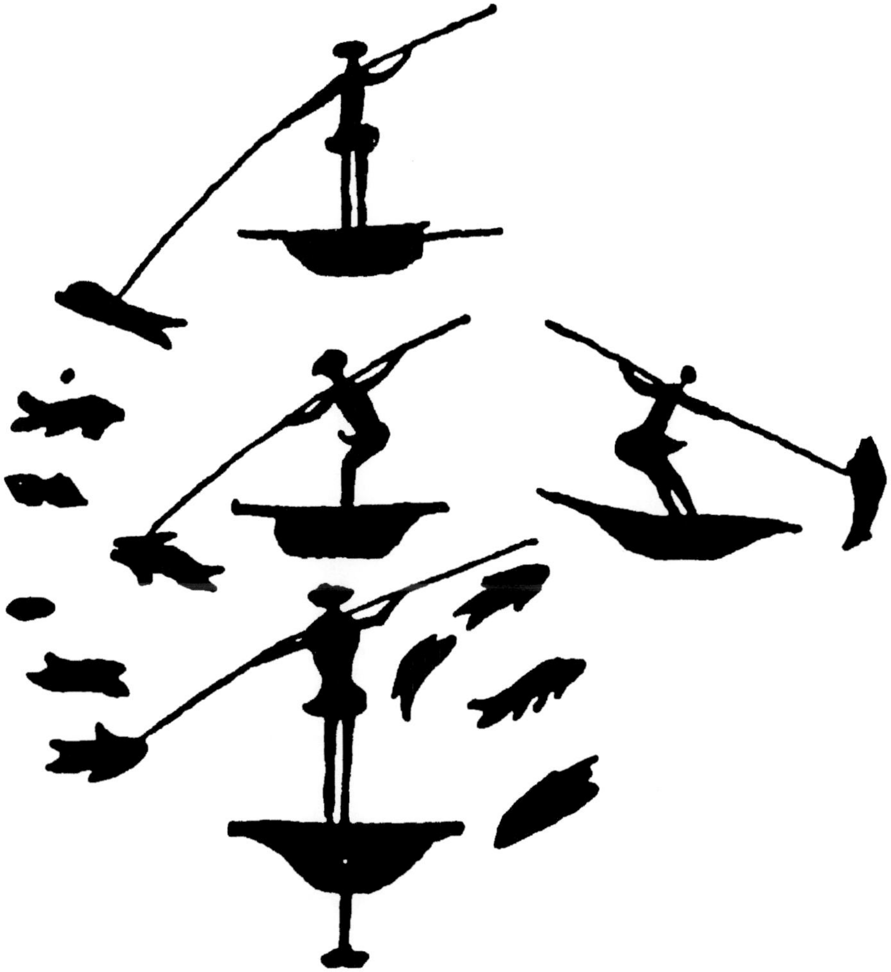

Fig. 95
Team fishing. Rock paintings of Evolved Hunters-Gatherers, Kenegha Poort, N.E. Cape Province, South Africa.
Source: Tracing by A.J.H. Goodwin in A.R. Willcox, 1984, p.198. (WARA Archive W00268)
Area Code: D-IV. Cat.: C-V.

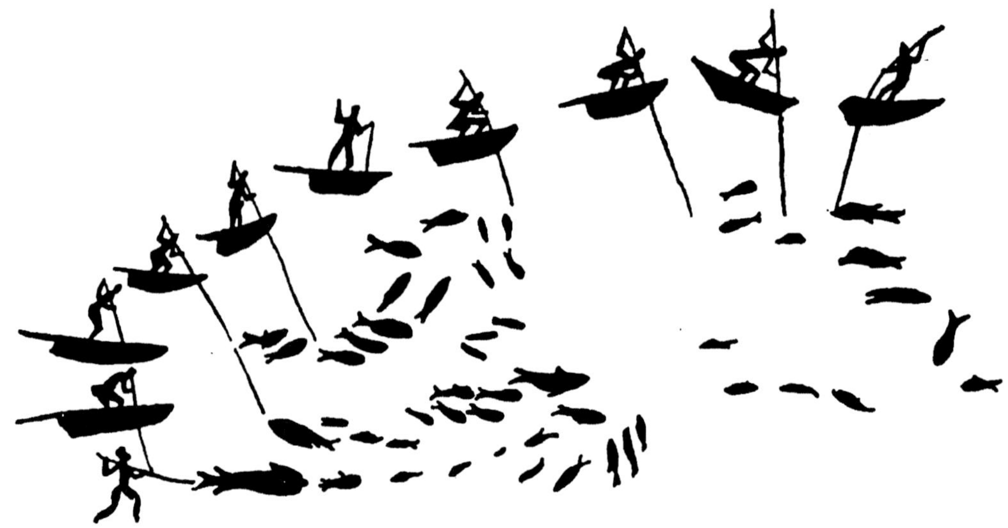

Fig. 96
Team fishing. Rock painting of Evolved Hunters-Gatherers, Mpongweni Mountain, Underberg, Natal, South Africa.
Source: Tracing by W.W. Battiss, in W.R. Wilcox, 1984, p. 198. (WARA Archive W00269)
Area Code: D-IV. Cat.: C-V.

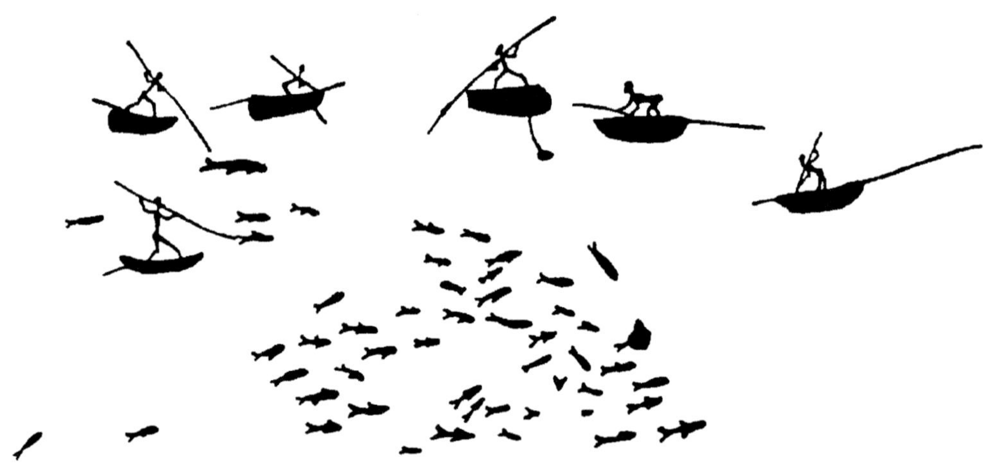

Fig. 97
Team fishing. Rock paintings of Evolved Hunters-Gatherers, Tsoelike River, Lesotho
Source: Tracing by P. Vinnicombe, in A.R. Wilcox, 1984, p. 198. (WARA Archive W00270)
Area Code: D-IV. Cat.: C-V.

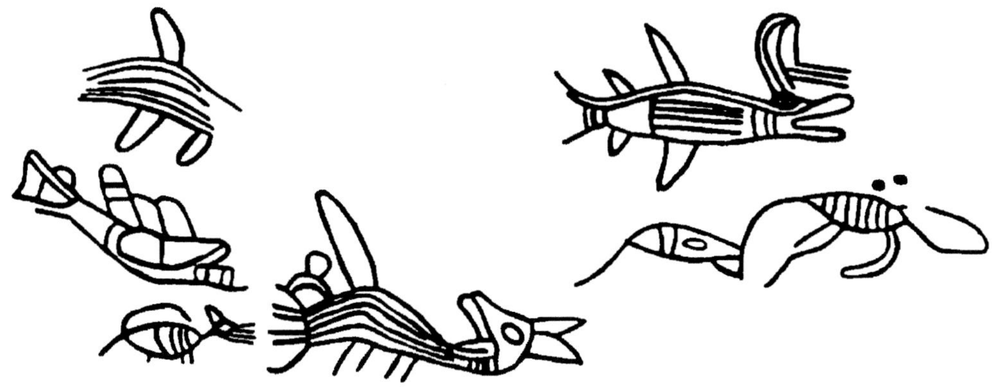

Fig. 98
Mythic beings populate the waters of the Ocean. Englishman River, British Columbia, Canada. A large number of deeply engraved imaginary fishes cover a vertical rock wall over 120 m. long. The site is considered to have been a place of shamanic performances, of visions and of initiation rites.
Source: B. & R. Hill, 1974, p. 120. (WARA Archive W00275)
Area code: F-I. Cat.: C-V.

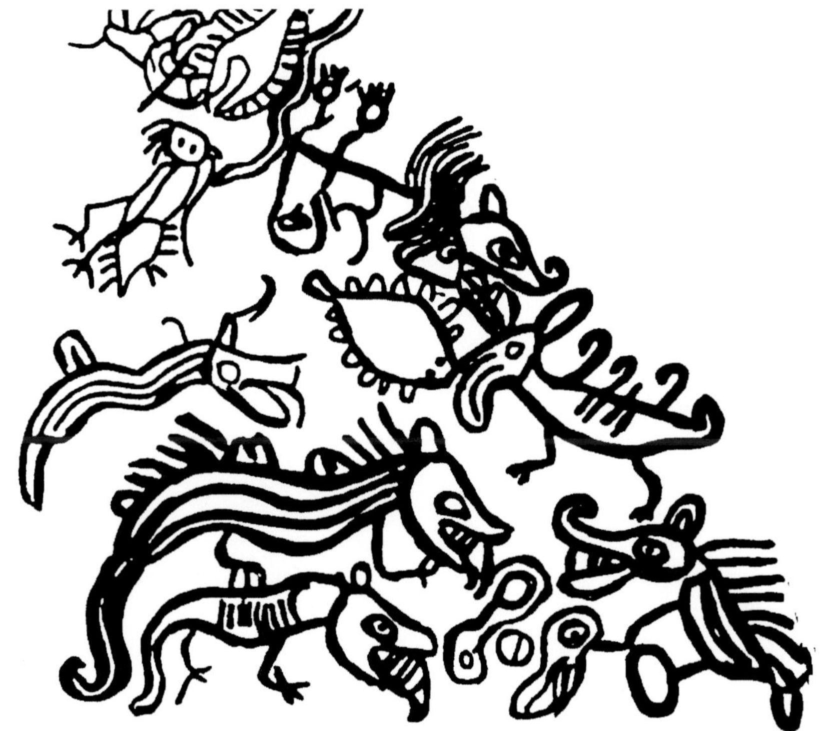

Fig. 99
Sea monsters of fishermen. Rock engravings of Nanaimo, British Columbia, Canada. In several areas around the Pacific sea spirits have been painted and engraved. As we know from more recent wood carvings and totem poles, they are likely to represent powerful spirits whose deeds, characters and qualifications have been transmitted by myths and popular tales.
Source: B. & R. Hill, 1974, p. 101. (WARA Archive W00274)
Area code: F-I. Cat.: C-V.

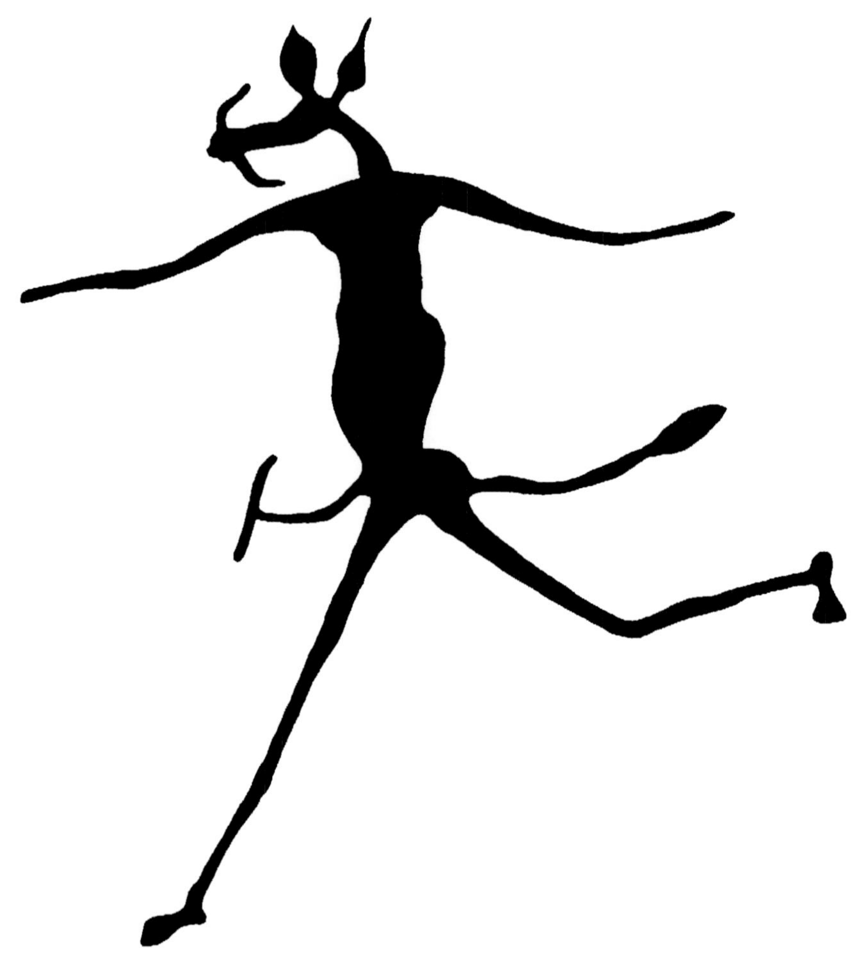

F. Late Hunters

Fig. 100
Strange beings populate the bush. Rock painting of Ruchera Cave, Mtoko, Zimbabwe. An anthropozoomorphic being is running fast.
Source: E. Goodall, 1959, p. 87. (WARA Archive W00241)
Area Code: D-IV. Cat.: C-I.

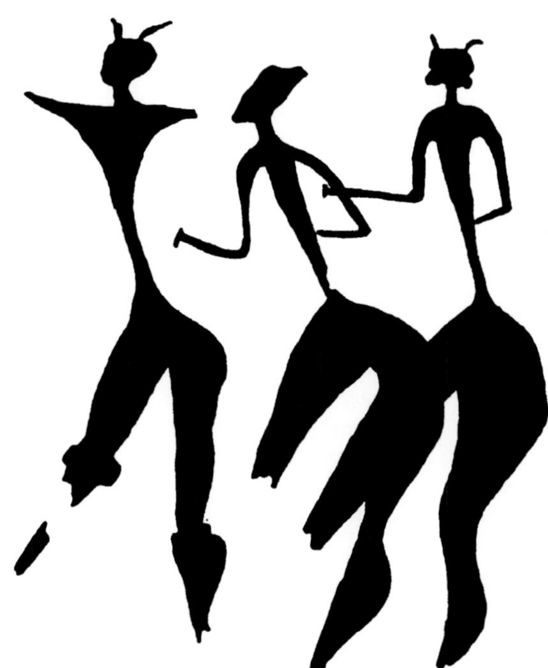

Fig. 101
Status symbols on the head. Rock painting of Cueva Saltadora, Valltorta, Castellon, Spain. Each one of these three human figures is being defined by the attributes that decorate his/her head. The central figure seems to wear a hat while the two others have feathers.
Source: A. Beltran, 1980, p. 39. (WARA Archive W00237)
Area code: E-I. Cat.: C-I.

Fig. 102
Rock paintings of Evolved Hunters in the Lavante area, Spain. Two anthropo-zoomorphic figures carrying weapons. Source: A. Beltran, 1980, p.42; E. Anati, 1989, p. 204. (WARA Archive W00238)
Area Code: E-I. Cat.: C-I.

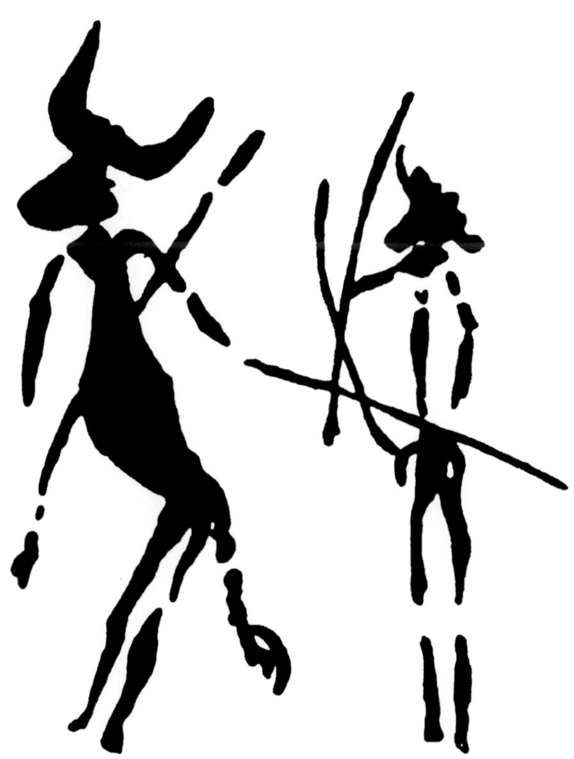

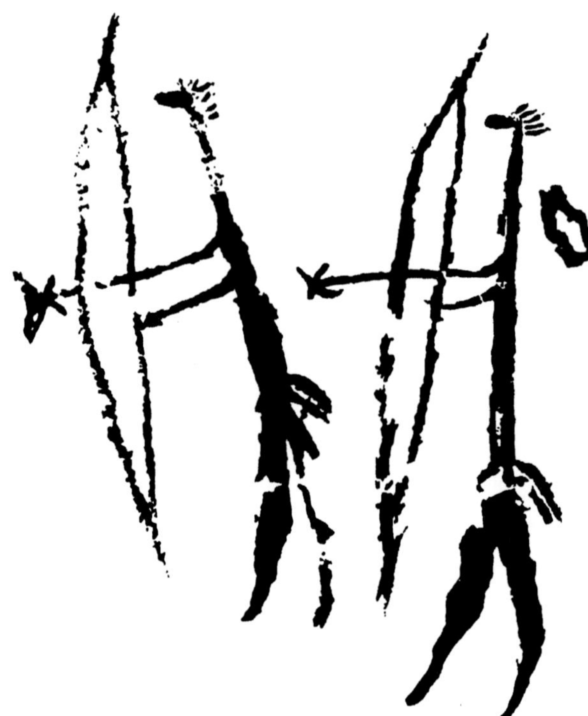

Fig. 103
Masked bowmen from Mosange, Tanzania. This rock painting in dark brown describes two beings with peculiar (animal?) faces and crests or head decorations. The long bows with arrows are not necessarily an indication of the male sex. The two lines in the back are usually an indicator of females. Behind the right figure an oval shaped ideogram is likely to be the indicative of the identity of the depicted beings.
Source: Drawn after a photograph in A.R. Willcox, 1984, p. 115. (WARA Archive W00239)
Area code: D-II. Cat.: C-I.

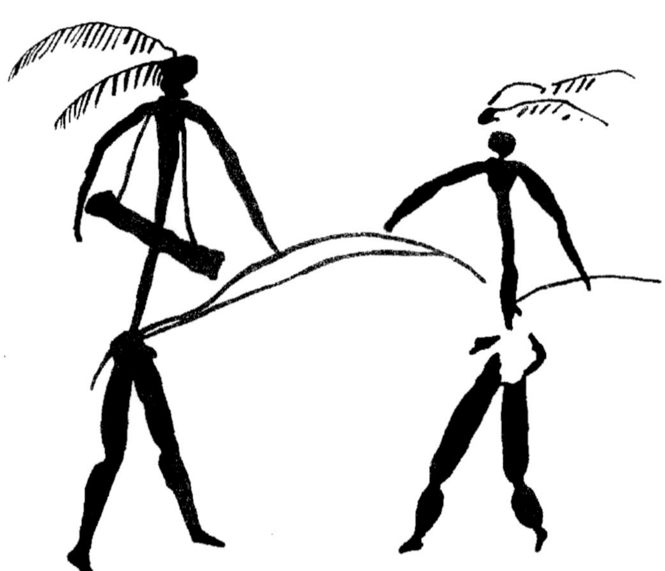

Fig. 104
Evolved Hunters meet. Rock paintings of Zimba, Zimbabwe. The direction of feet shows that they are walking toward each other. The head-dresses indicate that they are of the same category or rank. However there are some differences. One has the head-dress attached to the head, the other has it above his head. One of them has longer feathers and is depicted in a larger size, indicating that is more important than the other. The larger one has a bow and a quiver, the other one holds a stick .
Source: E. Goodall et al. 1959, p. 22. (WARA Archive W00240)
Area code: D-V. Cat.: C-I.

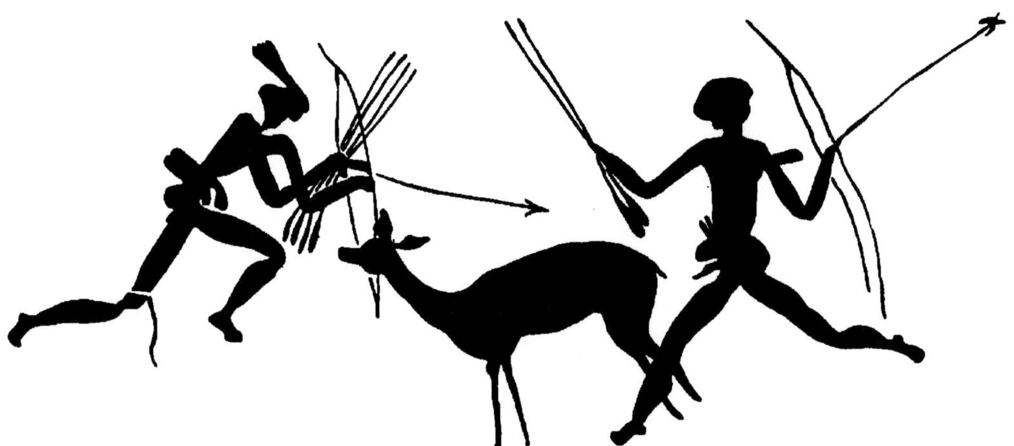

Fig. 105
Bow and arrow hunting of the Evolved Hunters; Msana, Zimbabwe. The entire space available on a small flat and smooth surface in a rock shelter has been used to paint this scene.
Source: E. Goodall, 1959, p. 19. (WARA Archive W00242)
Area code: D-V. Cat.: C-I.

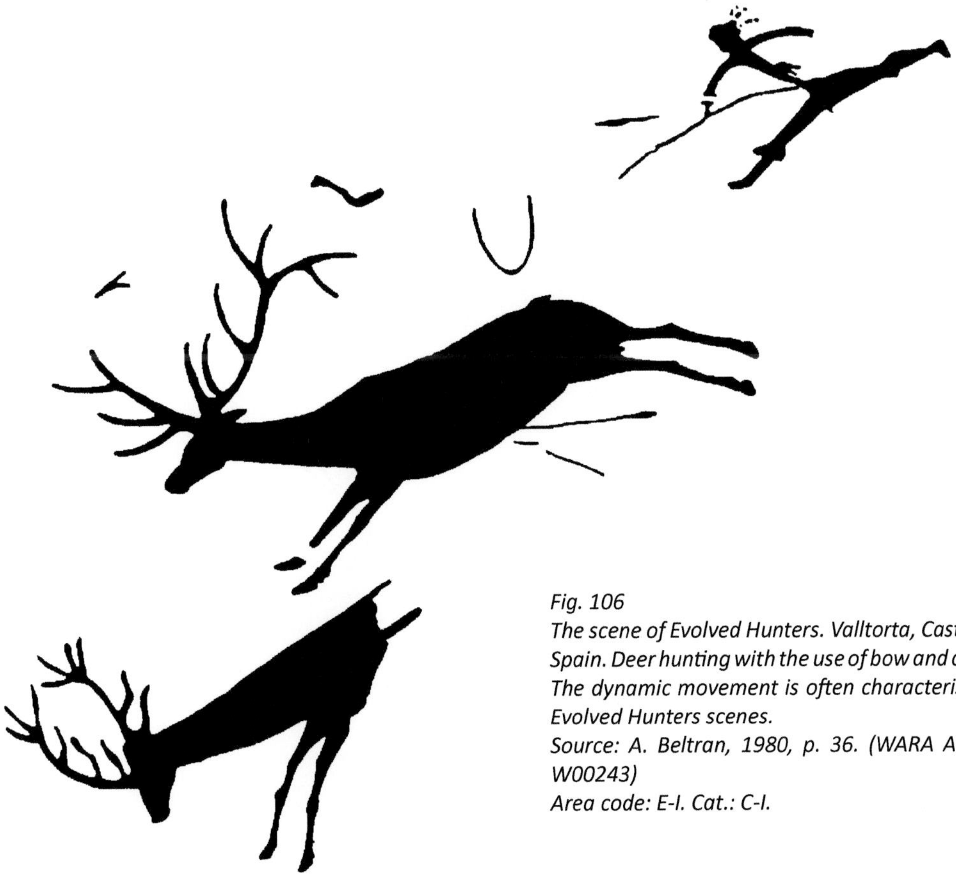

Fig. 106
The scene of Evolved Hunters. Valltorta, Castellon, Spain. Deer hunting with the use of bow and arrow. The dynamic movement is often characteristic of Evolved Hunters scenes.
Source: A. Beltran, 1980, p. 36. (WARA Archive W00243)
Area code: E-I. Cat.: C-I.

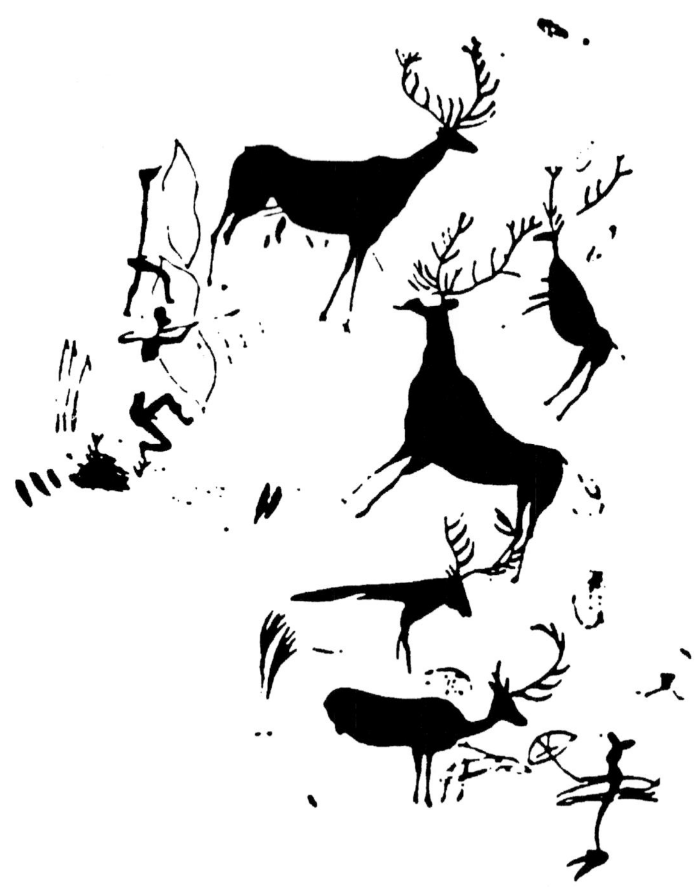

Fig. 107
The descriptive scene commemorates moments rather than messages. Rock painting of Evolved Hunters, Alpera, Albacete, Spain. The hunted are more important than the hunters in the early phases of Evolved Hunters. At the center of the scene are the animals. The bowmen are at the sides, and they are proportionally smaller. Source: Tracing by Cabre in A. Beltran, 1980, p. 24. (WARA Archive W00245) Area Code: E-I. Cat.: C-I.

Fig. 108
The trajectory of the arrow. Rock paintings of Benasal, Castellon, Spain. The arrow is shown in the air and then wounding the prey.
Source: Tracing of Gonzales Prats in A. Beltran, 1980, p. 29. (WARA Archive W00246)
Area Code: E-I. Cat.: C-I.

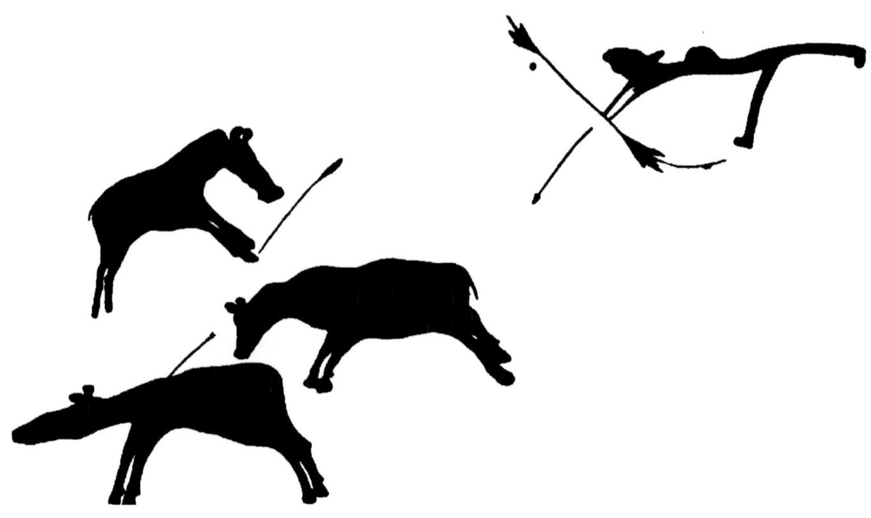

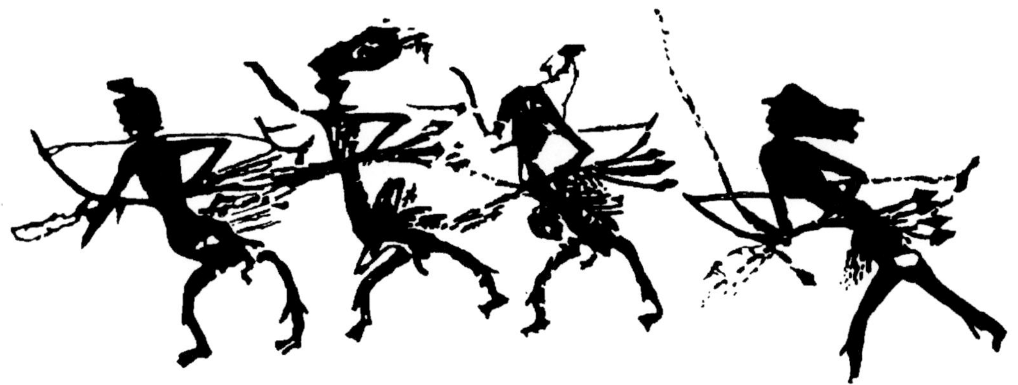

Fig. 109
Sense of humor of Evolved Hunters. Rock paintings of El Boro, Quesa, Valencia, Spain. Four bowmen walk in a row. Their movements are shown in a sort of slow motion dance. The theatrical result may well be intentional.
Source: Tracing by Gonzales Prats in A. Beltran, 1980, p. 45. (WARA Archive W00249)
Area Code: E-I. Cat.: C-I.

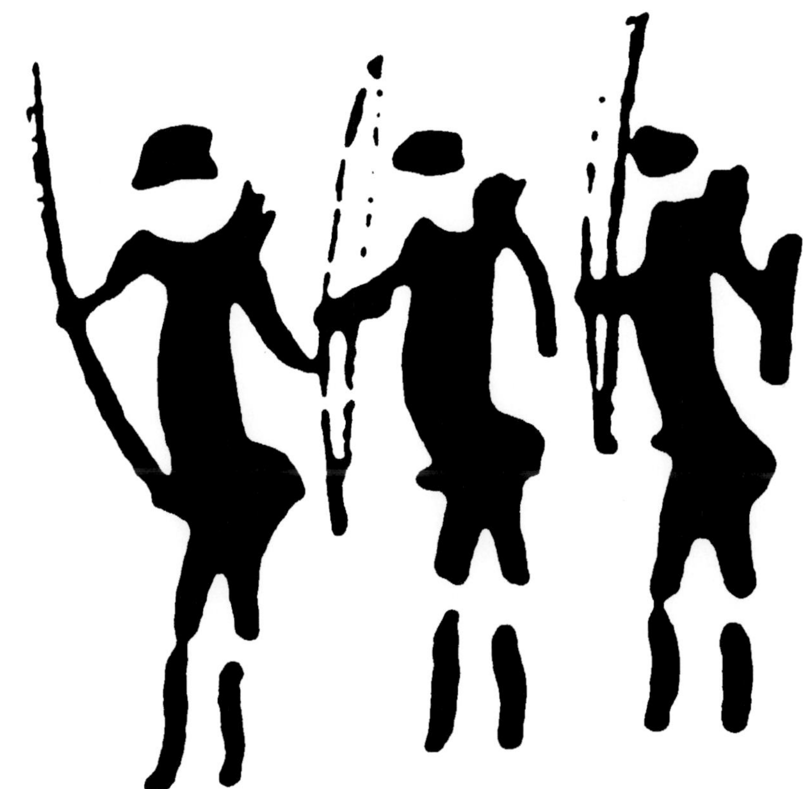

Fig. 110
Three bowmen. Rock paintings of Evolved Hunters, Mt. Vumba, Mozambique. Source: Tracing by O.R. de Olivera in A.R. Wilcox, 1984, p. 146. (WARA Archive W00250)
Area Code: D-III; Cat.: C-I

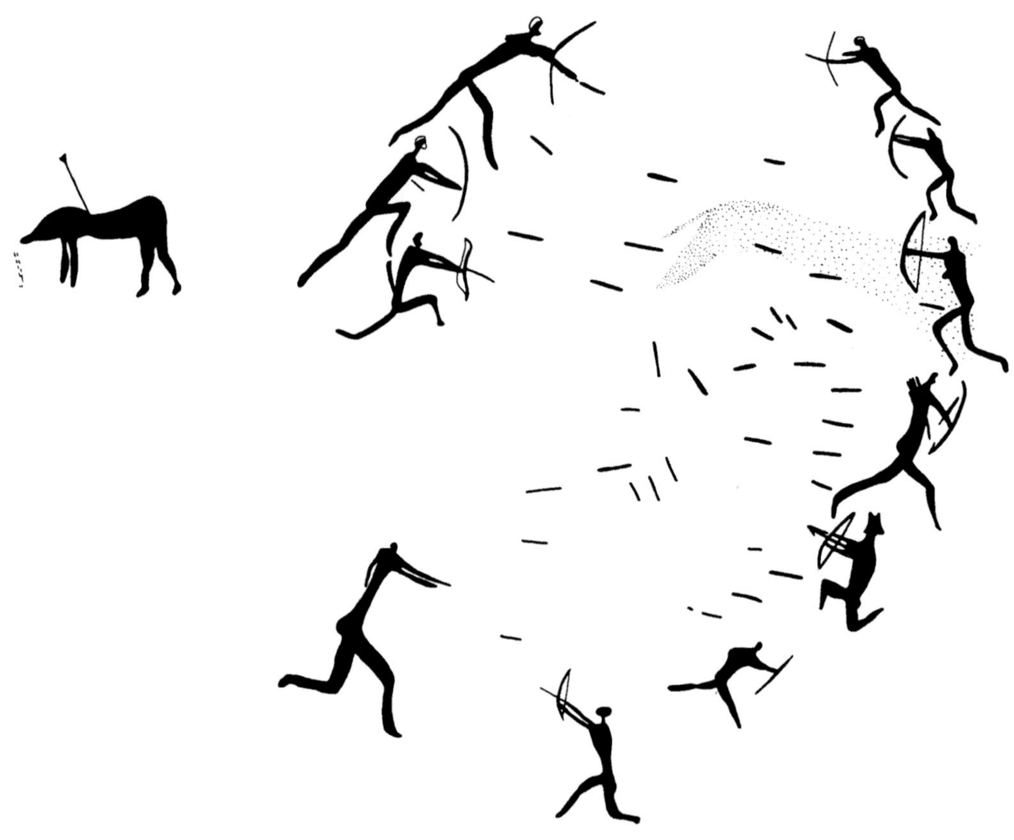

Fig. 111
Rock painting of Evolved Hunters. De Rust, Cape Province, South Africa. A scene of fight using the bow, between two rival groups. Arrows are flying while the two teams are well organized one in front of the other. The most numerous group seems to be made by small people. Probably the cause of the conflict is a wounded animal bleeding from the mouth. Its hind legs seem to be human.
Source: J.D. Lewis-Williams, 1983, p. 35. (WARA Archive W00247)
Area code: D-V. Cat.: C-I.

Fig. 112
Dynamic human representation of the Evolved Hunters. Rock paintings of Cueva del Civil, Valltorta, Castellon, Spain. The elegance and stylization of shapes is often characterizing the hunters using bow and arrow. Human figures of the dynamic style have been accumulated in this panel. At least three different groups of paintings are overlapping each other.
Source: Tracing by U. Obermaier, in A. Beltran, 1980, p. 38. (WARA Archive W00248)
Area code: E-I. Cat.: C-I.

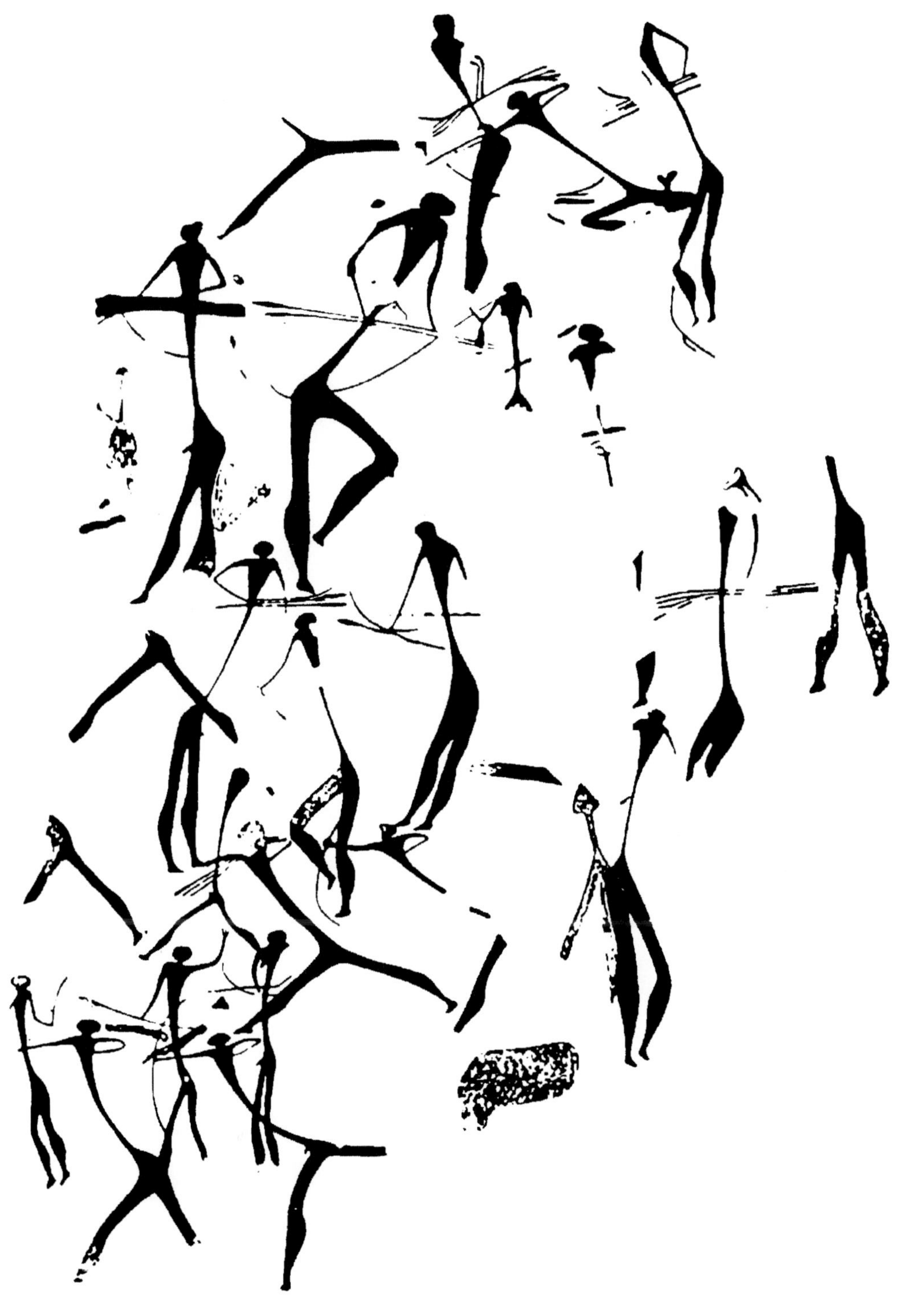

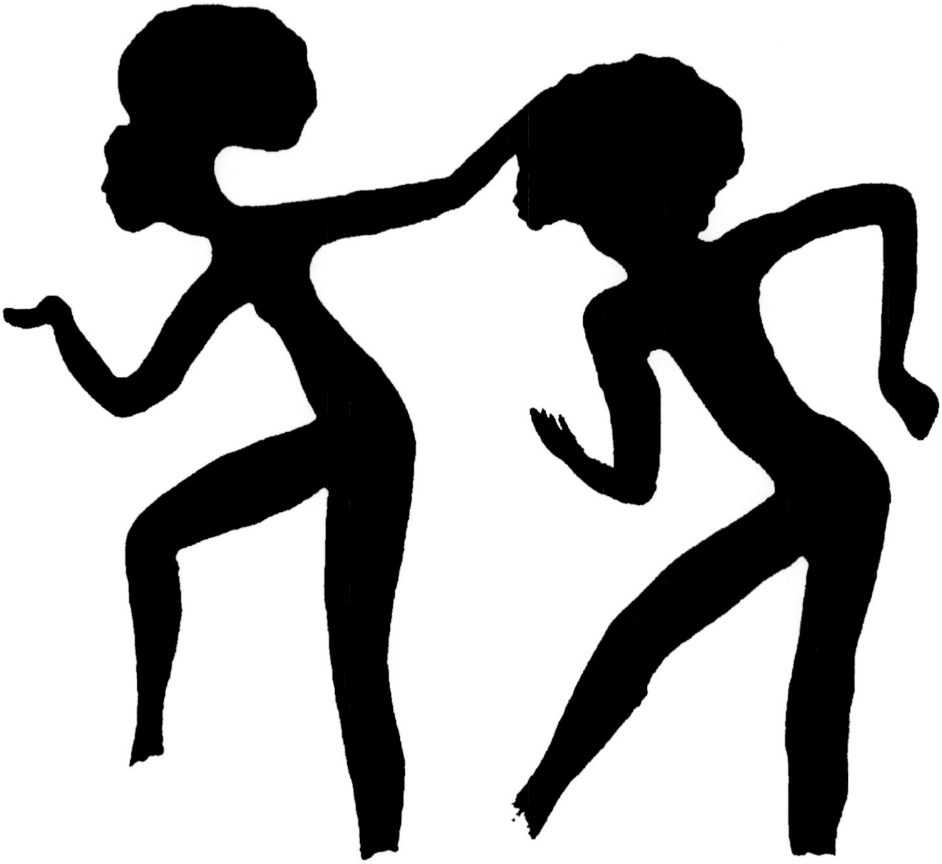

Fig. 113
Dancing girls. Rock paintings of Evolved Hunters, Wed Mertoutek, Hoggar, Algeria. Rhythm and style make this scene easily suitable to modern European aesthetic.
Source: Drawing from a photograph, EA-62. (WARA Archive W00235)
Area Code: C-II. Cat.: C-I

Fig. 114
Rock painting of Evolved Hunters from Cueva Remigia, Valltorta, Spain. A group of armed people with bow and head-dress, indicating the arrows display, each one, a different profile and a different concern for details. The organization of the people in a row, marching with a rhythms indicates the presence of co-ordination. Proto-Neolithic phase from the Levante area.
Source: Tracing by J. Porcar, in E. Anati, 1992, fig. 61. (WARA Archive W00236)
Area code: E-I. Cat.: C-I.

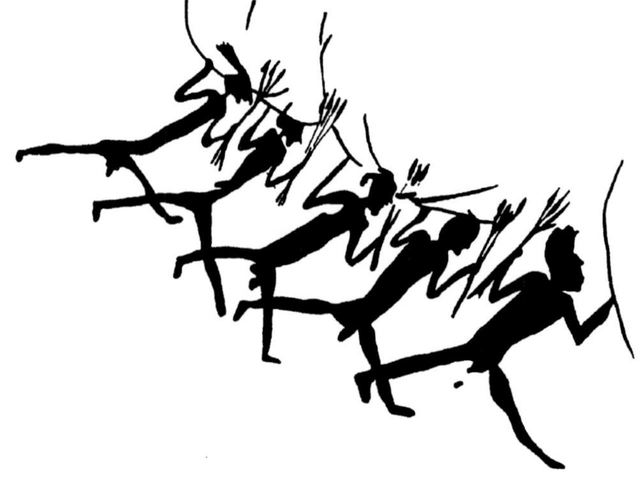

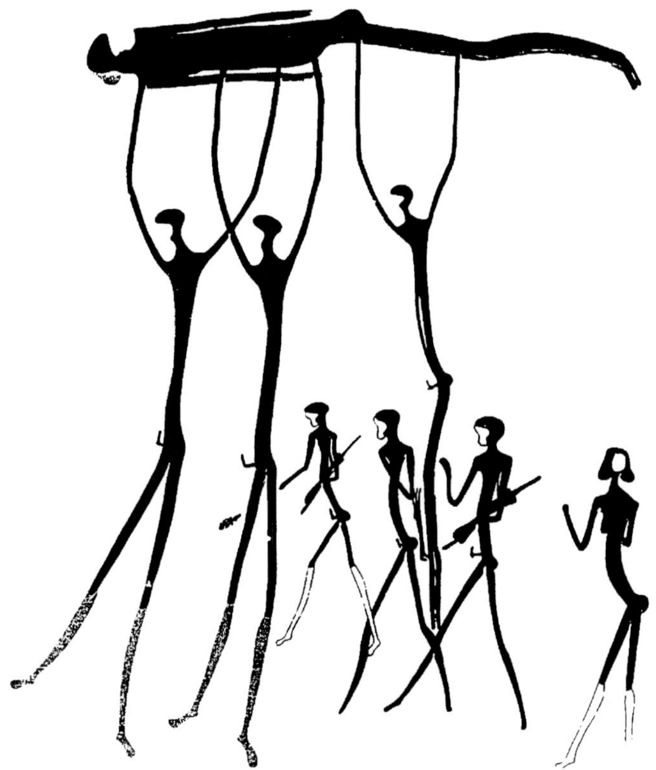

Fig. 115
A narrative mortuary scene of Evolved Hunters. Zisab Gorge, Brandberg, Namibia. The difference in size of the carriers and the followers is noteworthy. It may indicate the different importance of the two types of participants in the event.
Source: Tracing by H. Pager, in E. Anati, 1989, p. 47. (WARA Archive W00252)
Area code: D-V. Cat.: C-I.

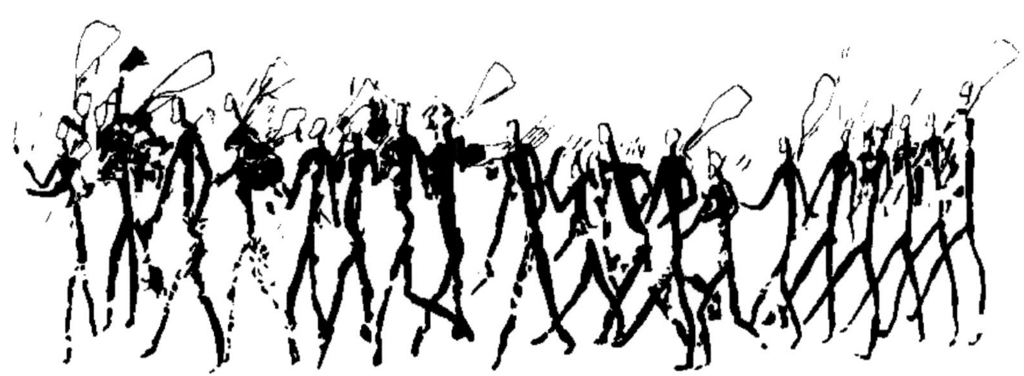

Fig. 116
The team. Rock paintings of Lesotho highlands. A team dance is showing 19 adults moving with the same cadence: expression of social solidarity and team sense.
Source: Tracing by L.A. Smits (WARA Archive W00254)
Area Code: D-IV. Cat.: C-I.

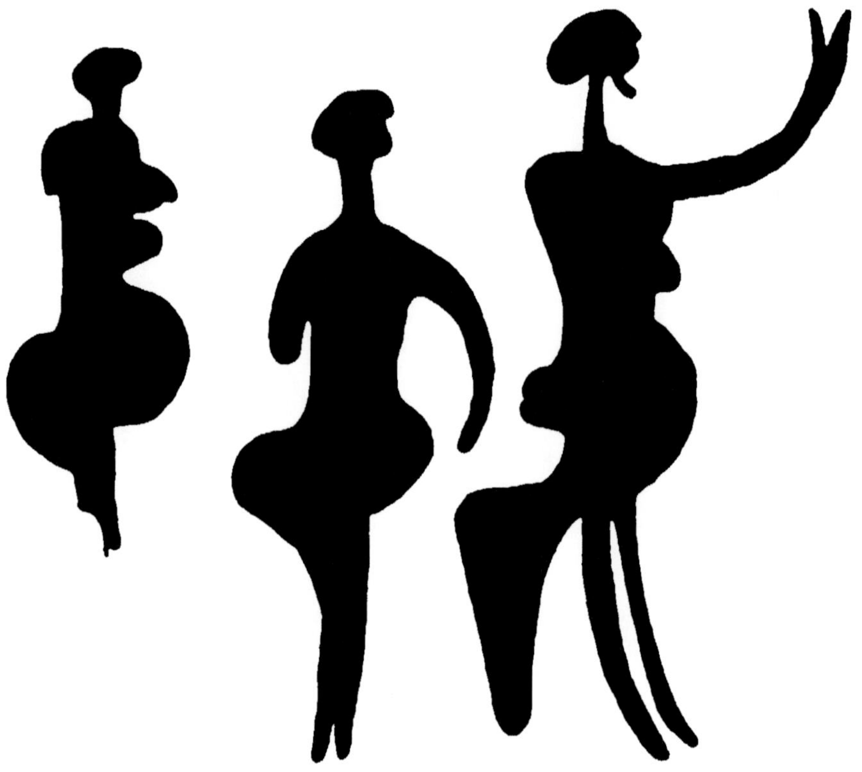

Fig. 117
Rock paintings of Late Hunters from Matebele, Zimbabwe. Two pregnant women follow a bearded being, dressed with a long skin: he is addressing with his arm in an interlocutory posture. Source: C.K. Cooke, 1959, p. 154. (WARA Archive W00251)
Area code: D-IV. Cat.: C-I.

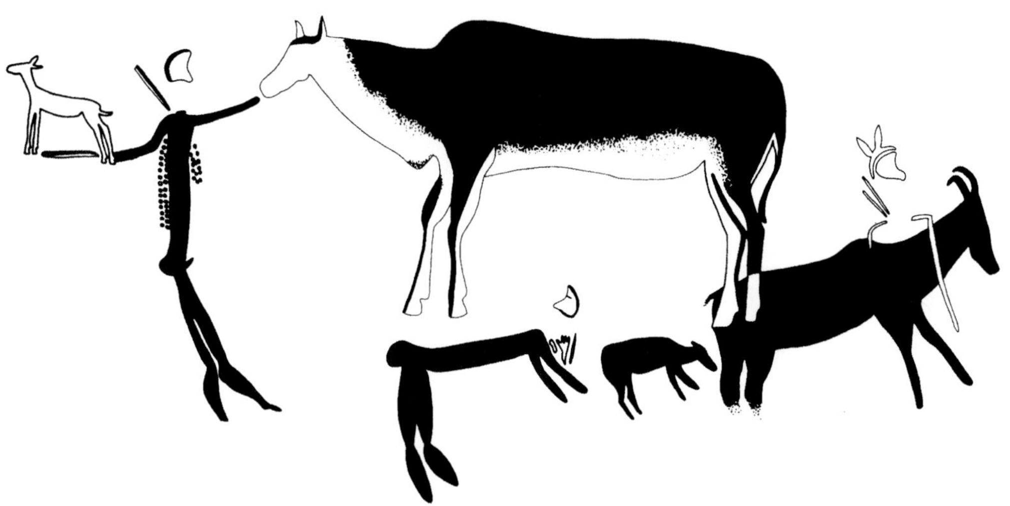

Fig. 118
Dominating the spirit of the animal. Rock painting of Giant's Castle, Drakensberg, Natal, S. Africa. The left side human figure displays the ability of the medicine man to catch the spirit of the antelope by putting his hand in front of its nose. The man figure below is performing a medianic dance and is in trance. His head is separated from the body.
Source: J.D. Lewis-Williams, 1983, p. 59. (WARA Archive W00255)
Area code: D-V. Cat.: C-I.

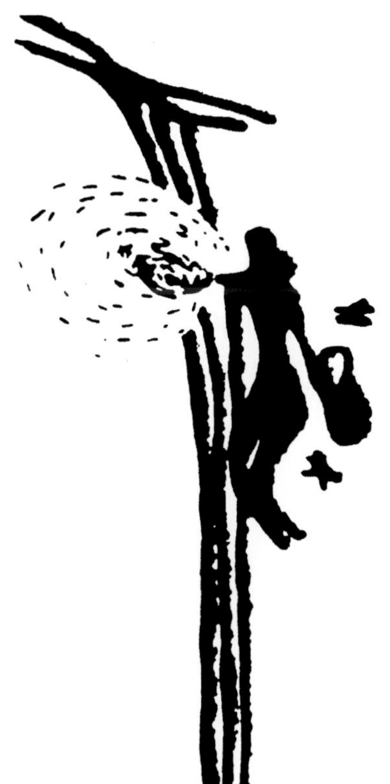

Fig. 119
The collection of honey is an economic activity of Hunters-Gatherers. Rock paintings of Cueva de la Araña, Bicorp, Valencia, Spain. The man is climbing on ropes to reach the beehive.
Source: Tracing by Hernandez Pacheco in A. Beltran, 1976, p. 54. (WARA Archive W00256)
Area Code: E-I. Cat.: C-I

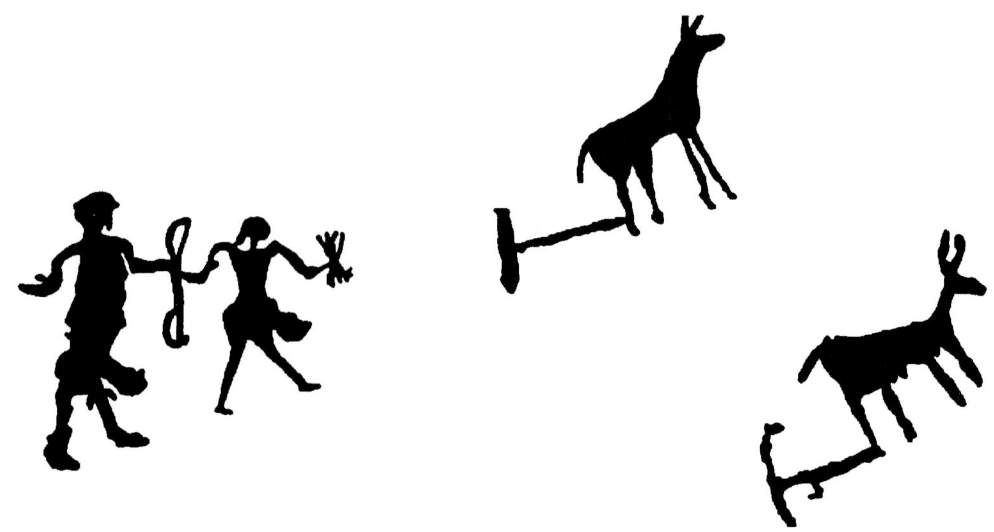

Fig. 120
The use of leg traps for hunting among Evolved Hunters. Jebel Uwenat, Egypt. The double bent bow of one
of the two human figures indicate a proto-dynastic age, a period in which different kinds of people coexisted
in Egypt. Late Hunters may be contemporary to Pastoralists, Incipient agriculturists and Proto-urban groups.
Source: tracing by CCSP from H. Winkler, 1938, vol. I, pl. XVIIIb (WARA Archive W00257)
Area code: C-II. Cat.: C I-II.

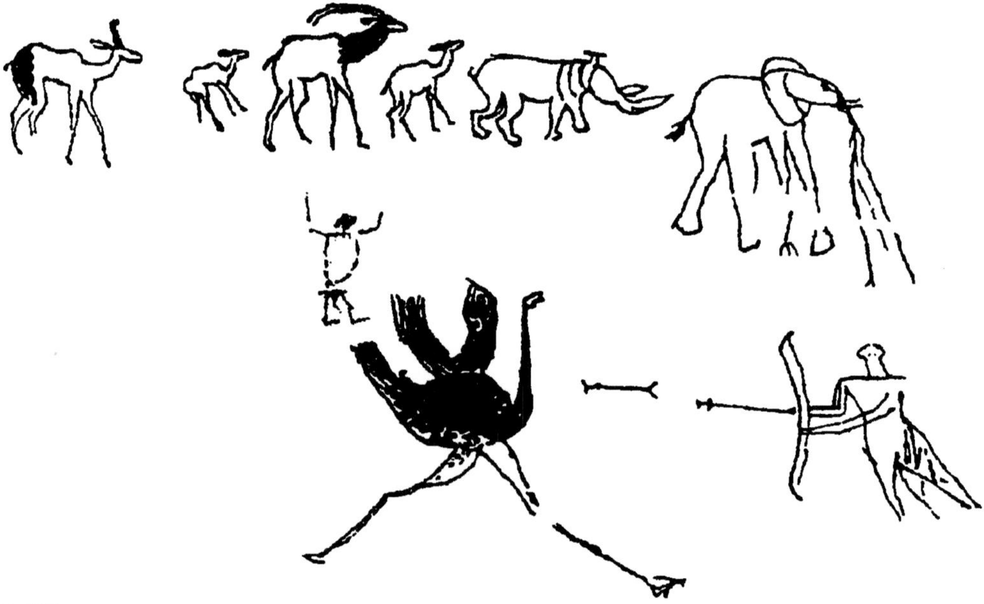

Fig. 121
The 'Late Hunter' makes a choice. Rock engraving of Jebel Uwenat, Egypt. A variety of possible game is 'listed'
on the upper part of the panel. In the lower part the choice is made and an ostrich is being hunted. This animal
occupies a central and dominant part in the panel The arrow,which has a peculiar arrow-head, is repeated
twice to indicate its trajectory. The human figure above the ostrich is an observer he may well be the maker
of the drawing.
Source: Drawn from a photograph by H. Winkler. (WARA Archive W00258)
Area code: C-IV. Cat.: C-I.

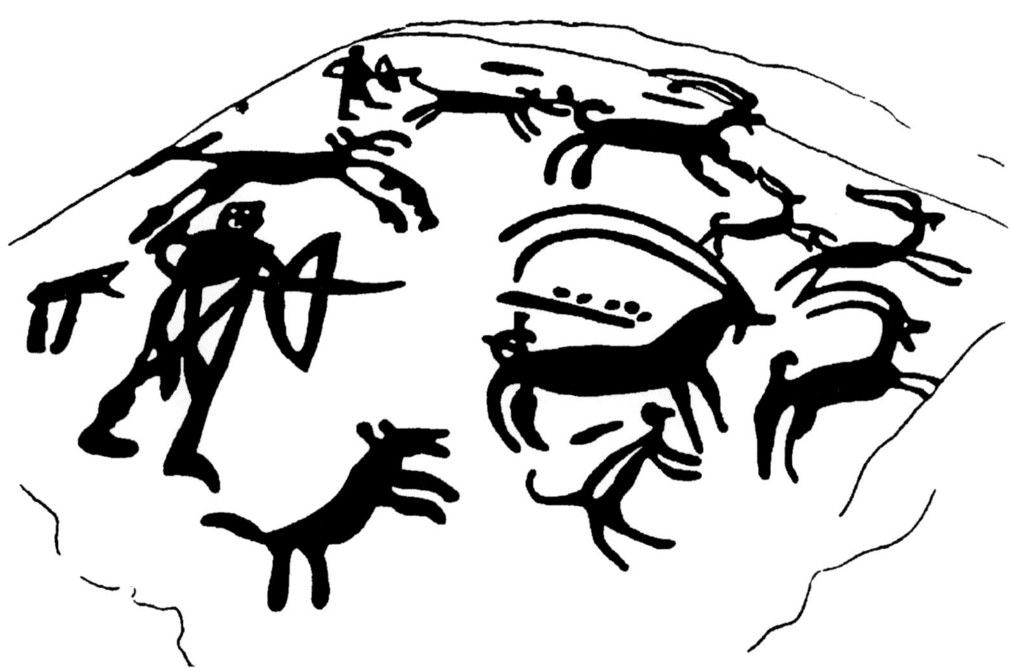

Fig. 122
Evolved Hunters using the bow and arrow are helped by dogs. Rock engraving of a hunting scene from Wadi Ramliye, Central Negev Desert, Israel. The arrow is repeated in the air to show the trajectory. Dots near the arrow are a sign of action. In many cases dots and series of dots seem to represent the verb 'to do' or some of its extensions, like 'to be well aimed' or 'to reach the goal'.
Source: E. Anati, 1979, p. 42. (WARA Archive W00259)
Area code: B-III. Cat.: B-II.

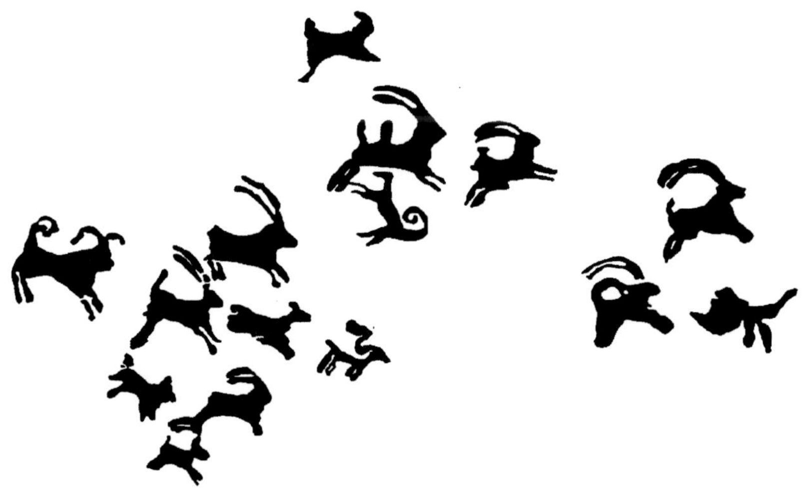

Fig. 123
A scene of Evolved Hunters. Rock engravings of Wusitaikou, Inner Mongolia. Wild goats are being attacked by a dog. The dog is at the center of the scene.
Source: Chen Zhao Fu, 1988, p. 171. (WARA Archive W00260)
Area code: A-II. Cat.: C-II.

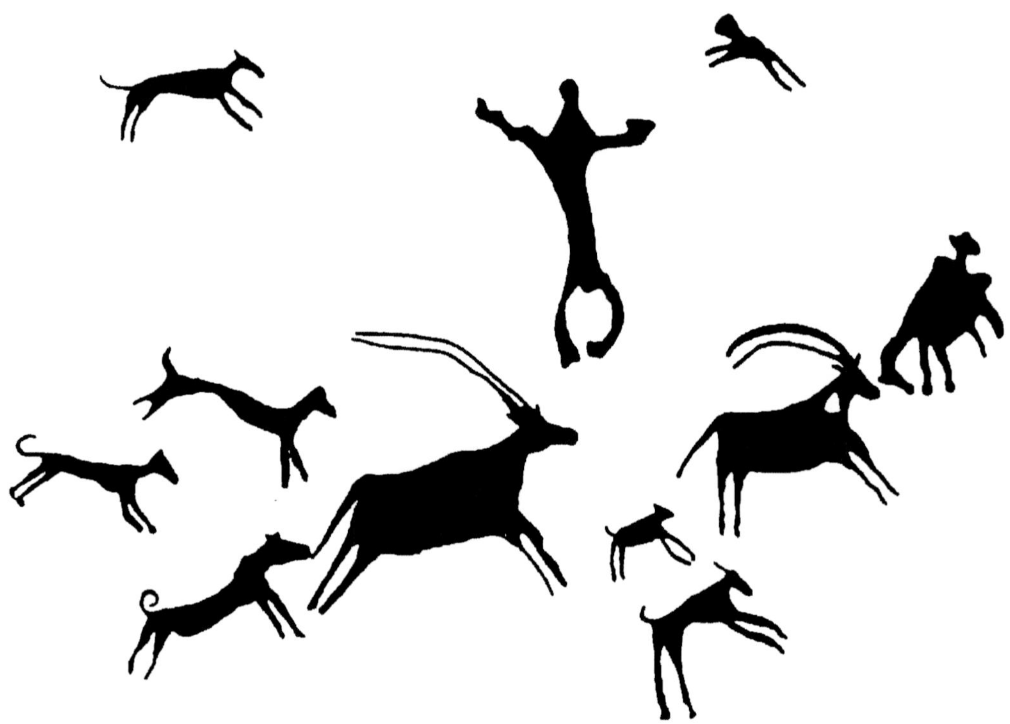

Fig. 124
Domestic dogs take care of the hunt. Jilf Kebir, Egyptian Sahara. The human being is at the center of the scene, more as a spectator than as a protagonist.
Source:Drawn after a photograph of H. Rhotert, 1952, pl. XXVII. (WARA Archive W00261)
Area code: C-IV. Cat.: C-II.

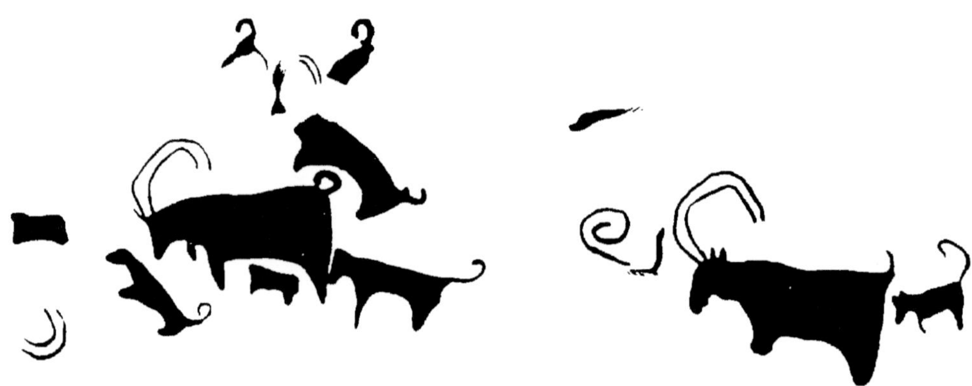

Fig. 125
Dogs attacking wild caprines. Rock engraving of Evolved Hunters from Kilwa, Saudi Arabia.
Source: E. Anati, 1979, p. 39. (WARA Archive W00262)
Area code: B-III. Cat.: C-II.

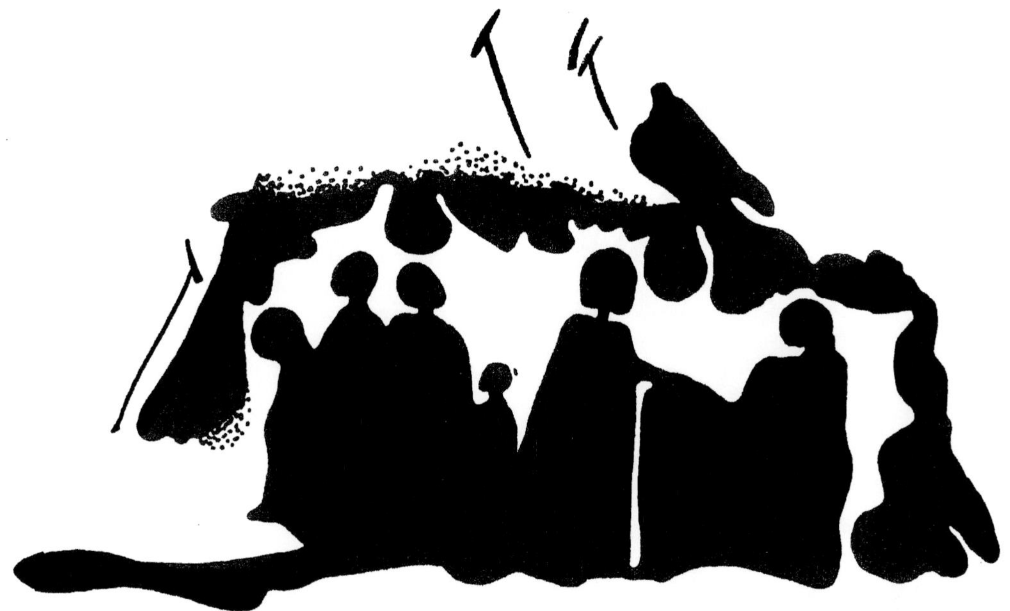

Fig. 126
Evolved Hunter's social life. Rock painting in red from Cedarberg, south-west Cape Province, South Africa.
Six people are close together in a rock-shelter. Above them, bags and other objects are suspended from the
ceiling. To the left and above, three ideograms are depicted, one for every two human figures. A sort of 'arm-
line' relies the figure with the largest head (probably the leader) with the most prominent female figure (with
breasts), to the right. The three ideograms are likely to indicate the sexual relationship between the people
represented. From left to right they are: Bâtonnet and closed lips; bâtonnet and closed lips; bâtonnet and
open lips.
Source: J.D. Lewis-Williams, 1983, p.15. (WARA Archive W00233)
Area Code: D-IV. Cat.: C-I.

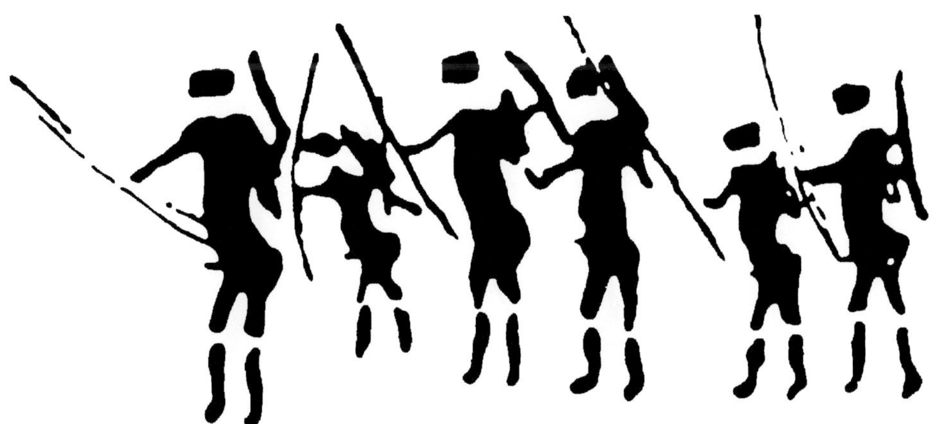

Fig. 127
Evolved Hunters on the trail of hunting. Rock paintings of Evolved Hunters, Mt. Vumba, Mozambique.
Source: Tracing by O.R. de Olivera in A.R. Wilcox, 1984, p. 146. (WARA Archive W00234)
Area Code D-III; CAT.: C-I

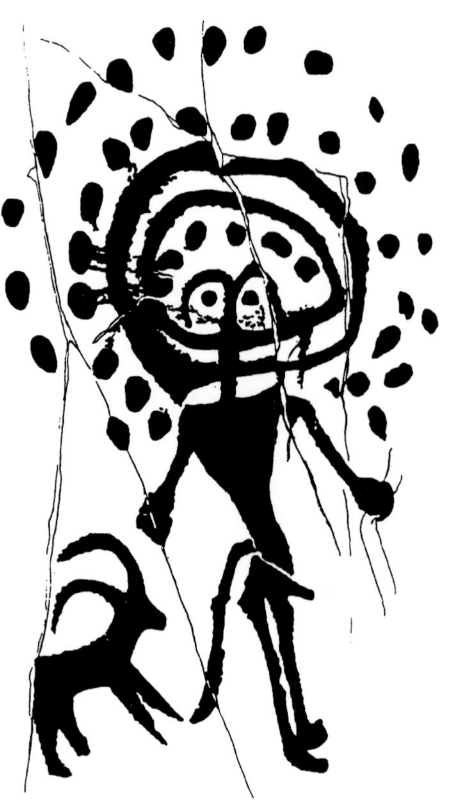

Fig. 128
Rock engraving of late Evolved Hunters. Tamgali, Kazakistan. The tailed anthropomorphic being is standing near a tail-less animal, which is likely to be his ideogram and indicate his identity. The anthropomorphic being has an owl-like 'oculi-face'. Around the face there are two disks and numerous dots, as if some ideas or thoughts were coming out.
Source: E. Anati, 1989, p. 220.
(WARA Archive W00263)
Area code: A-I. Cat.: C-III.

Fig. 129
Evocation of a myth? Tamgali, Kazakistan. Anthropo-zoomorphic beings interplay in a descriptive scene. Two anthropomorphic wolves are holding hooks, or have hook-like hands. They approach a small tailed being with a feather on his head.
Source: E. Anati, 1989, p. 31. (WARA Archive W00264)
Area code: A-I. Cat.: C-III.

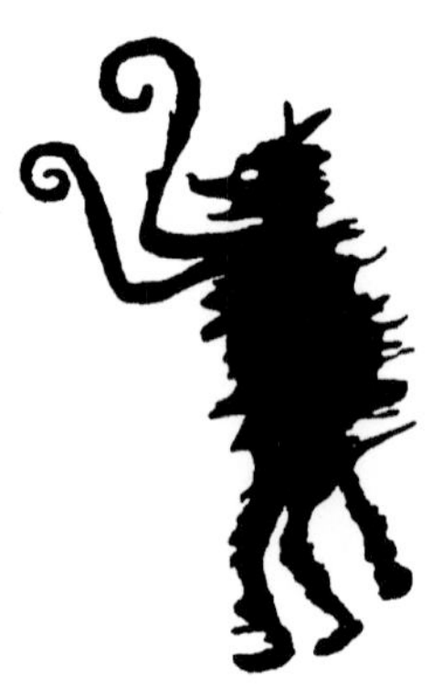

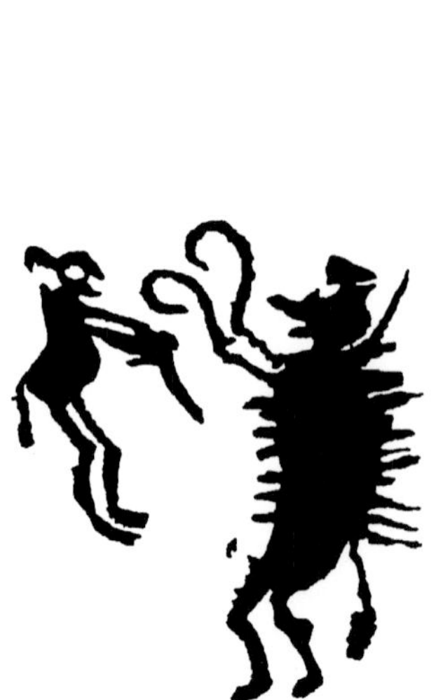

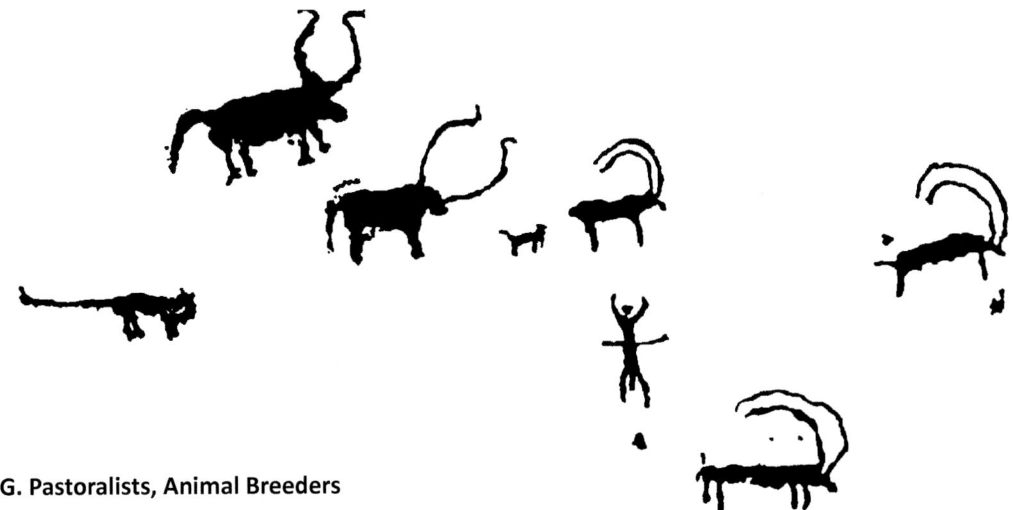

G. Pastoralists, Animal Breeders

Fig. 130
The danger of wild felines for both domestic and wild animals (and man). Rock engravings of hunting-and-pastoral people from Wadi Huwara, Egyptian Sinai. Long horned oxen, one dog and antelopes are moving away from a lion. The human figure is in a 'praying' position. These kind of rock engravings are likely to have a commemorative character.
Source: E. Anati, 1979, p. 44. (WARA Archive W00276)
Area code: B-III. Cat.: D-I.

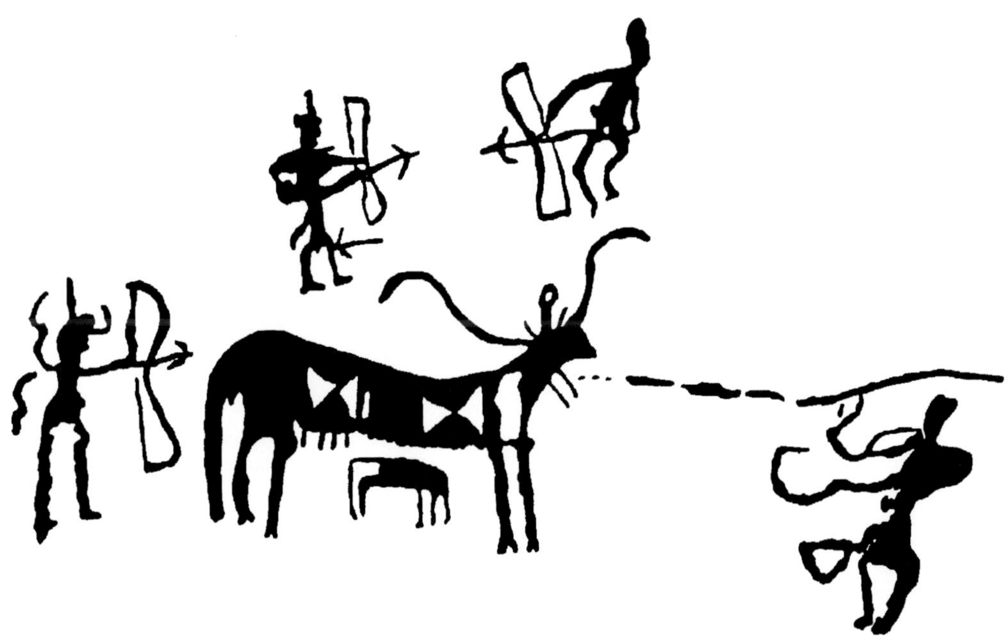

Fig. 131
Story-telling among pastoralists. Rock engraving of hunting and pastoral people from Jebel Uwenat, Egypt. While three people are fighting with each other with bows and arrows a fourth man is attacking a domestic ox with a spear. Between the horns and on the body, the ox has ideograms of identification.
Source: Drawn from a photograph of H. Winkler. (WARA Archive W00277)
Area code: C-IV. Cat.: D-I.

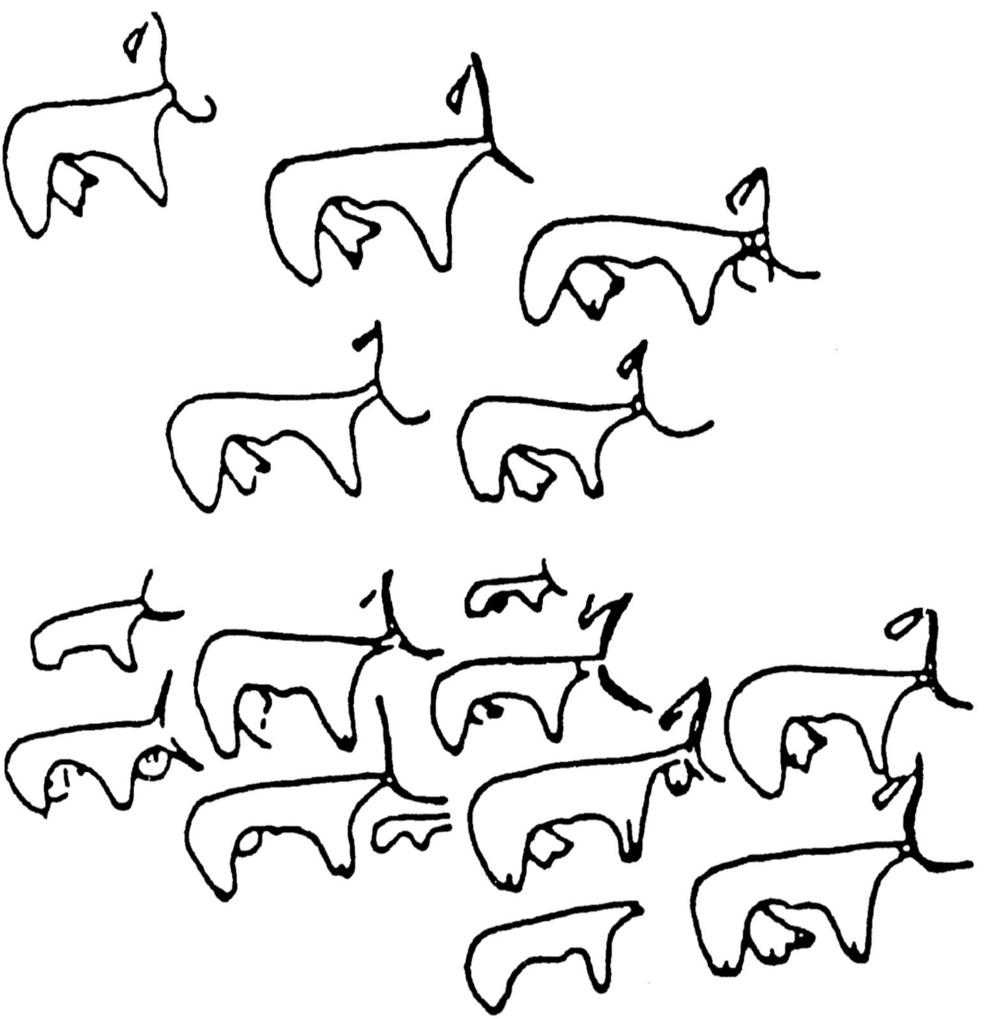

Fig. 132
The herd of oxen. Rock engravings from Chabbé Sidamo, Ethiopia. Cows with huge udders are followed by calves.
Source: Tracing by F. Anfray, 1967. (WARA Archive W00282)
Area Code: G-III. Cat.: D-II.

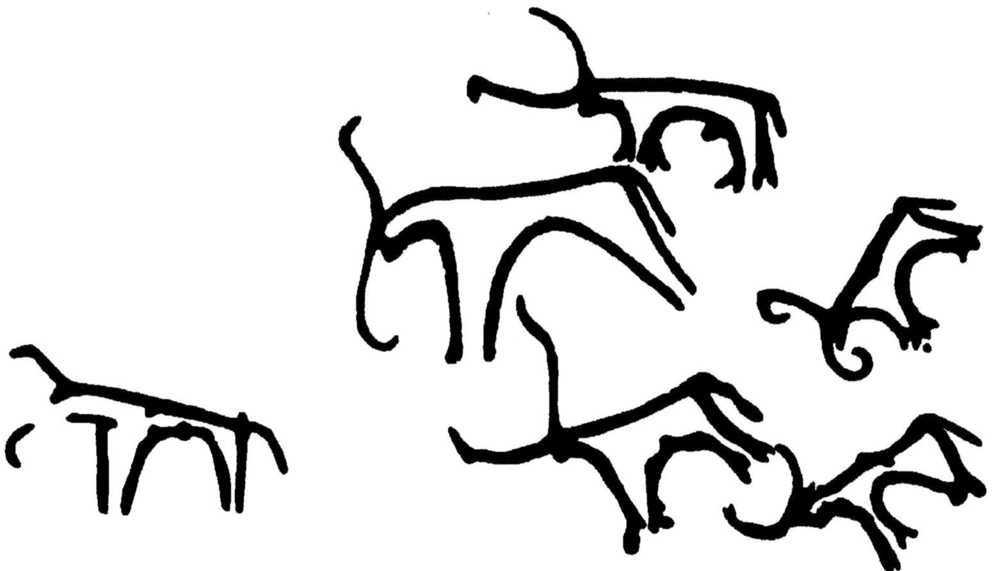

Fig. 133
A herd of long-horned bovines. Pastoral rock paintings of Wadi Nashriya, Sayala, Nubia, Egypt. The long horns are exaggerated in their proportions and are given idealized shapes
Source: Redrawn from M. Bietak and R. Engelmayer, 1963, taf. XXVII. (WARA Archive W00283)
Area Code: C-IV. Cat.: D-II.

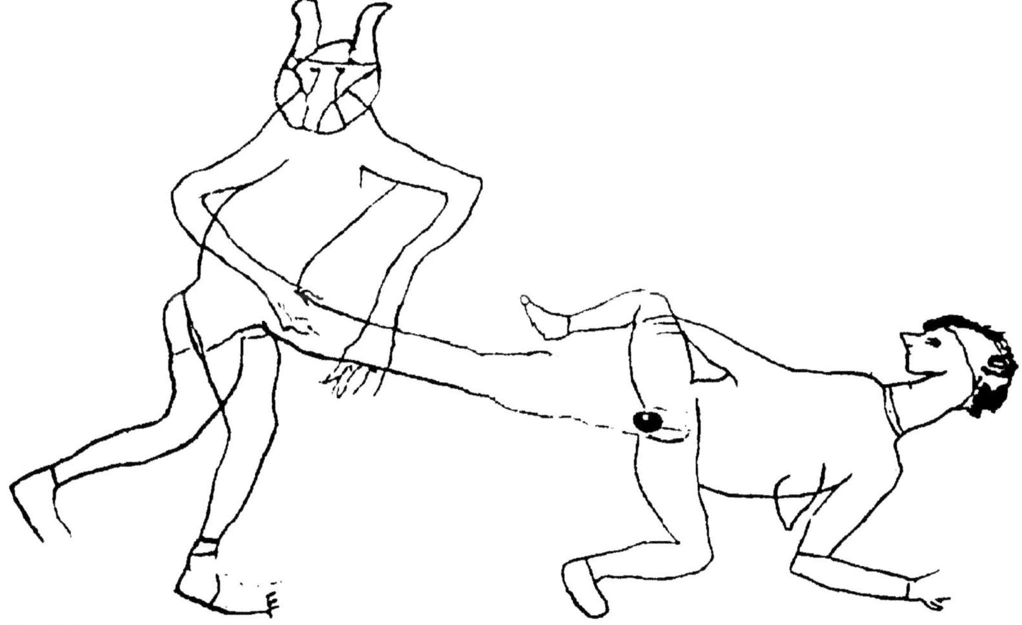

Fig. 134
The 'powerful feline' and the sleeping beauty. Pastoral engraving from Ti-n-lalan, Tadrart Acacus, Libya. Pastoral people often depict the presence of dream-like myths. The crude realistic style is sometimes present in the rock engravings but very rarely appears in the rock paintings which are usually more refined. Early phase of Pastoral Neolithic, size of tracing m. 2.70 by 1.80.
Source: F. Mori, 1975, p. 358. (WARA Archive W00284)
Area Code: C-II. Cat.: D-II.

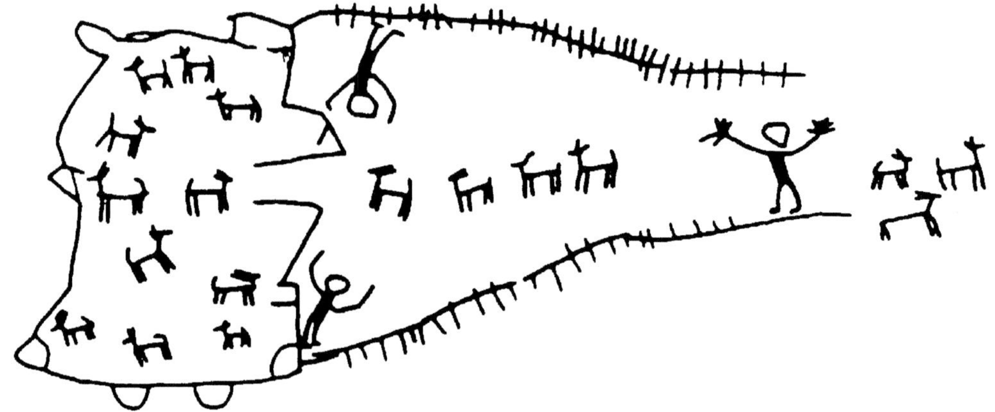

Fig. 135
Assembling the animals in the enclosure. Rock engraving of transhumant pastoralists from Rujum Hani, Jordan.
Source: E. Anati, 1979, p. 57. (WARA Archive W00285)
Area code: B-III. Cat.: D-II.

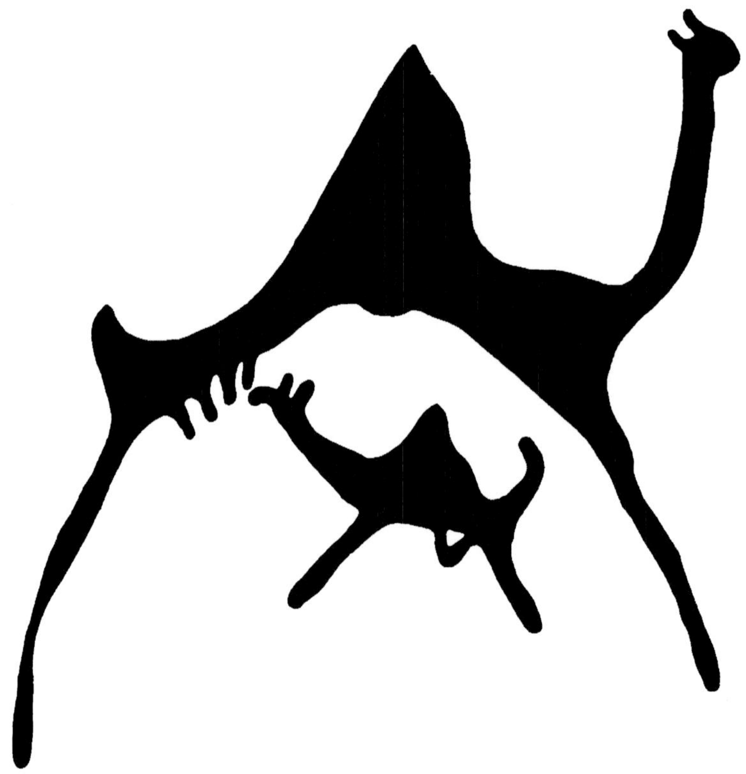

Fig. 136
Nursing camel in rock engraving of late semi-sedentary seasonal pastoralists. Nahal Odem, Southern Negev, Israel. The interest of pastoralists often focus on details of daily events .
Source: E. Anati, 1979, p. 62. (WARA Archive W00286)
Area code: B-III. Cat.: D-II.

146

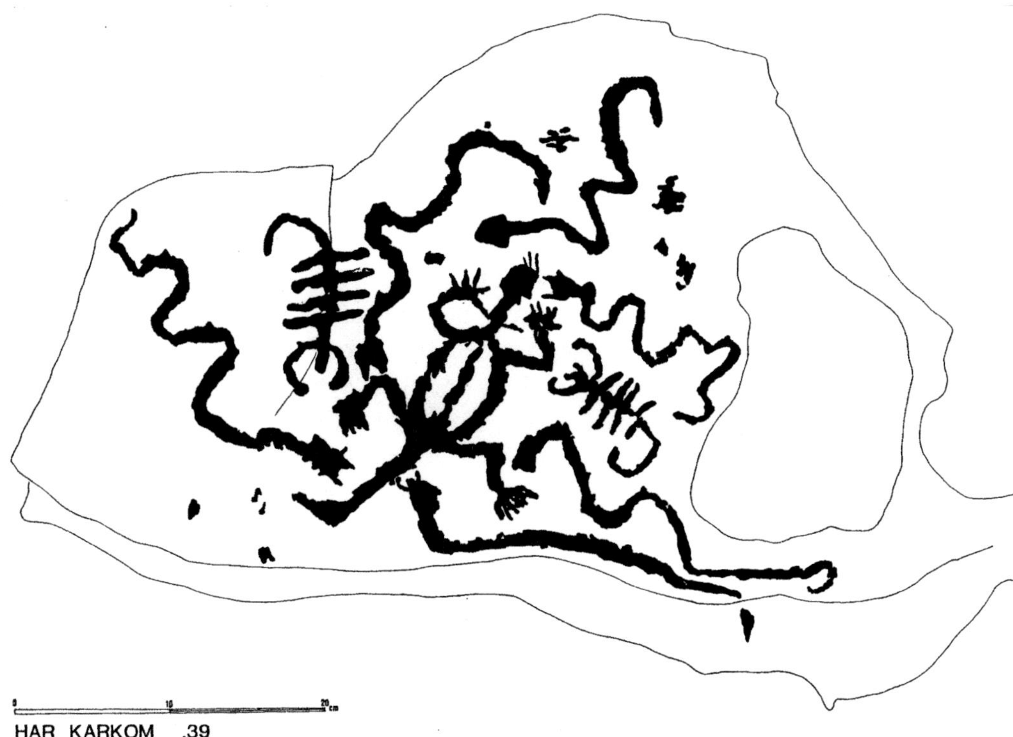

Fig. 137
Har Harkom Negev desert, Israel. Rock engraving from the Bronze Age Pastoralists representing a group of poisonous animals.
Source: tracing by E. Anati (WARA Archive W06003)
Area Code: B-III; Cat. D-II.

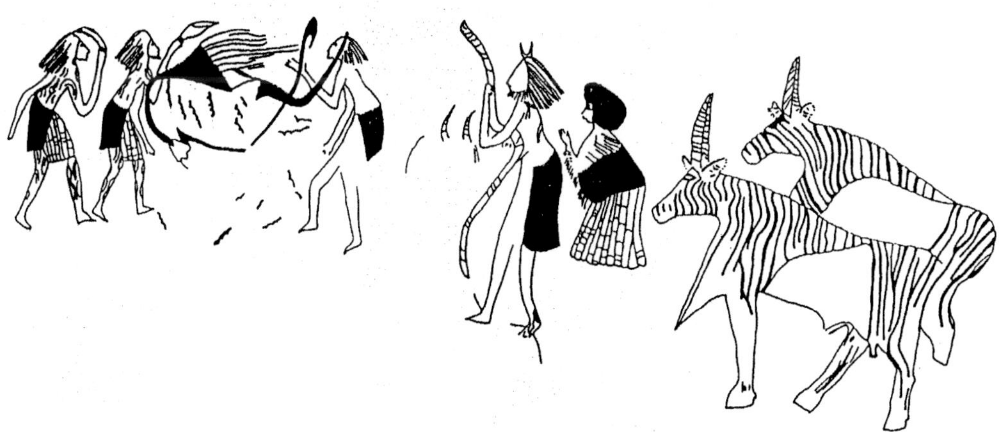

Fig. 138
Pastoral rock painting of Quan Derbaouen, Tassili-n-Ajjer, Algeria. It describes a rite of assigning the task of fire preservation.
Source: R. Kuper. (WARA Archive W07133)
Area Code: C-II; Cat. D-II.

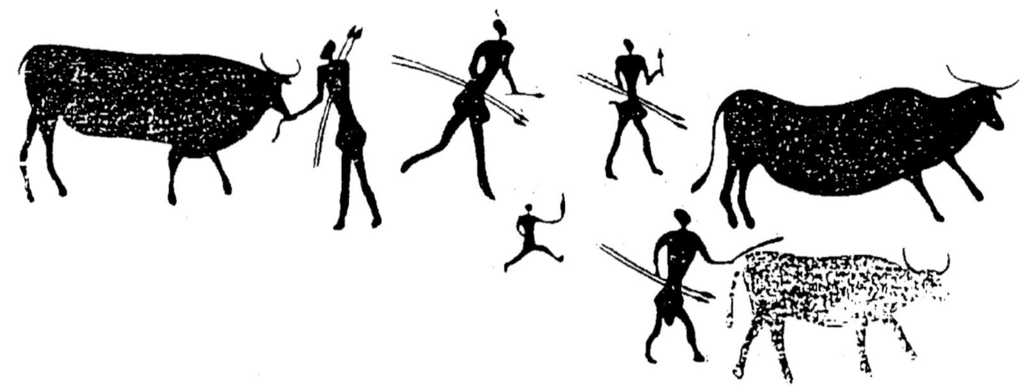

Fig. 139
The relationship between man and his animals. Rock paintings from South Africa (site unspecified). This scene describes pastoral people on the move. A man is giving some food or medicine to a bovine while the others are continuing on their way.
Source:Tracing by M.H. Tongue, 1909. (WARA Archive W00280)
Area code: D-V. Cat.: C-II.

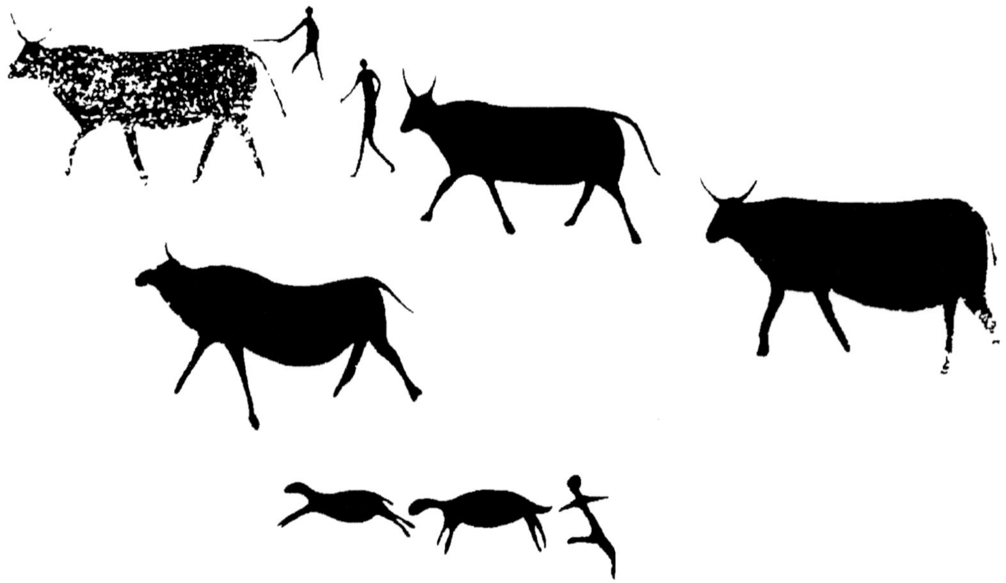

Fig. 140
Rock paintings of nomadic pastoralists. These are likely to come from the same area as the previous drawing. South Africa.
Source:Tracing by M.H. Tongue, 1909. (WARA Archive W00281)
Area code: D-V. Cat.: D-II.

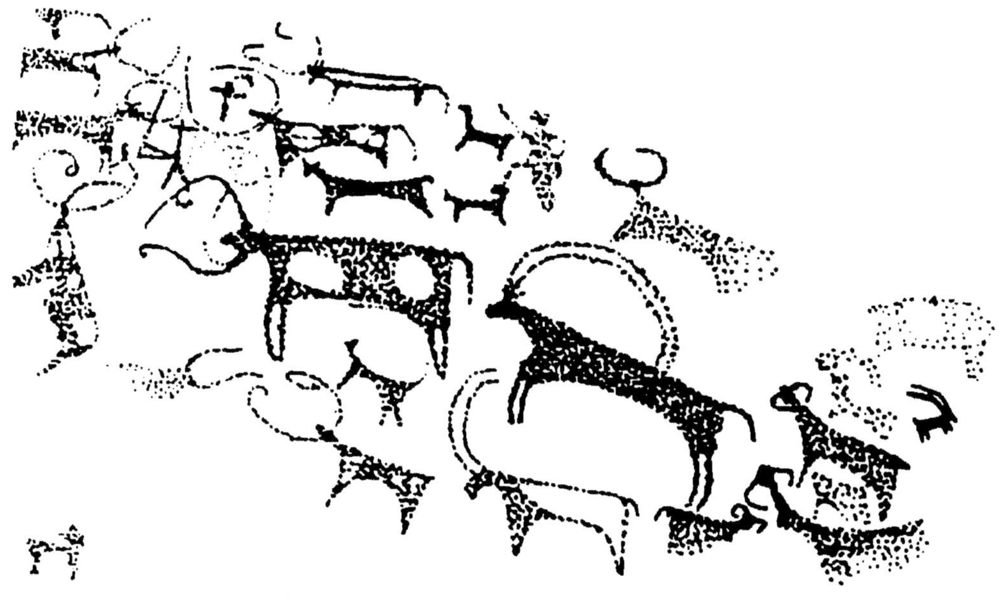

Fig. 141
Rock engravings of pastoral people from Hijaz, Saudi Arabia. Bovines, caprines and ovines are taken care of by man. The size of the animals is bigger than that of the humans. Source: E. Anati, 1979, p. 39. (WARA Archive W00278)
Area code: B-IV. Cat.: D-II.

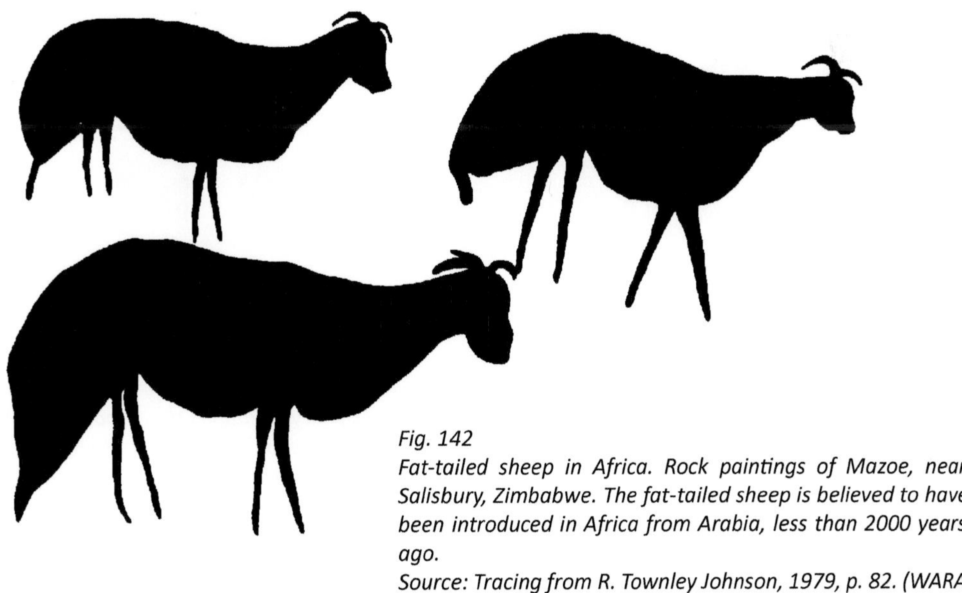

Fig. 142
Fat-tailed sheep in Africa. Rock paintings of Mazoe, near Salisbury, Zimbabwe. The fat-tailed sheep is believed to have been introduced in Africa from Arabia, less than 2000 years ago.
Source: Tracing from R. Townley Johnson, 1979, p. 82. (WARA Archive W00279)
Area code: D-V. Cat.: D-II.

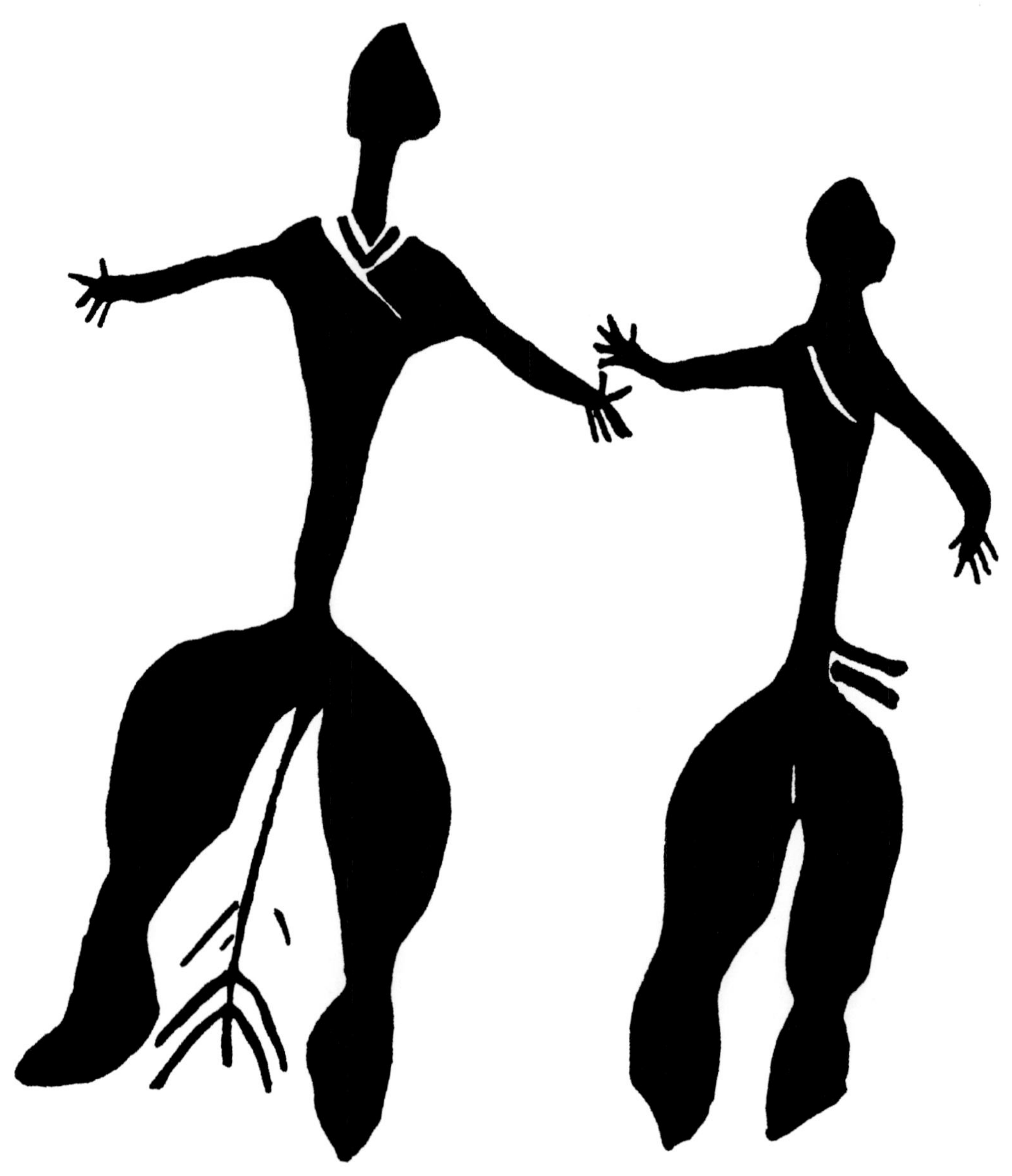

H. Mixed Economy

Fig. 143
Symbols for male and female. Rock engravings of Incipient Agriculturists of Gobustan, Azerbaijan maintain ideograms of Early Hunters, indicating the persistence of a millenary tradition. The 'arbolet' or 'branch', indicates the male sex, while the two parallel lines by the side of the woman, or 'lips', indicate the female sex. This may well be an indication of the names given to the sexual organs by those people.
Source: E. Anati, Gobustan, Azerbaijan, 2001, rock No. 42. (WARA Archive W00287)
Area Code: E-III. Cat.: E-I.

Fig. 144
Incipient Agriculturalists. Rock paintings of Dos Aguas, Spain. Women with large gowns are naked on the upper part of the body. They are using digging sticks?
Source: A. Beltran, 1980, p.43. (WARA Archive W00288)
Area Code: E-I. Cat.: E-I..

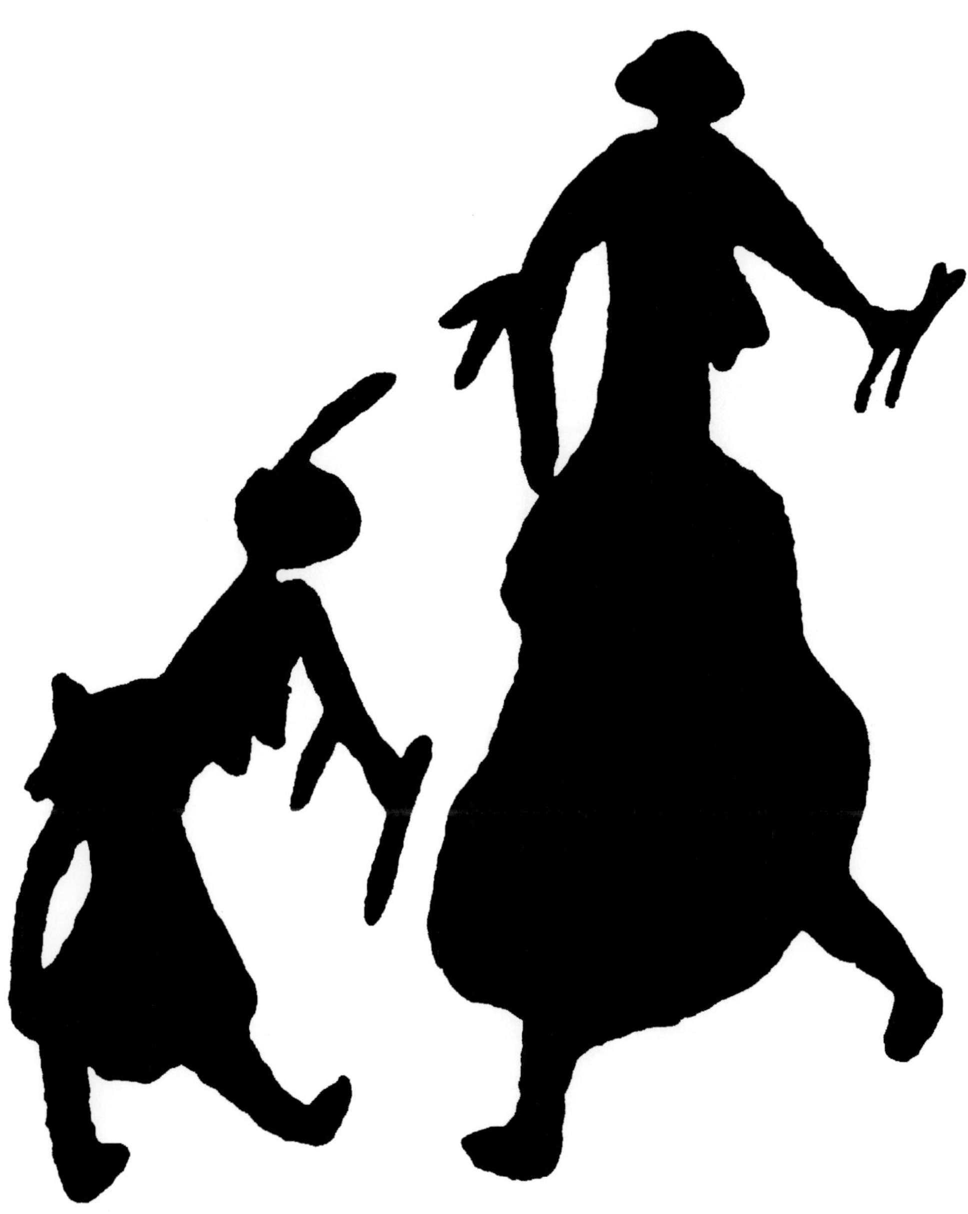

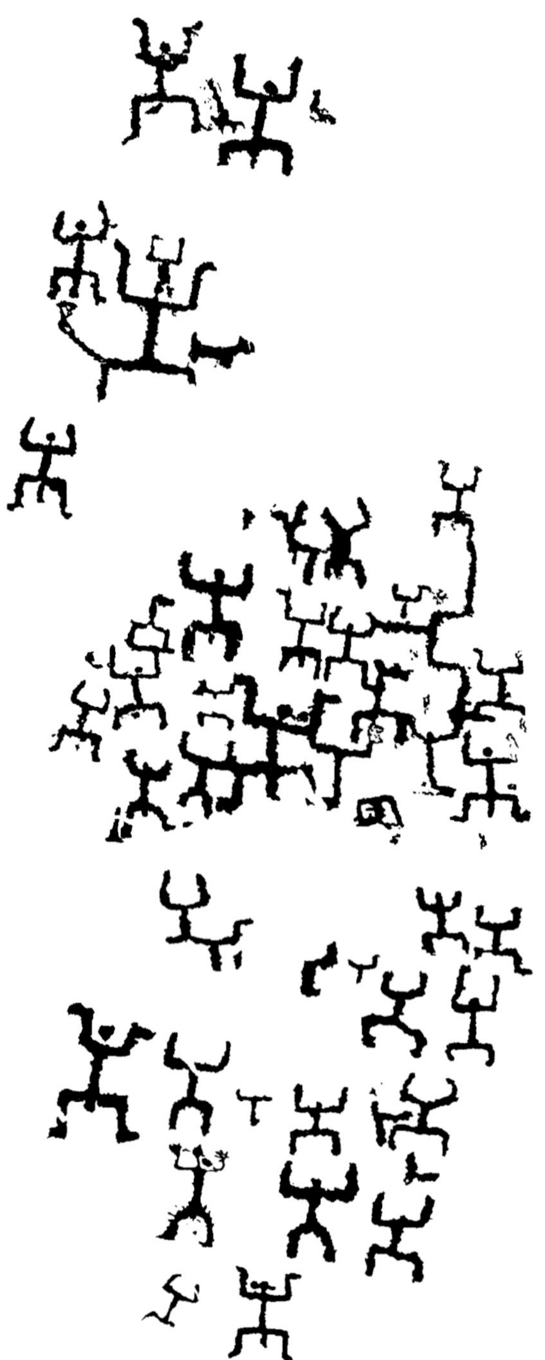

Fig. 145
A social event. Rock engravings at Naquane, Valcamonica, Italy. A composition of schematic anthropomorphic figures. Bottom center, an anthropomorphic figure has an animal head (masked?). Immediately above it, a human figure with large hands is emitting energy rays from his body. He has been considered as a shaman. Several couples may be seen composed of one headless figure and one headed figure. In several tribal societies, this kind of 'couple' indicates the separation of 'body and soul' of the same individual.
Source: E. Anati, 1976, p. 60. (WARA Archive W00293)
Area Code: E-I. Cat.: E-I.

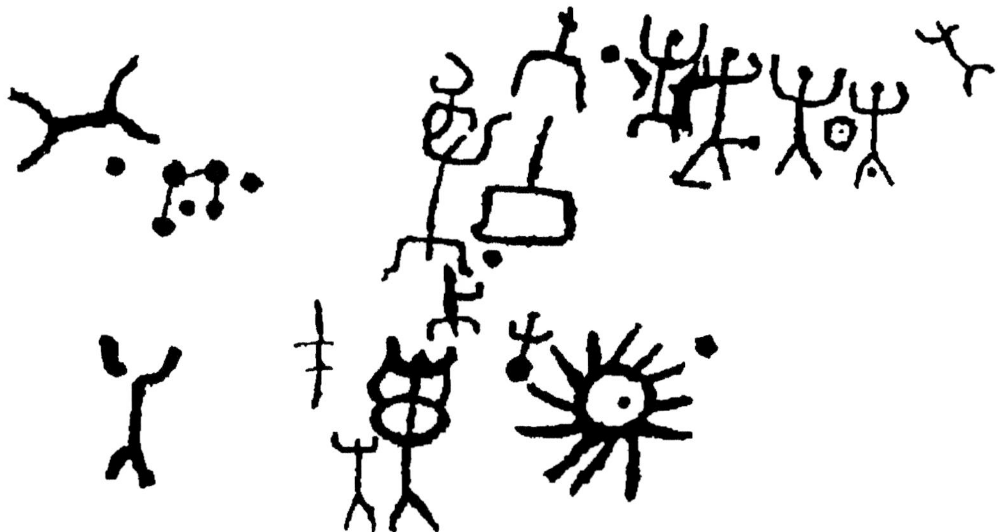

Fig. 146
Rock engravings of people with complex economy. Coren del Valento, Valcamonica, Italy. The panel seems to represent a scene of solar cult. Neolithic period, ca. 4000 BC.
Source: E. Anati, 1982, p. 162. (WARA Archive W00294)
Area code: E-I. Cat.: E-I.

Fig. 147
An appeal to supernatural forces by Incipient Agriculturists. Rock engravings of Kamooally, Hawaii, USA (North Pacific). The human figure with upraised arm (in 'worship' posture) is addressing to ideograms above. A disk which is likely to mean 'sky', an axe or some other tool, which is emanating energy (the dots) might indicate the kind of power he is addressing to, and more ideograms. By the side of the human figure there is a larger ideogram, which is indicating who is the worshipper. It is likely to be a badly depicted rectangular shape meaning 'land' or 'territory' identifying the individual who may represent the maker of the engraving. In such case the anthropomorph would be 'a man from the land' or a 'land owner'.
Source: Drawn from a photograph by J.H. Cox & E. Stasack 1970, p. 8. (WARA Archive W00295)
Area code: F-II. Cat.: E-I.

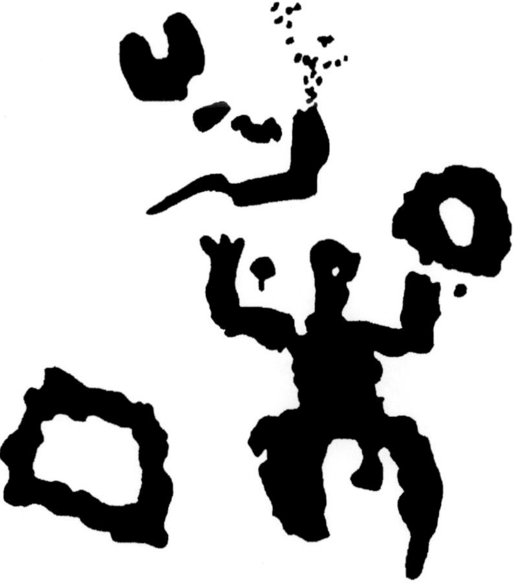

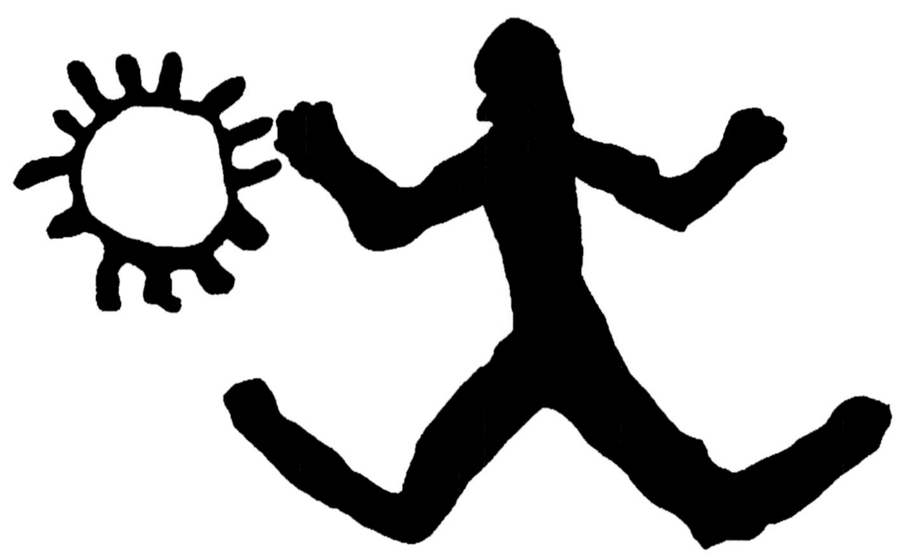

Fig. 148
An appeal to supernatural forces by Incipient Agriculturists. Red rock painting from Carrizo Plain, California, USA. The worshipper is genuflected and addresses to a sun disk with 13 rays.
Source: Drawn from a photograph by J.A. Van Tillburg, 1983, pl. 11. (WARA Archive W00296)
Area code: H-III. Cat.: E-I.

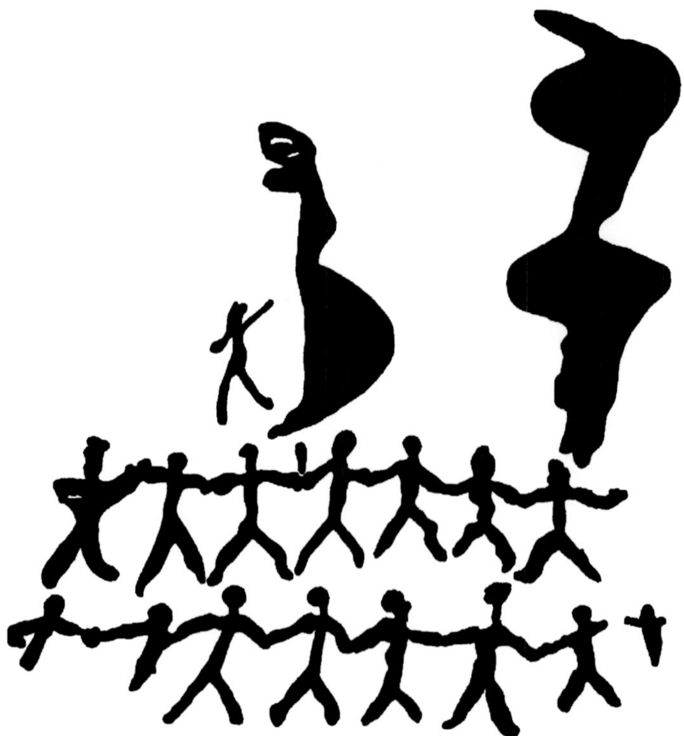

Fig. 149
The cloudy spirits. Rock engravings of incipient Agricalturalists of Gobustan. Two rows of people hold hands and dance (?) while an isolated person seems to address one of the two cloudy spirits above them. The scene seems to evoke a ceremony.
Source: Drawn from a photograph of I.M. Djafarsade, 1973, rock n°46
Area Code: E-III. Cat.: D-I

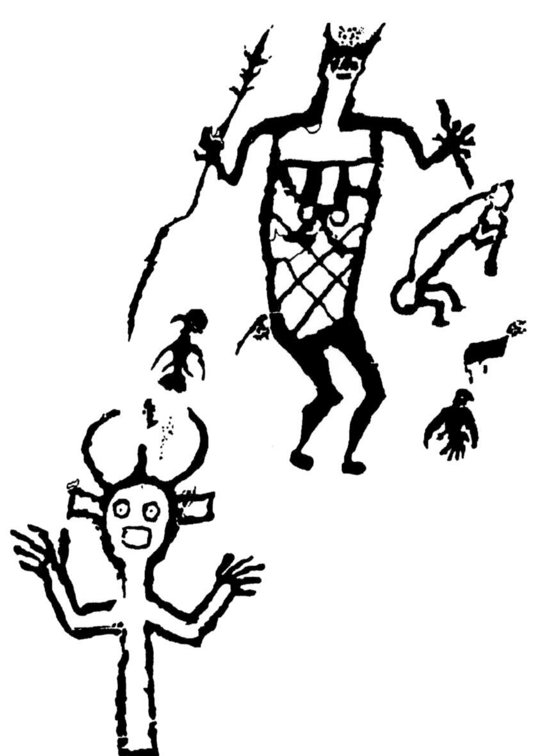

Fig. 150
Narrative rock engraving evocating a myth, of people in an early phase of complex economy. Comanche Gap, New Mexico, USA. The spirit in the lower left side of the panel has, above him, an ideogram which identifies him. He is sending a mythic ancestor on his way. The ancestor, upper anthropomorphic figure, is holding corn in his hand. Near his legs he has his own ideogram of identification. He is shown the way by Kukupeli (a mythic positive spirit of the Great Plains), who is playing a flute (telling stories).
Source: Drawn from a photograph by E. Anati, in E. Anati, 1989, pl. 35. (WARA Archive W00298)
Area code: F-II. Cat.: E-I.

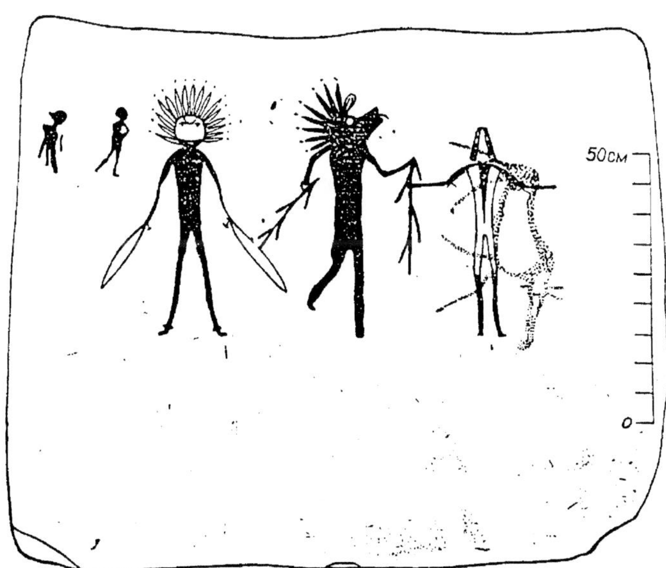

Fig. 151
Paintings on slab of Early Agriculturists evocate mythic ancestors. Cist tomb, Karakul, Siberia. This slab is one of several cist tombs from the Chalcolithic age. The central 'spirit' is apparently giving an 'arbolet' (symbol of masculine energy) to the being on is right, walking in his direction and turning the face to the feather-decorated anthropomorph to his left. The dotted elk, to the right, belong to an earlier phase.
Source: B.D. Kubarev, 1988, p. 49. (WARA Archive W00299)
Area code: A-I. Cat.: A-IV; E-II.

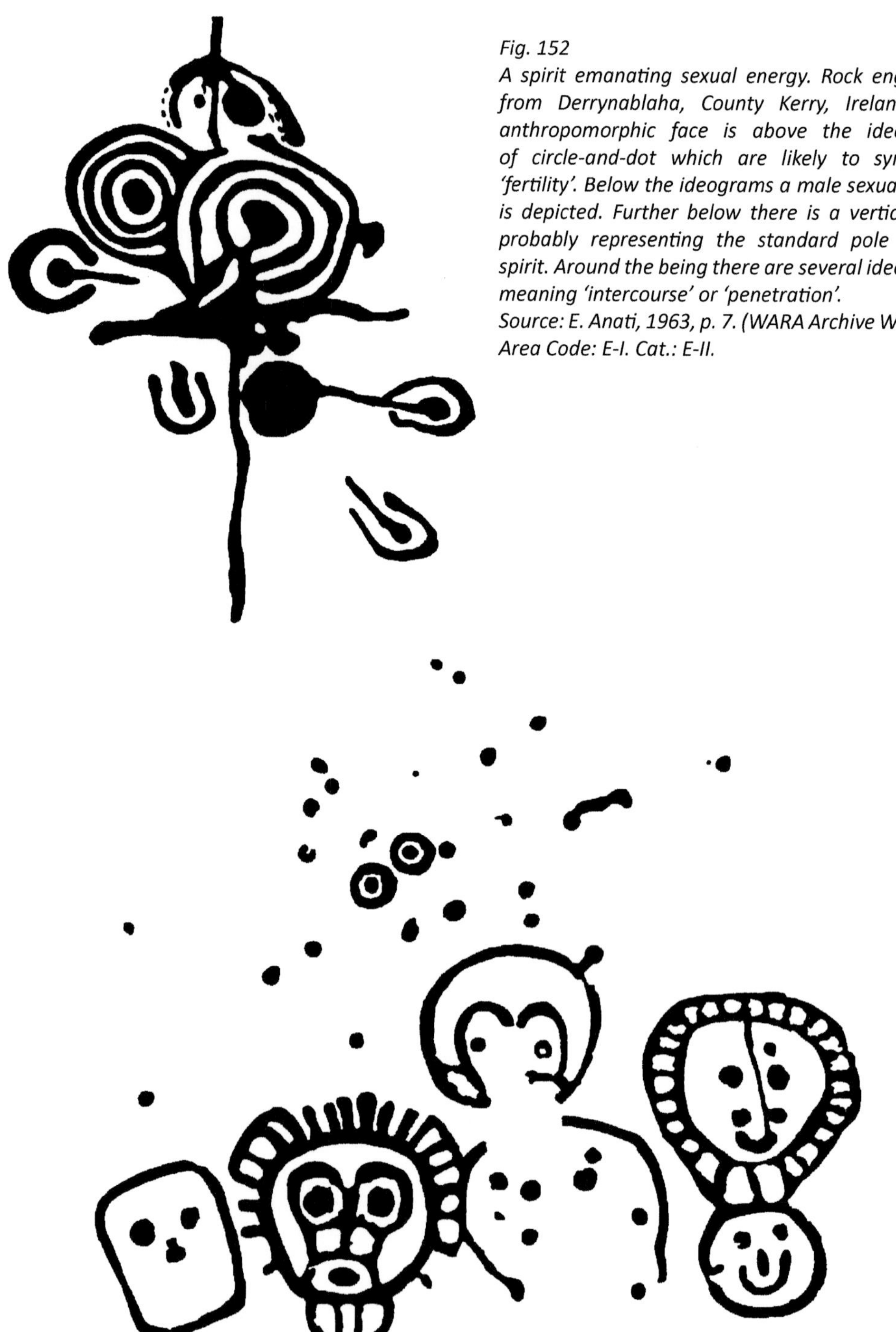

Fig. 152
A spirit emanating sexual energy. Rock engraving from Derrynablaha, County Kerry, Ireland. The anthropomorphic face is above the ideograms of circle-and-dot which are likely to symbolize 'fertility'. Below the ideograms a male sexual organ is depicted. Further below there is a vertical line, probably representing the standard pole of the spirit. Around the being there are several ideograms meaning 'intercourse' or 'penetration'.
Source: E. Anati, 1963, p. 7. (WARA Archive W00300)
Area Code: E-I. Cat.: E-II.

Fig. 153
Spirits on the rocks. Rock engravings of Incipient Food Producers from Helan Shan,
Ningxia, China. Each one of the masks appears to have its own personality. The surrounding rock surface is covered by cup-marks. The rock surface is steeply oblique.
Source: Chen Zhao-Fu, 1988, p. 162. (WARA Archive W00301)
Area code: A-II. Cat.: E-I.

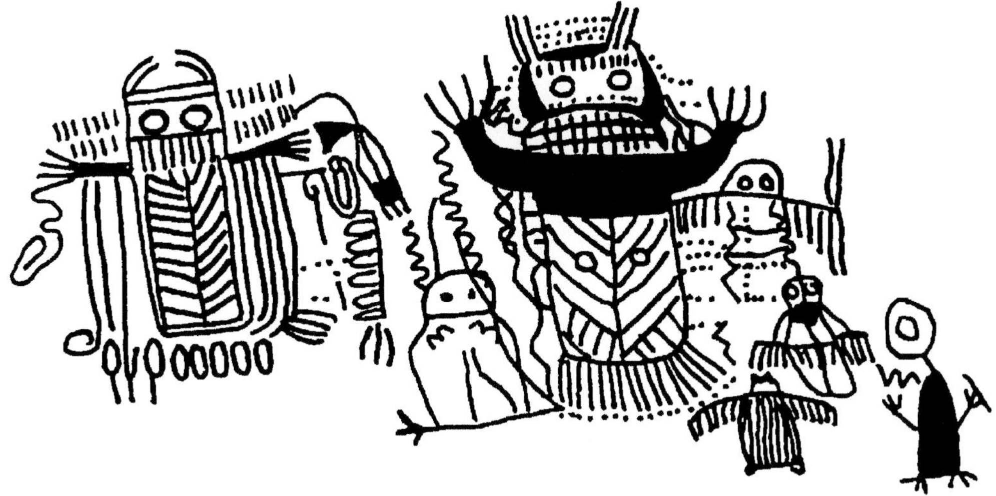

Fig. 154
The powerful spirits of the Shoshoni nation. Rock engravings of Dinwoody Lake, Wyoming, USA. Like other tribes of North America, the Shoshoni used to evocate ancestral spirits in front of rock surfaces on which the spirits were depicted. According to their tradition 'the spirits are inside the rocks' and these images 'have always been there'. Each spirit can be recognized by the shape and the ideograms that accompany him.
Source: C. Grant, 1983, p. 47. (WARA Archive W00302)
Area code: F-II. Cat.: E I-II.

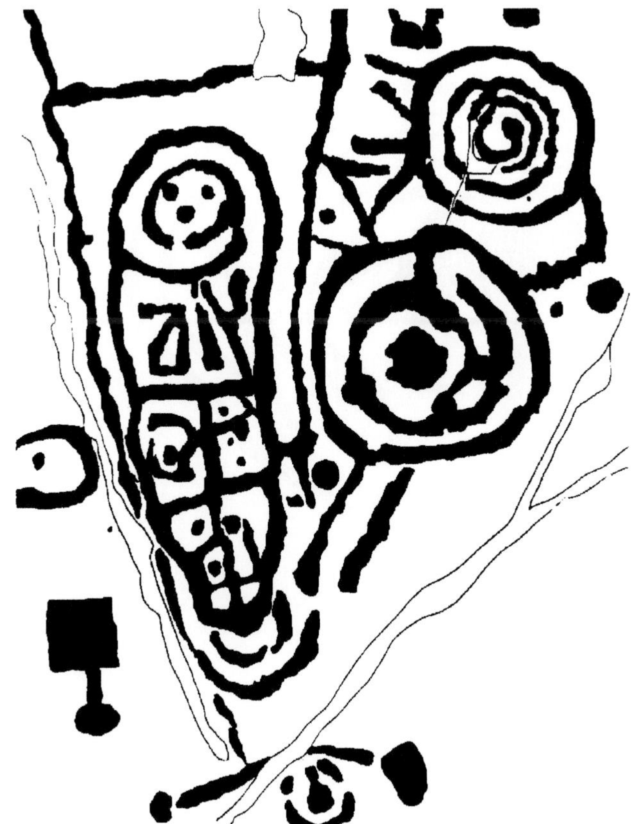

Fig. 155
The so-called 'Sonico Idol'. Rock engraving of Early Agriculturists, form Sonico, Valcamonica, Italy. A vaguely anthropomorphic 'baby-god' is surrounded by its ideograms. The 'body' of the anthropomorph is subdivided by horizontal lines. The upper one separates the mask-like rounded head (sky) from the upper part of the body which is made of two rectangles (territory). Inside them are the indicative symbols, among which a bucranium and an axe. The lower part, vaguely triangular, has a net-like pattern with dots (the underworld).
Source: E. Anati, 1982, p. 183. (WARA Archive W00303)
Area code: E-I. Cat.: E-II.

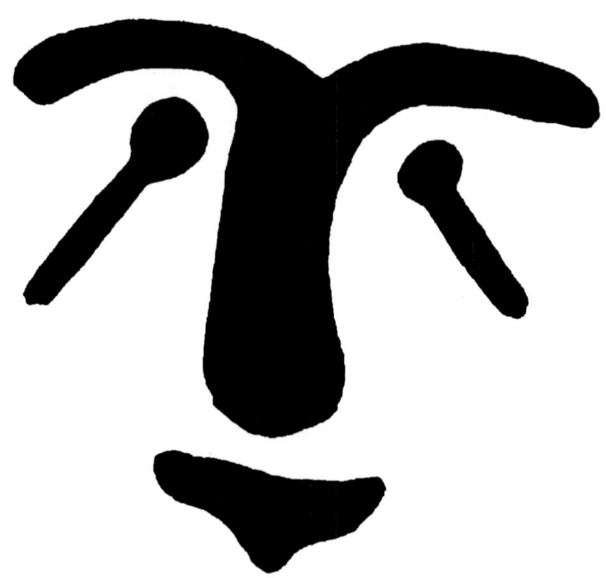

Fig. 156
The crying mask. Rock engraving of Incipient Complex Economy. Afofrak, British Columbia, Canada. Numerous masks from the same period in British Columbia display a larm pattern and are currently called 'crying masks'. Behind this representation there is a mythic tale of a spirit who regretted his bad deeds.
Source: B. and R. Hill, 1974, p. 241. (WARA Archive W00322)
Area Code: F-I. Cat.: E-II.

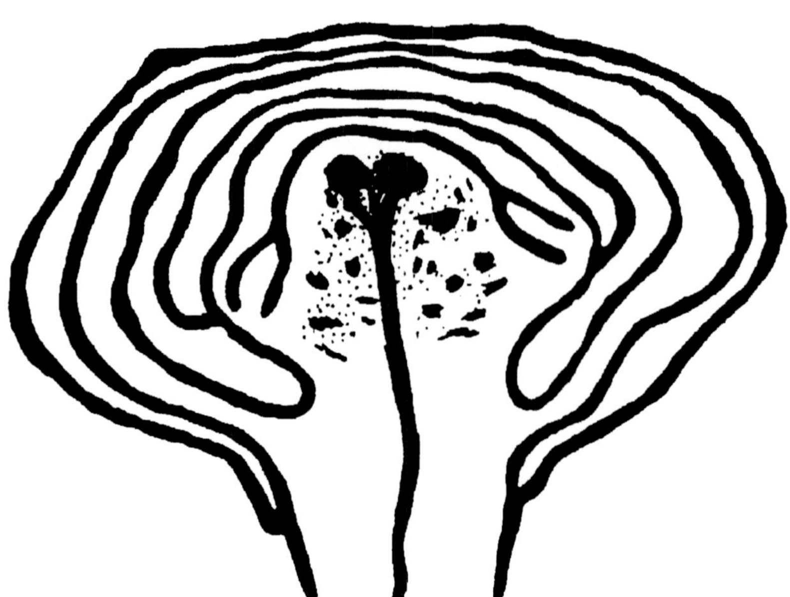

Fig. 157
The face of the Spirit. Rock engraving of complex economy from Laxe do Pombal, Galacia, Spain. The labyrinth shape surrounding the occuli-face is likely to be an indication that the being is from the world of the dead. The dots around the occuli may represent messages or ideas emanating from the being.
Source: E. Anati, 1968, p. 21. (WARA Archive W00305)
Area Code: E-I. Cat.: E-II.

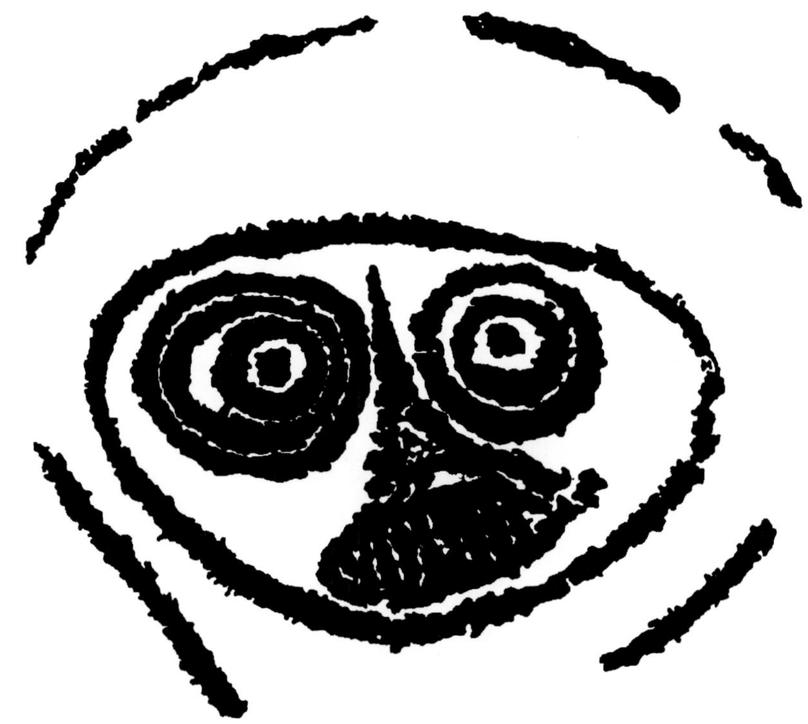

Fig. 158
The power of the rock. A spirit-mask engraved near Fulford Harbour, Salt Spring Island, British Columbia, Canada. The eyes are different from each other, one with two rings, the other with three. The mouth is supposed to be that of a predatory fish.
Source: Drawn from a photograph, cf. B. & R. Hill, 1974, p. 86. (WARA Archive W00306)
Area code: F-I. Cat.: E-II.

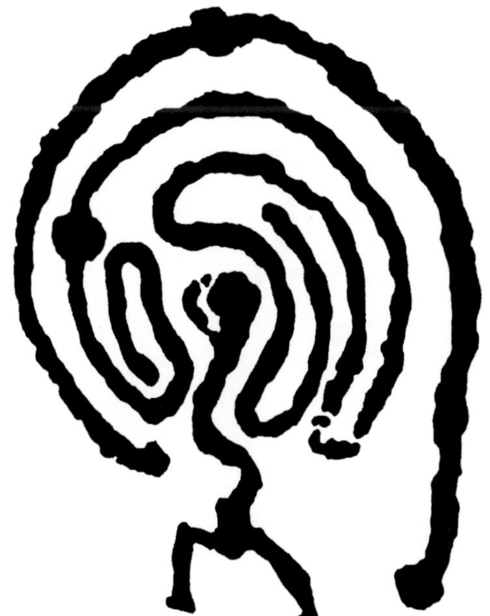

Fig. 159
Penetrating the labyrinth. Rock engraving of Complex Economy from Laxe da Rotea de Mende, Campo Lameiro, Galacia, Spain. The labyrinth is likely to represent the world of the dead but is often identified with the feminine sexual organ. The being may be a shaman seeking communication with the spirits. The sexual penetration is identified with a visit to the world of the spirits, where children reincarnate the ancestor's rebirth.
Source: E. Anati, 1968, p. 89. (WARA Archive W00307)
Area Code: E-I. Cat.: E-II.

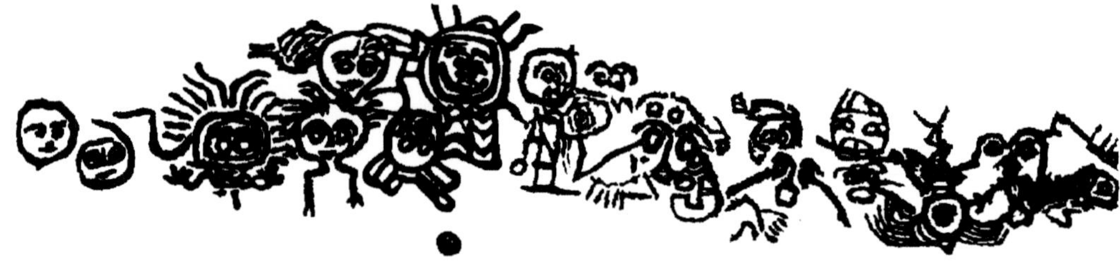

Fig. 160
Shamans Pool, Kulleet Bay, British Columbia, Canada. Over 20 'masks' are represented here, each one different from the others, in a place which is still considered to be sacred
Source: Drawn from a photograph in B. and R. Hill, 1974, p. 94. (WARA Archive W00319)
Area Code: F-I. Cat.: E-II.

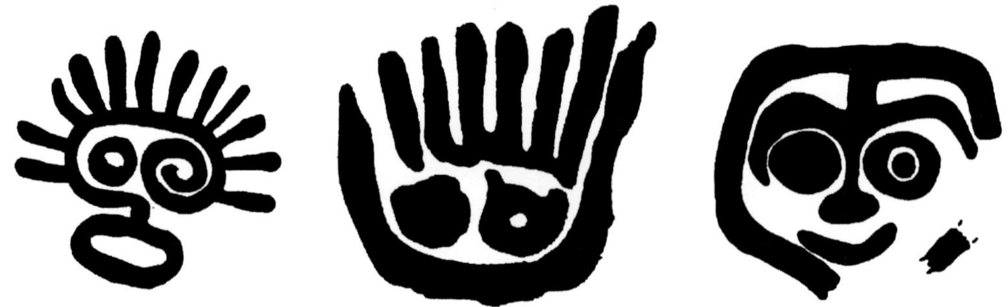

Fig. 161
The eloquent eye of people with Incipient Complex Economy. Deeply engraved mask figures from British Columbia, Canada. When the eyes in facial figures are different they convey a message. A recurrent message is 'I, spirit, can see things you do not see'. But they can also indicate the identity of a special spirit who can see or preview supernatural events.
Source: B. & R. Hill, 1974, p. 275. (WARA Archive W00320)
Area code: F-I. Cat.: E-II.

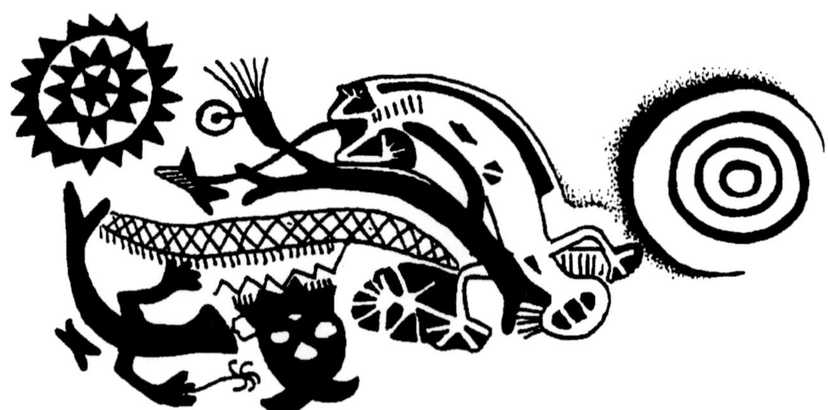

Fig. 162
Psychedelic cave paintings of the Chumash. Santa Barbara, California, USA. Ritual caves of the Chumash Indians of California are richly decorated in red, yellow and black with images of spirits and with ideograms of celestial and terrestrial energies which evocate visions. They are said to have been executed by shamans while under the effect of hallucinogens.
Source: C. Grant, 1983, p. 35. (WARA Archive W00321)
Area code: F-III. Cat.: E-III.

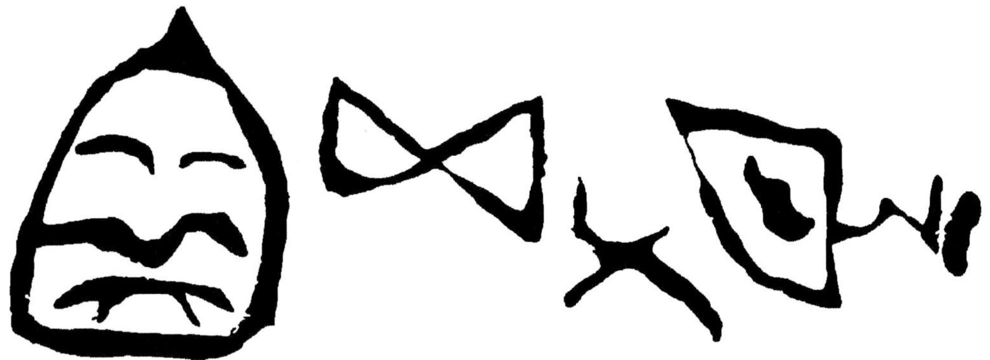

Fig. 163
An ideographic sequence. Helan-Shan, Ningxia, China. This is likely to be a 'written' message. The subject, the mask, is followed by a row of ideograms.
Source: Chen Zhao-Fu, 1988, p. 46. (WARA Archive W00308)
Area code: A-II. Cat.: E-II.

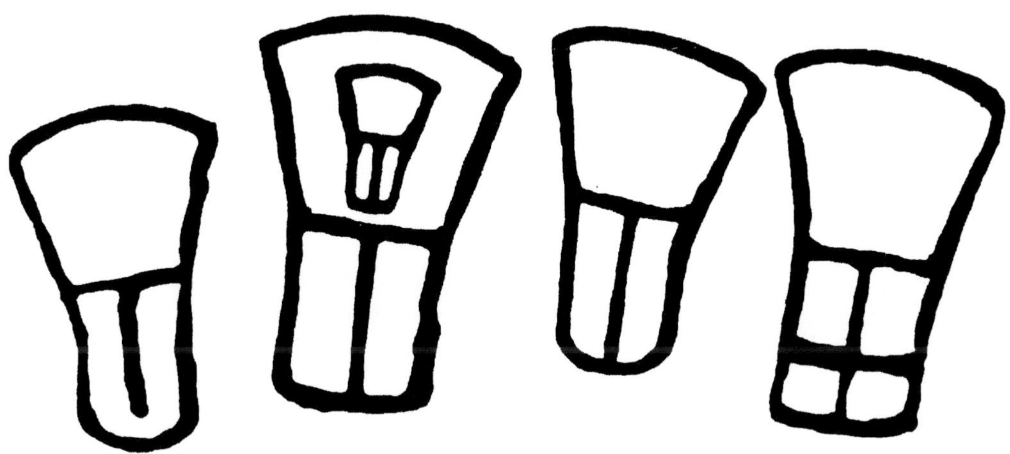

Fig. 164
Wealth represented by copper. Rock engravings of Complex Economy with Metallurgy. Beaumont Island, British Columbia, Canada. The rock engravings represent copper ingots offered to special guests in the potlatch ceremony in the occasion of an important marriage or the death of a chief, when the host, to gain political and social prestige is displaying his wealth. The habit is still reported in accounts of the 19th century and the shape of copper ingots was still the same.
Source: B. & R. Hill, 1974, p. 276. (WARA Archive W00309)
Area code: F-I. Cat.: E-II.

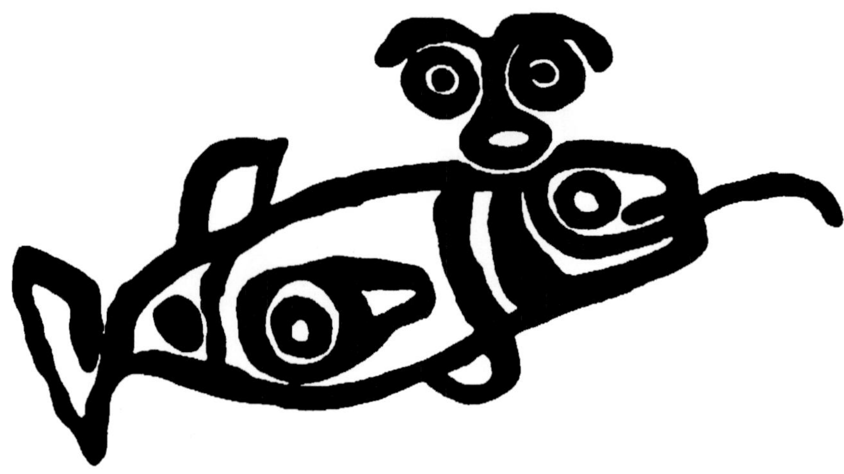

Fig. 165
The 'Lord of fishes'. Rock engraving of Incipient Complex Economy. Return Channel, British Columbia, Canada.
The image or mask of an ancestral spirit is like a second face of a spirit-fish which is identified by the ideogram
engraved on its body. The long tongue out of the mouth indicates 'breathing' or 'emanating vital energy'.
Source: B. & R. Hill, 1974, p. 166. (WARA Archive W00310)
Area code: F-I. Cat.: E-II.

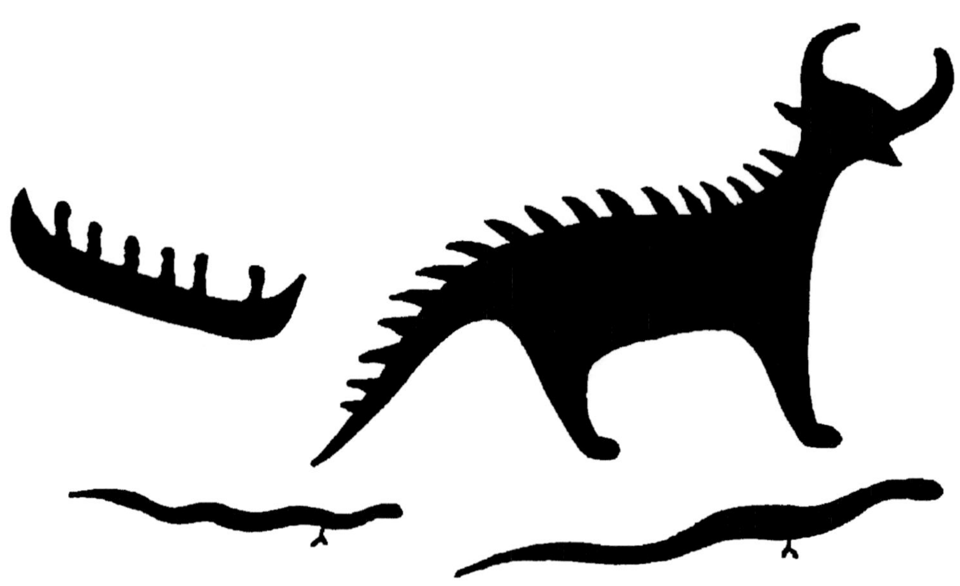

Fig. 166
A mysterious journey of the Algonquian people. Agawa, Ontario, Canada. This painting in red on a vertical
rock washed by the waves of Lake Superior is supposed to be over 2000 years old and is still regarded with
reverence by the local tribes. According to tradition it evocates the story of a group of people, on a canoe
over Lake Superior who met the spirits of the underworld, Mishipizbiw the spirit of the black panther, and the
Great Legged Snake.
Source: Tracing by Selwyn Dewdney, 1962, p. 85. (WARA Archive W00311)
Area code: F-I. Cat.: E-II.

162

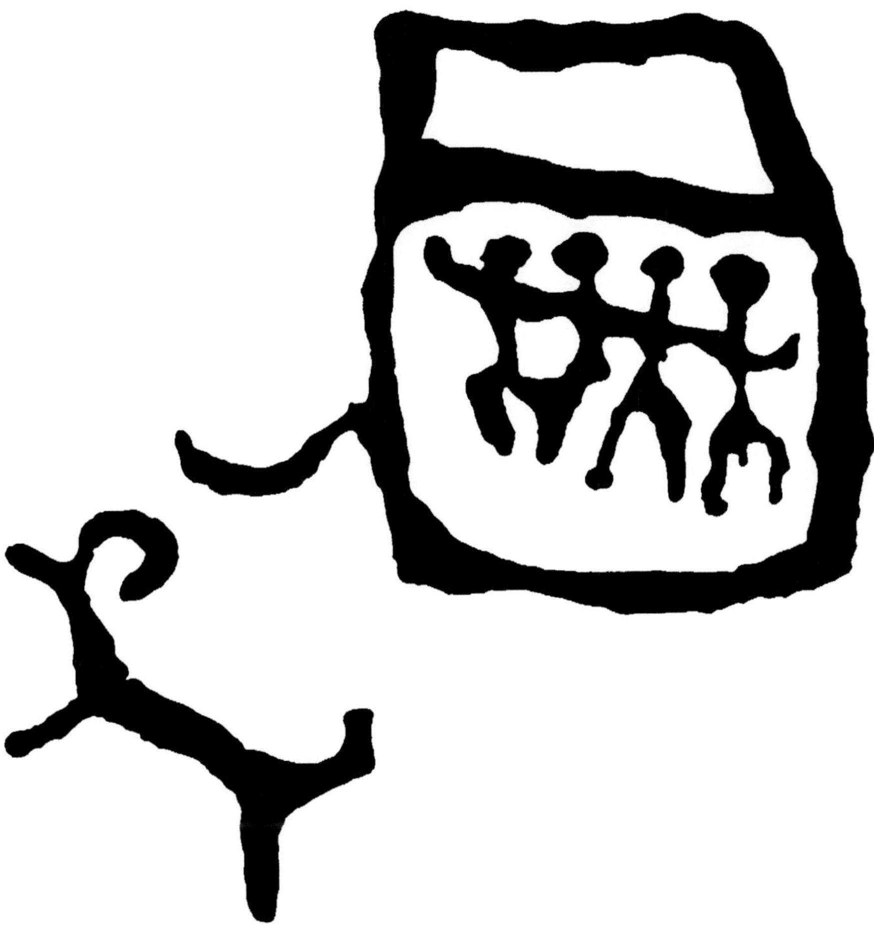

Fig. 167
Historical records: commemoration or wishful thinking? Rock engravings of Helan Shan, Ningxia, China. The rectangle means 'land' or 'territory'. The same meaning is preserved in early Chinese writing. The message of this depiction is something like: 'The four clans of (our) people are in the territory while the clan of the goat (breeders) is out'. It seems to reveal the presence of contrasts between Agriculturists and Pastoralists.
Source: Chen Zhao-Fu, 1988, p. 178. (WARA Archive W00312)
Area code: A-II. Cat.: E-II.

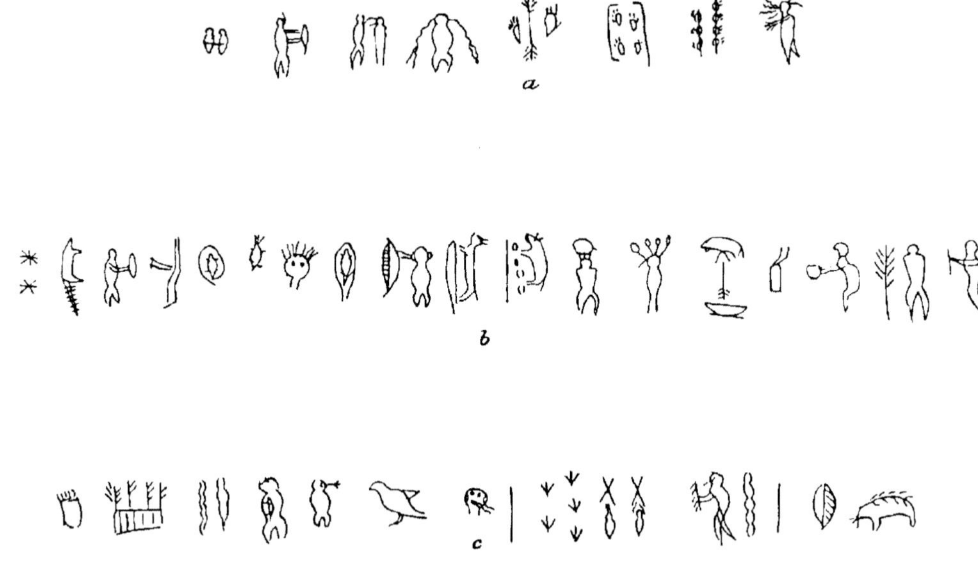

Fig. 168
Graphic memorization of a story which is evocated by a song of the Ojibwa tribe, near Red Lake, Canada.
Source: G. Mallery, 1888, vol. I, p. 245. (WARA Archive W00313)
Area code: F-I. Cat.: E-II.

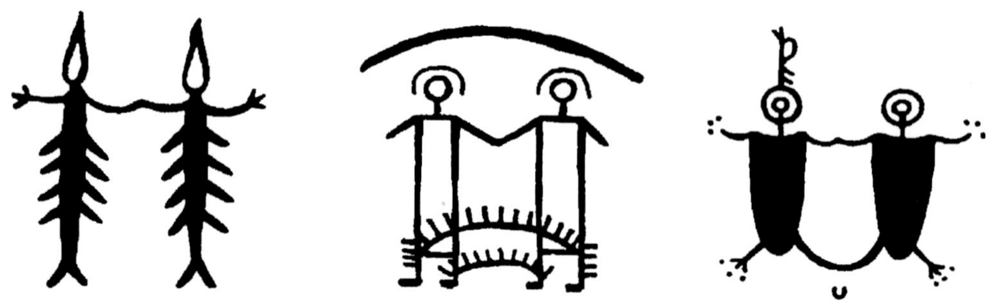

Fig. 169
The 'Mythic Twins coming from the sea'. Three rock engravings from the State of Washington, USA, and from British Columbia, Canada, evocate a myth of origin which is recorded on many rock engravings of the Western Coastal area of North America. A similar myth is also recorded in the rock art of the Siberian Far East.
Source: C. Grant, 1983, p. 26. (WARA Archive W00314)
Area code: F-II. Cat.: E-II.

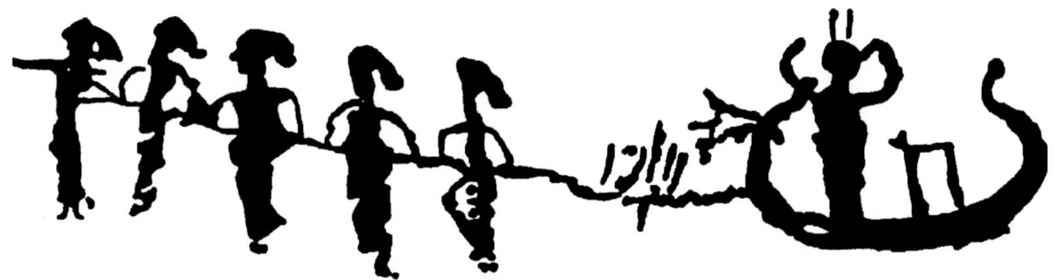

Fig. 170
Proto-dynastic rock engraving from the Nile Valley describes an event: the arrival on boat of a praying being (a priestess?) with a head decoration. The boat is carried (on shore?) with a rope by five women . Some ideograms are engraved between the boat and the women.
Source: H. Winkler, 1938, vol. I, pl. XII/a. (WARA Archive W00290)
Area code: C-IV. Cat.: E-I.

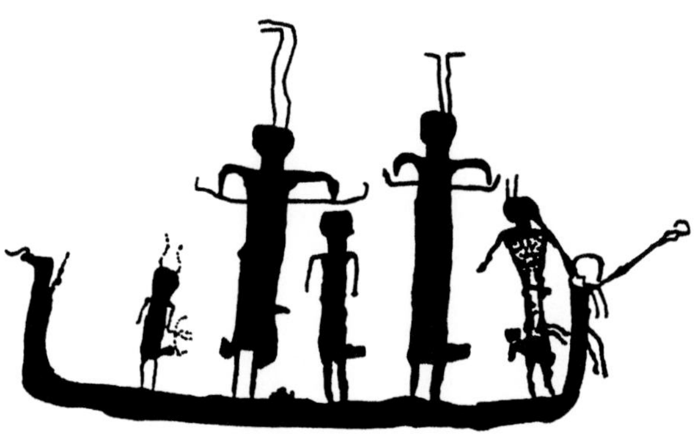

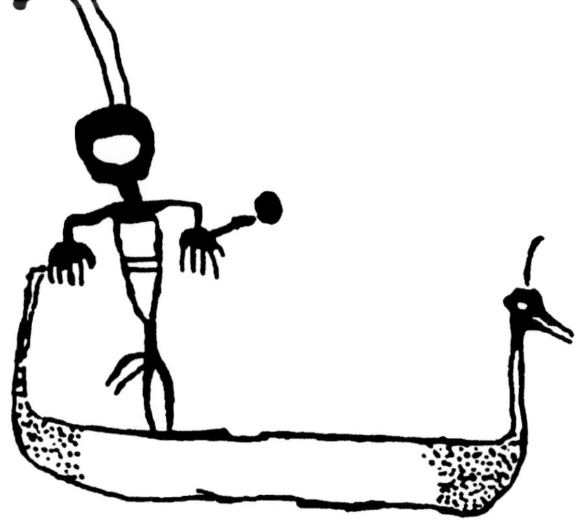

Fig. 171 and 172
Strange people arriving on boats. Rock engravings from the Upper Nile Valley, Nubia, Egypt. Two representations of elaborate boats with anthropomorphic beings displaying their weapons: bows in fig. A and a mace in fi g B. In both cases they represent pre- or proto-Dynastic weapons. The beings have some kind of elongated 'antennae' on their head, which are their identification symbol. These images may commemorate an event or a myth.
Source: Drawn from photographs in H. Winkler, 1938, vol. I, pl. XXII. (WARA Archive W00291 – W00292)
Area code: C-IV. Cat.: E-I.

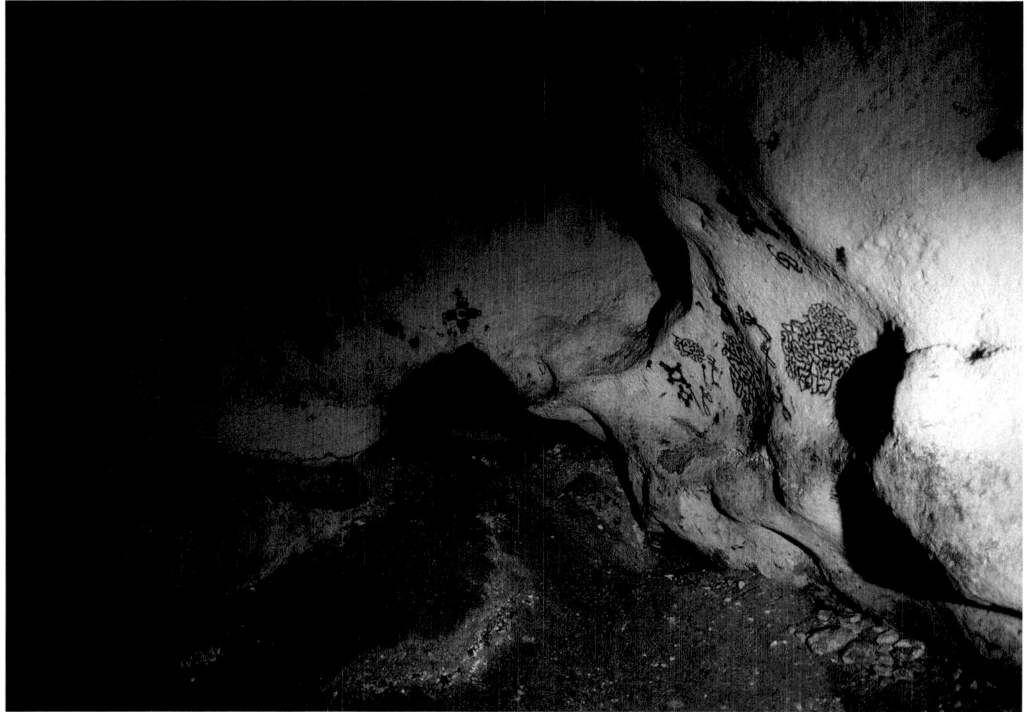

Fig. 173
Porto Badisco Cave, Lecce, Italy. Neolithic paintings mark the wall of a passage leading to a major hall of the cave.
Source: Photo E. Anati EA 2000: IX-9 (WARA Archive W05119)
Area code: E-I. Cat.: E I-II.

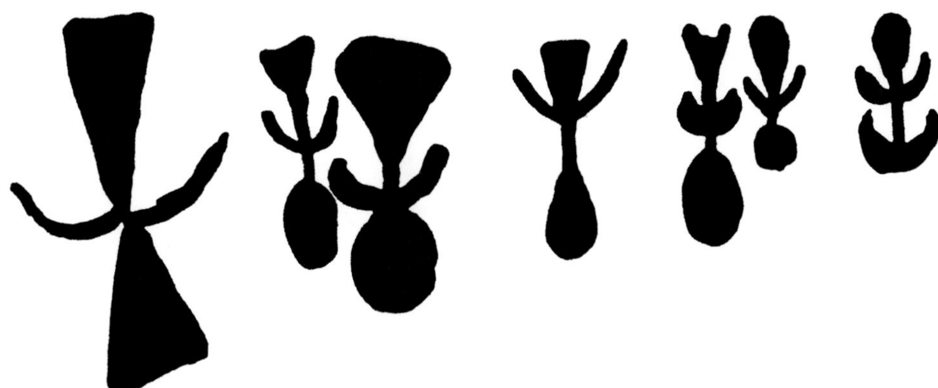

Fig. 174
La Sierpe, Valence, Espagne. Rock paintings of hunting and incipient agriculture societies likely to represent spirits or ancestral spirits.
Source: H. Breuil, 1915. (WARA Archive W05411)
Area Code: E-I; Cat: C-III.

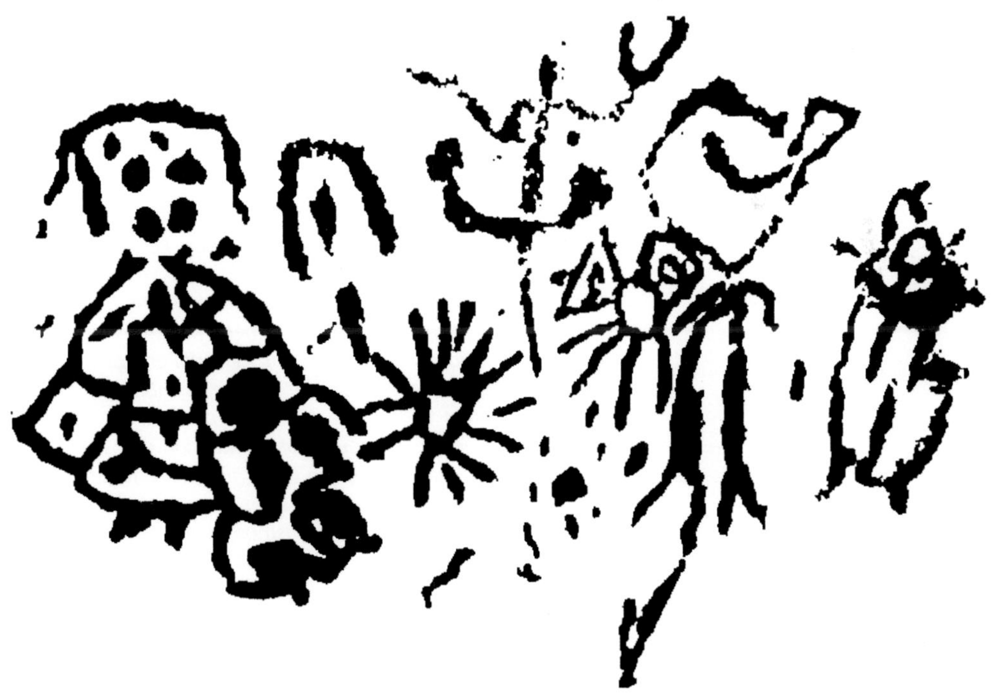

Fig. 175
Porto Badisco Cave, Lecce, Italy. A composition of apparently abstract signs reflect the ideology of its makers, and their state of mind.
Source: Drawing CCSP from a photo by E. Anati (WARA Archive W05469)
Area code: E-I. Cat.: E I-II.

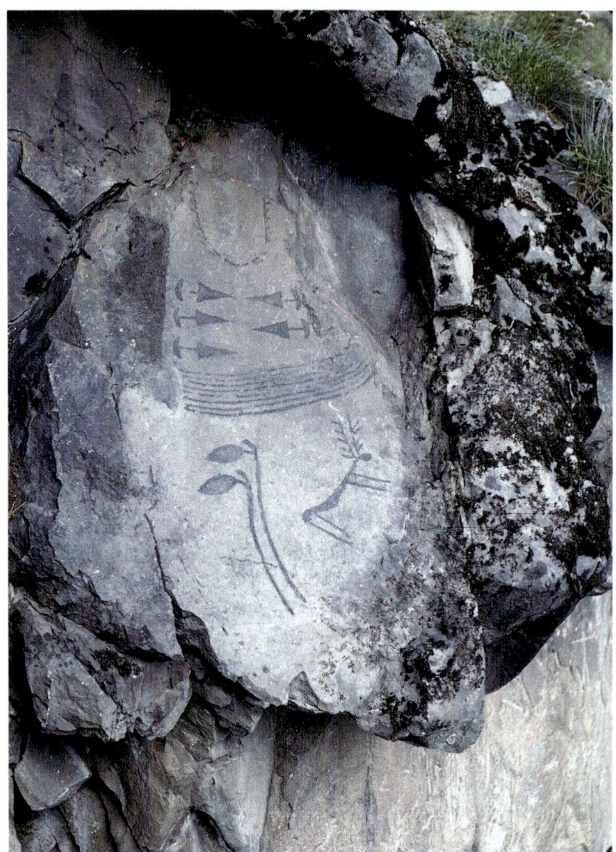

Fig. 176
A rock engraving from Valcamonica, Italy. A symbolic composition of the Chalcolithic Age, ca. 3000 BC, from Paspardo. The surface has obviously been selected because of its shape. The composition of the engravings is adapted to the shape of surface. See following figure.
Source: E. Anati 1982, p. 217. (WARA Archive W05642)
Area Code: E-I. Cat.: D-II.ù

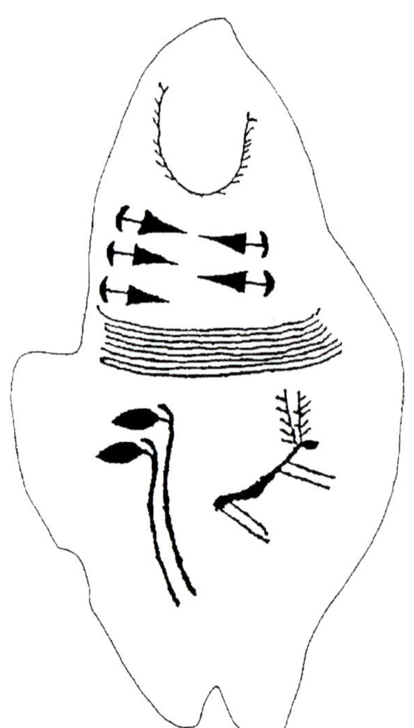

Fig. 177
Rock engraving of people with Complex Economy. Paspardo, Valcamonica, Italy.
Chalcolithic period, late 4th millennium BC. 'Anthropomorphic' composition of ideograms. The 'head' is represented as solar antlers which symbolize 'sky' or 'celestial energy'; in the bust area are depicted five copper daggers symbolizing the power of chiefhood in life; the belt with parallel lines symbolizes the river or 'water', source of purification and passage from life to the underworld; the lower limbs are foliated halberd, (sacrificial tools), and to the right there is a deer, messenger of the underworld. The composition represents a cosmic 'body' enveloping the sky, the earth of the living and the world of the dead.
Source: E. Anati, EA-64. (WARA Archive W00304)
Area code: E-I. Cat.: E-II.

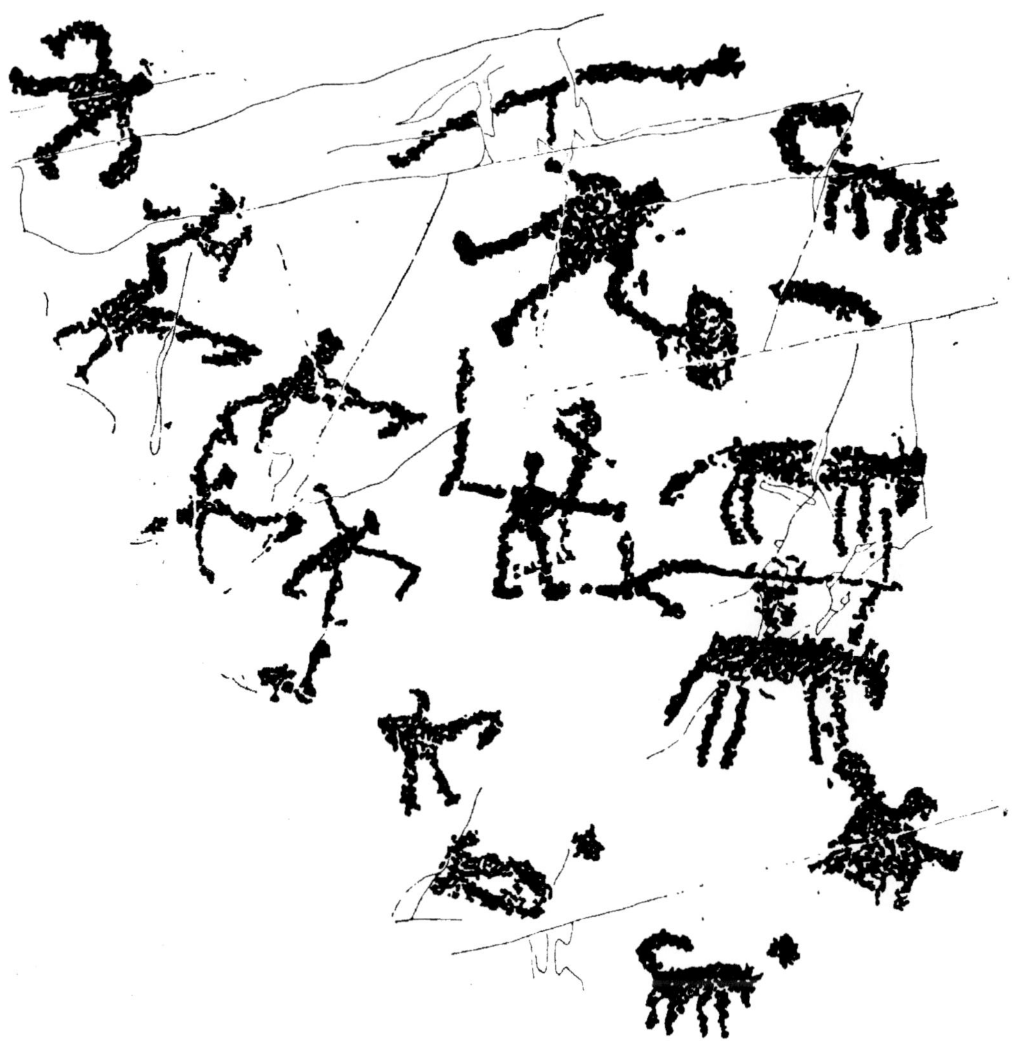

Fig. 178
Rock engravings of an agricultural scene belonging to the Iron Age (middle of the 1st millennium BC). A team work of people shoveling is following a plough. The figure of a warrior with spear and shield in the upper part is representing a mythic spirit which is frequently represented in the Iron Age rock engravings of Valcamonica. Source: Anati, Camonica Valley, 1979. (WARA Archive W00373) Area code: E-I. Cat.: E-II.

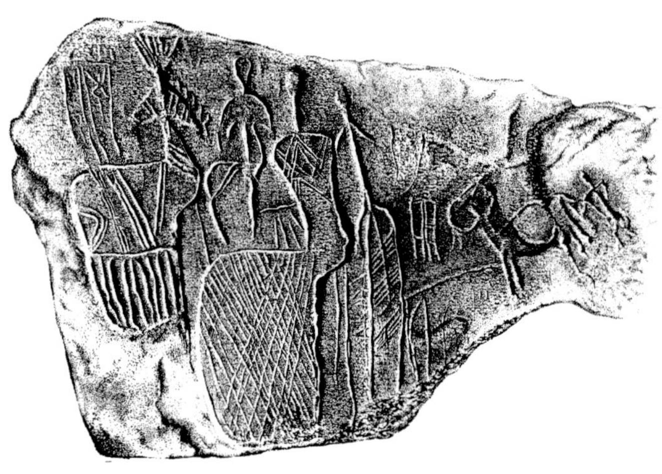

Fig. 179
Elaborate dresses of oasis dwellers. Rock engravings on a rock slab found near Jebel Uwenat, Upper Egypt. Two elegantly dressed women are being attended by two others who are more modestly dressed. On both sides of the scene the same ideogram is repeated: it represents schematically two human beings near to each other and is likely to mean 'union' The two elegant women are likely to be preparing for a ceremony (marriage?). The scene may be attributed to Incipient Agriculturalists of early Neolithic culture. To the right there is a human figure with a bovine made by a different hand. It reflects a Pastoral style and is later. Jebel Uwenat, which is today in the middle of a dry stony desert, may have been a fertile zone when the women were engraved.
Source: Drawn from a photograph by H. Winkler. (WARA Archive W02018)
Area code: C-IV. Cat.: D-I; E-III.

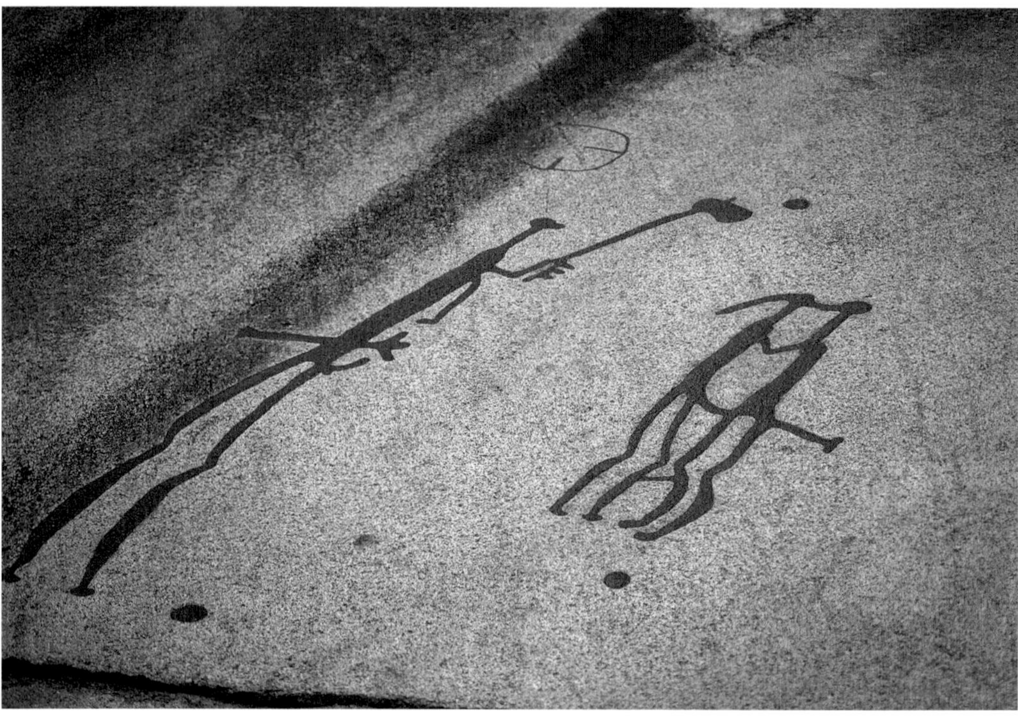

Fig. 180
Rock engravings of a group with complex economy at Vitlycke, Tanum, Sweden. A couple is mating under the protection of a being of much bigger size which is ithyphallic and holds an axe above them. The point, in three different places of the scene, has the meaning 'to do'. The point at the foot of the couple is likely to mean 'to copulate' near the foot of the big being is likely to mean 'to go', near the axe it is likely to emphasize the metaphor of the perforated axe head penetrated by the handle.
Source: photo by E. Anati, 1974, E-9
Area Code: E-II. Cat.: D-II.

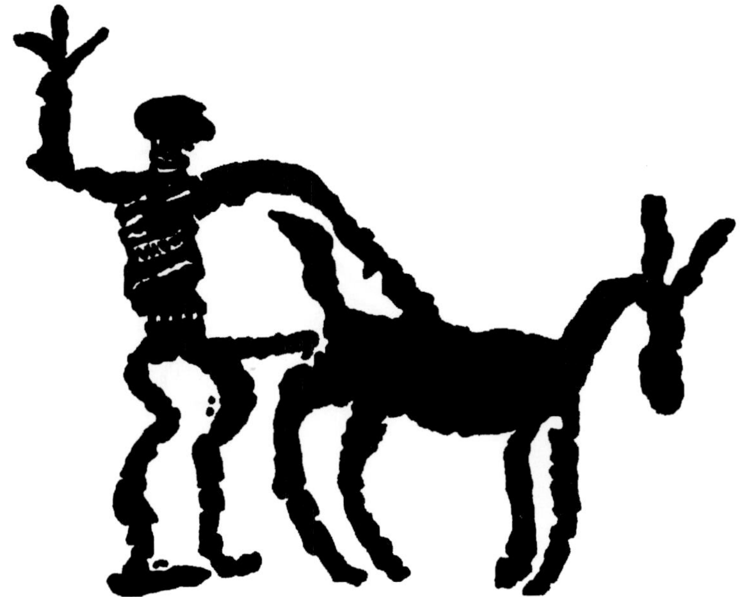

Fig. 181
Search of communion with the animal world. Coren del Valento, Valcamonica, Italy. The Iron age people of Valcamonica tried, in various ways, to provoke the power of nature.
Source: E. Anati, 1976, p. 128
Area Code: E-I. Cat.: D-II

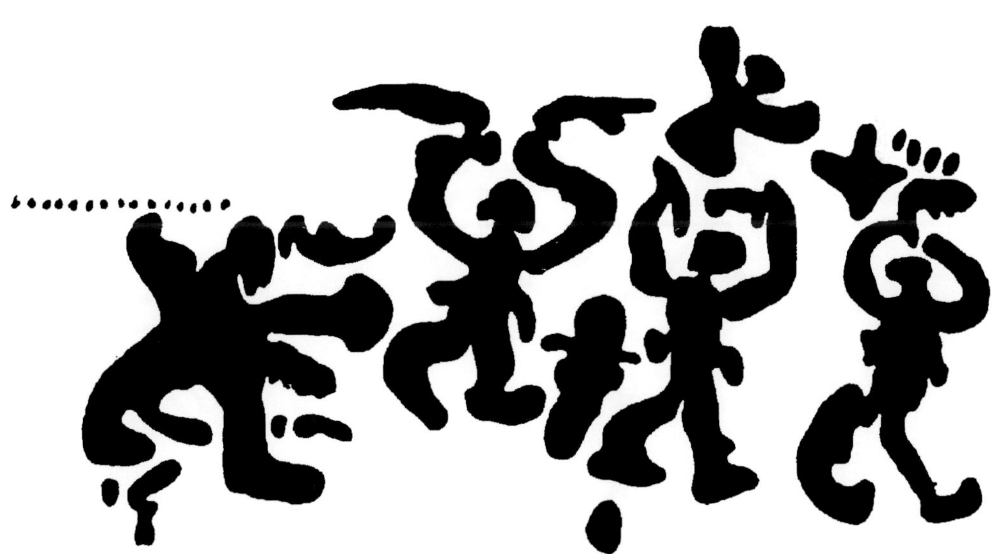

Fig. 182
Rock engraving of people with Complex Economy. Valcamonica, Italy. A male and three females dance and produce sounds and rhythms. These are expressed by the ideograms.
Source: E. Anati, 1989, p. 208
Area Code: E-I. Cat.: D-II

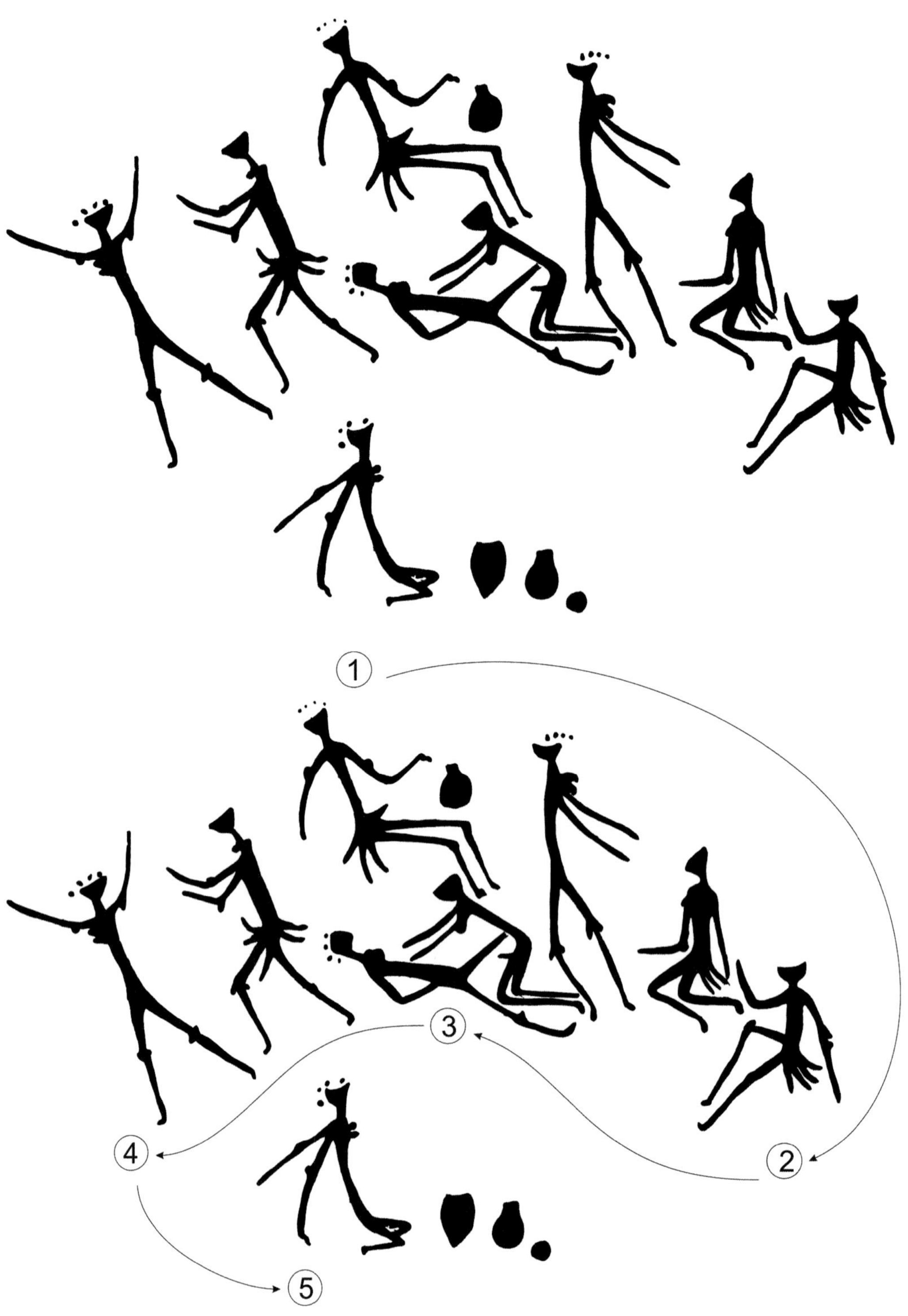

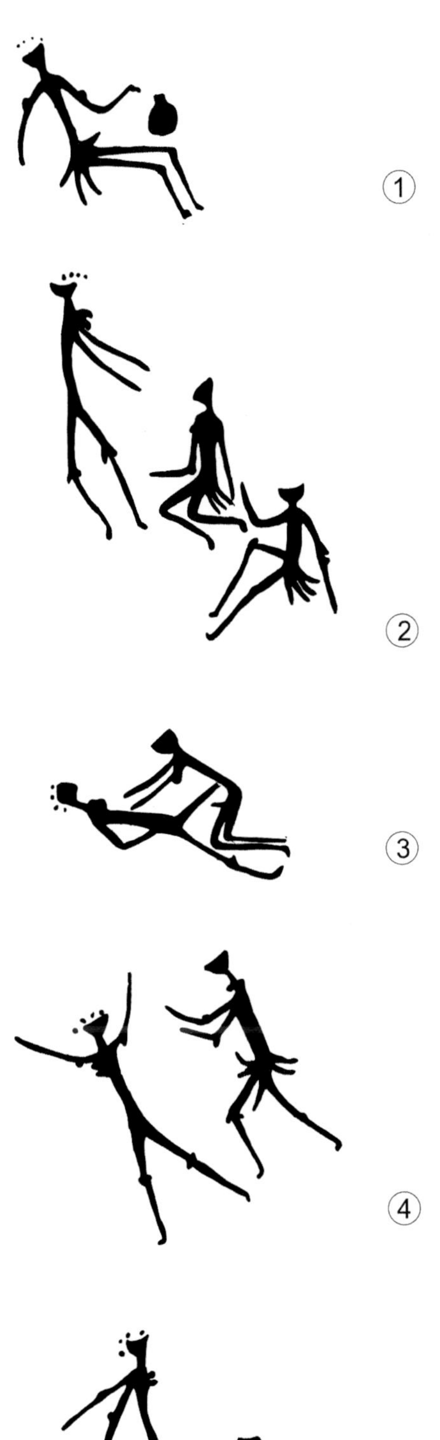

Fig. 183 a - b - c
The story of 'The Girl with the Jar'. The Tassili n'Ajjer, Algeria. Rock paintings of evolved hunters or early Pastoralist telling the story of a girl, concentrating in one pictures five moments. The girl is always indicated with four dots on her head and is defined by her relation with pottery jars. A man is trying to seduce her and she runs away, finally going back to her jars. To be noted that the beginning and the end of the story are in the middle, and the story is turning around. The picture may illustrate a myth or a popular story.
Source: E. Anati 2003, p. 159. (WARA Archive W06862)
Area Code: CII. Cat: C-III.

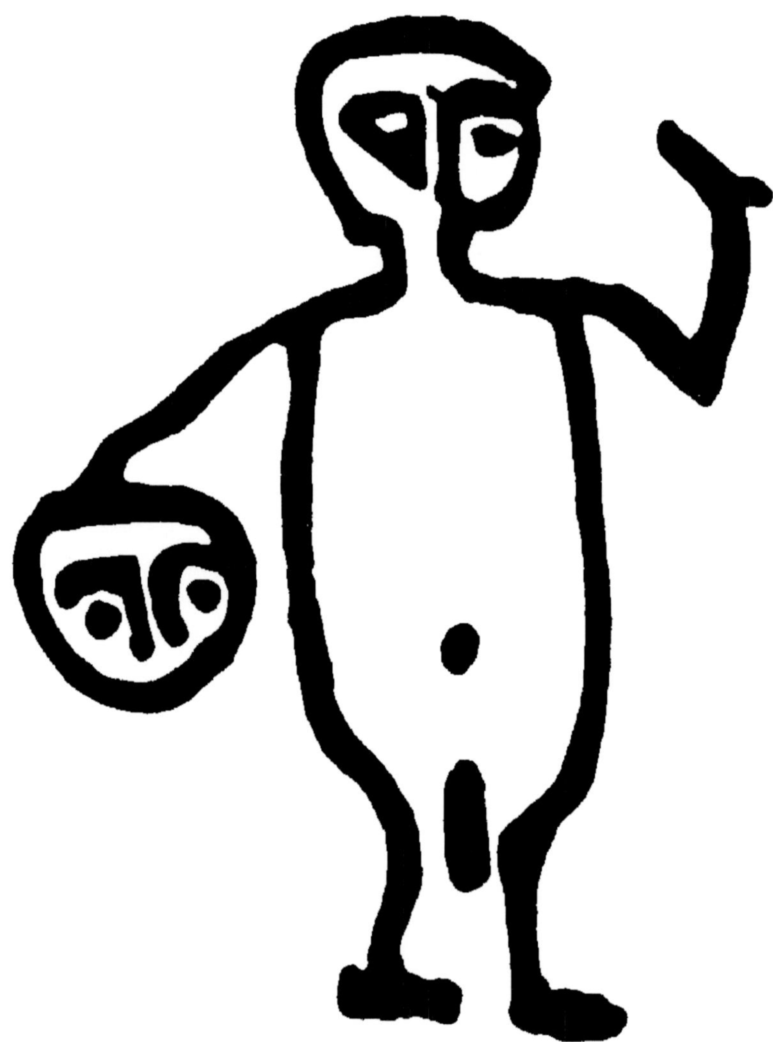

Fig. 184
A masked man and his true face. Incipient Complex Economy. Rock engraving from Clo-oose, British Columbia, Canada. A masked man is holding his true face so the question arises: 'which one is the true face? The one you have been born with or the one you put on?' This question is probably still asked by many people in our own society.
Source: B and R. Hill, 1974. p. 280. (WARA Archive W00323)
Area Code: F-I. Cat.: E-II.

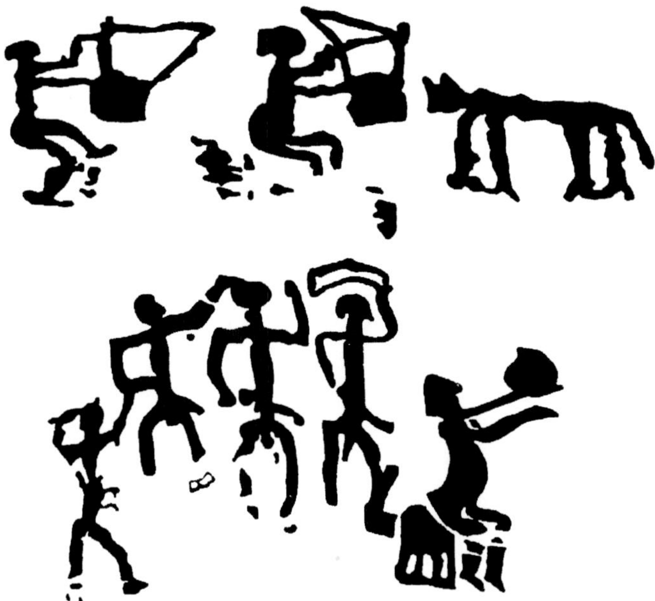

Fig. 185 a - b
Two scenes of dance and music. Rock engravings of Pastoralists-Agriculturists-Traders having knowledge of metal. Wadi Harash, Central Negev, Israel. The asymmetric lyre, the chair and other elements allow to establish a date in the 2nd millennium BC. The two players in the upper scene dance in front of an animal. Both scenes are depicted on the same rock and are likely to be related to each other.
Source: E. Anati, 1979, p. 50. (WARA Archive W00317)
Area code: B-III. Cat.: E-II.

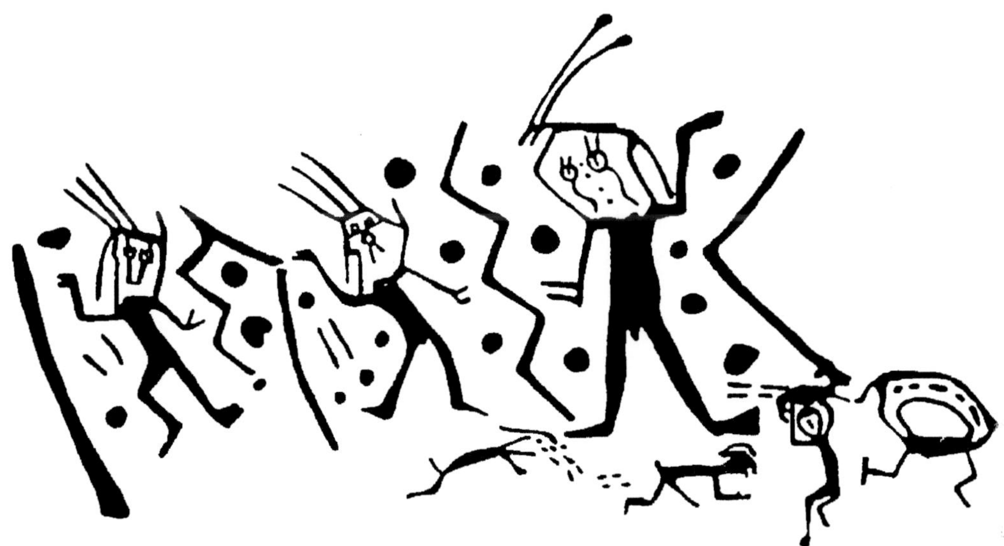

Fig 186
Rock engravings of Incipient Food Producers. An early phase of the 'Complex Economy' group. Toro Muerto, Perù. A scene of dance and music where rhythms and sounds are represented graphically with dots and lines around the dancers. Each dancer has a different mask which indicates his identity (or the identity he represents in the dance).
Source: A. Núñez Jiménez, 1986, vol. 4, p. 469. (WARA Archive W00318)
Area code: G-II. Cat.: E-I.

BIBLIOGRAPHY: REFERENCES IN THE CAPTIONS OF ILLUSTRATIONS

ANATI Emmanuel

1963   New petroglyphs at Derrynablaha, County Kerry, Ireland, *Journal of the Cork Historical & Archaeological Society*, vol. LXVIII/2O7-2O8, pp. 1-15, 12 figs, IV pls.

1968   *Arte rupestre nelle regioni occidentali della penisola Iberica*, Archivi, vol. 2, Capo di Ponte (Edizioni), 135 pp., 143 figs.

1972   *Arte Preistorica in Anatolia*, SC, vol. 4, Capo di Ponte (Edizioni), 51 pp., 46 figs.

1974   *Sectors J-Q. Qahra Range to Najran*, Rock-Art in Central Arabia, vol.4: Corpus of the Rock Engravings, Part 3, Publications de l'Inst. Orientaliste de Louvain, n.6, Louvain-la-Neuve, (Inst. Orientaliste de L'Univ. Catholique de Louvain), 2O6 pp., figs. 1O6-319.

1976   *Evolution and Style in Camunian Rock Art*, Archivi, vol. 6, Capo di Ponte (Edizioni), 181 pp., 161 figs.

1979   *L'arte rupestre del Negev e del Sinai*, Milano (Jaca Book).

1982   *I Camuni. Alle radici della civiltà europea*, Milano (Jaca Book).

1984   The State of Research in Rock Art, *BCSP*, vol. 21, pp. 13-56.

1989   *Origini dell'arte e della concettualità*, Milano (Jaca Book).

1992   *Le radici della cultura*, Milano (Jaca Book).

BELTRAN Antonio

1980   *Rock Art of the Spanish Levant*, Cambridge (Cambridge University Press).

1988   L'art Préhistorique Espagnol. Nouveaux horizons et problèmes de la question, *BCSP*, vol 24, pp. 13-44.

BIETAK M.

1963   *Eine Frühdynastische abri-siedlung mit felsbildern aus Sayala-Nubien*, Wien (Osterreichische Akakdemie der Wissenschaften, Philosophisch-Historische Klasse denkscriften).

BOVIO MARCONI J.

1955   Nuovi graffiti preistorici nelle grotte di M. Pellegrino, *BPI*, vol. 64, 1954-55, pp. 57-72.

BREUIL H.

1912   in Alcalde del Rio, H. Breuil & L. Sierra, *Les Cavernes de la Région Cantabrique* (Espagne) Monaco.

BREUIL H. & H. BEGUOEN

1958   *Les Cavernes du Volp* Paris (Travaux de l'IPH, Arts et Métiers Grafiques).

CAMPS Gabriel

1975   Symboles religieux dans l'art rupestre du Nord de l'Afrique, in E. Anati (ed.), *Les Religions de la Préhistoire*, Valcamonica Symposium '72, pp. 323-333.

CHEN Zhao-Fu
1988   *Cina. L'arte rupestre preistorica*, Milano (Jaca Book).

CLEGG J.K.
1983   Australian Rock art and Archaeology, *BCSP*, vol. 20, pp.55-80

COOKE C.K.
1959   Rock Art in Matabeleland, in E. Gooddall, C.K. Cooke & J. Desmond Clark, *Prehistoric Rock Art of the Federation of Rhodesia and Nyasaland*, Glasgow (University Press).

COX Halley & Eward STASACK
1970   *Hawaiian Petroglyphs*, Honolulu, HI (Bishop Museum).

DEWDNEY S. & E. KIDD
1962   *Indian Rock Paintings of the Great Lakes*, Toronto (University of Toronto Press).

DJAFARSADE I.M.
1973   *Gubustan*, Baku (Institut Istorii, Akademia Nauk).

FERNANDEZ DISTEL Alicia
1990   Reseña, *SIARB*, n. 4, pp. 76-80.

FOCK Gerhard J. & Dora
1984   *Felsbilder in Südafrica*, Vol. II: *Kinderdam and Kalahari*, Köln (Institut für Ur- und Frühgeschichte der Universität Köln).

FROBENIUS Leo
1962   *Madsimu Dsangara. Südafrikanische Felsbilderchronik*, Graz (Akademische Druck), Vol. I.

GOODALL E.
1959   The Rock Paintings of Maashonaland, in E. Gooddall, C.K. Cooke & J. Desmond Clark, *Prehistoric Rock Art of the Federation of Rhodesia and Nyasaland*, Glasgow (University Press).

GRANT Campbell
1983   *L'arte rupestre degli indiani nord-americani*, Milano (Jaca Book).

GUIDON Niède
1984   *L'art rupestre du Piaui dans le contexte Sud-américain*, Paris (Université Paris I).

HILL B. & R.
1974   *Indian Petroglyphs of the Pacific Northwest*, Saanichton, BC (Hancock).

JOHNSON Townley
1986   *Major Rock Paintings of Southern Africa*, Cape Town (David Philip).

KUBAREV B.D.
1988   *Drevnie Rospisi Karakola*, Novosibirsk (Institut istorii, Akademia Nauk SSSR).

LEAKEY M.
1983   *Africa's Vanishing Art*, New York (Doubleday).

LEE Georgia
1986   Easter Island: Recent Archaeological Research, *BCSP,* Vol. 23, pp. 69-90.

LEROI-GOURHAN André
1981   *I più antichi artisti d'Europa*, Milano (Jaca Book).

LEWIS Darrell
1988   *The Rock Paintings of Arnhem Land*, Australia, Oxford (BAR).

LEWIS WILLIAMS J.D.
1983   *The Rock Art of Southern Africa*, Cambridge (Cambridge University Press).

MALLERY G.
1972   *Picture-Writing of the American Indians*, 2 vols., 1888 (and photostatic reprint, 1972), 1° ed., Washington (Government Printing Office), 1988; 2. ed. New York (Dover).

MORI Fabrizio
1975   Contributo allo studio del pensiero magico-religioso attraverso l'esame di alcune raffigurazioni rupestri preistoriche del Sahara, in E. Anati (ed.), *Les religions de la préhistoire*, Valcamonica Sympodsium'72, pp. 343-366.

NUNEZ JIMÉNEZ Antonio
1986   *Petroglifos del Peru*, vol. 4, La Habana (Editorial Cientifico-Técnica).

RAPHAEL Max
1945   *Prehistoric Cave Paintings*, The Bollingen Series, vol. IV, New York (Pantheon Books).

RESCH W.F.E.
1967   *Die Felsbilder Nubiens*, Graz (Akademische Druck).

RHOTERT H.
1952   *Libysche Felsbilder*, Darmstadt (L.C. Wittich).

SAMORINI G.
1989   Etnomicologia nell'arte rupestre sahariana (Periodo delle 'Teste Rotonde'), *BCN*, vol. VI/2, pp. 18-22.

SARRADET M.
1975   *L'art préhistorique du Perigord*, Studi Camuni, vol.6, Capo di Ponte (Ediz. del Centro).

SCHOBINGER J.& C. J. GRADIN
1985   *L'arte delle Ande e della Patagonia*, Milano, (Jaca Book).

STRIEDTER K.H.
1984   *Felsbilder der Sahara*, München (Prestel-Verlag).

VAN TILLBURG J.A. (ed.)
1983   *Ancient Images on Stone*, Los Angeles, CA (UCLA).

WELCH D.
1990   The Bichrome Art Period in The Kimberley, Australia, *Rock Art Research*, vol. 7/2, pp. 110-124.

WILLCOX A.R.
1984   *The Rock Art of Africa*, London (Croom Helm).

WINKLER H.A.
1938-39 *Rock-Drawings of Southern Upper Egypt*, London (The Egyptian Exploration Society), vol. I, 1938; vol. II, 1939.

ACKNOWLEDGEMENTS

The present publication is the preliminary result of a project aimed at producing a world data bank on rock art. It has been in progress since 1982 under the name of WARA or 'World Archives of Rock Art'. The project started as a tool to compile the 'State of Research in Rock Art' commissioned by UNESCO (United Nations Educational, Scientific and Cultural Organization). It was conceived in a cooperation between Raj J. ISAR of UNESCO, François LEBLANC then Director of the Secretariat of ICOMOS (International Council of Monuments and Sites), Luis MONREAL, then General Secretary of ICOM (International Council of Museums), and the present writer, then Chairman of CAR (ICOMOS International Committee on Rock Art). After the *State of Research in Rock Art* was published (1984) The WARA was hosted at the Centro Camuno di Studi Preistorici and grew thanks to contributions of colleagues from five continents. To them all go our thanks.

Special acknowledgments are due to the late Prof. Antonio BELTRAN , past Dean of Humanities, University of Zaragoza, Spain; Prof. Zhao-Fu CHEN, Central Institute of Nationalities, Beijing, China; Dr. Jean CLOTTES, my successor as Chairman of CAR, France; Dr. Jarl NORDBLADH, University of Gothenborg, Sweden; Prof. Juan SCHOBINGER, University of Mendoza, Argentina; Drs. Lucas SMITS, Professor Emiritus, Rome University, Lesotho; Dr. Kalles SOGNNESS, University of Trondheim, Norway; the late Prof. Vishnu WAKANKAR, University of Ujjain, India.

In 1988, Dr. Sante BAGNOLI, Chairman of Jaca Book publishing house, Milan, commissioned the book *'Origini dell'Arte e della Concettualità'* which was then published in Italian, French and German in 1989. The compilation of this book allowed me to gather the world data on the Hunters-gatherers rock art. In 1993 another 'State of Research in Rock Art' was commissioned by ICOMOS and a new synthesis became necessary. These experiences have been the core upon which this work has grown.

The present book was born as a series of lectures at the University of Lecce, Italy. It is basically a further elaboration of the main results presented by the two World Reports, 1983 and 1993. It was compiled at the Centro Camuno di Studi Preistorici, Italy and at the Maison des Sciences de l'Homme, Paris.

ABOUT THE AUTHOR
EMMANUEL ANATI

Emmanuel Anati is President of CISPE (International Centre for Prehistoric and Ethnologic Studies) and President of UISPP-CISENP (Union International des Sciences Préhistoriques et Protohistoriques – Commission Internationale Scientifique 'Les expressions intellectuelles et spirituelles des peoples sans écriture'). He is founder and Director of Centro Camuno di Studi Preistorici in Capo di Ponte, Italy. He has been Professor of Prehistory at Tel-Aviv University, Israel and Professor Ordinarius of Paleo-ethnology at the University of Lecce, Italy. He has taught in other universities and research institutes in Italy, France, the United Kingdom, Israel, the United States and Canada.

His main scientific interests are the art, ideology and religion of prehistoric and tribal cultures. He has conducted field research in Europe, the Near East, India, Australia and other countries. Anati's work in Valcamonica, where he founded and heads the CCSP (Centro Camuno di Studi Preistorici), has led to UNESCO's inclusion of the rock art of this Alpine valley in its list of *World Cultural Heritage*. In Valcamonica he created a school for specialization in prehistoric art, the only existing institute of its kind in this field.

On behalf of UNESCO and various governments he has carried out research and has served as consultant for the creation and development of archaeological reserves and parks, museums, major exhibitions and other field projects.

He is the founder of the International Committee on Rock Art (CAR) of the International Council on Monuments and Sites (ICOMOS). For nine years he served as the first Chairman of the Executive Board. He has organized international congresses and seminars on prehistoric and tribal art, planned and developed large exhibitions, and has stimulated a broad international movement in this discipline.

Anati has edited several prestigious publications. He is the director of the periodical, 'World Journal of Prehistoric and Tribal Art' (BCSP). He headed the series 'The Imprint of Man' for the Cambridge University Press, and the series 'Le Orme dell'Uomo' for Jaca Book, Milan. He has written over 70 volumes and numerous monographs for leading publishers in Europe and America. Works by Anati have been published in over twenty languages.

Among his publications are: *Palestine Before the Hebrews*, New York (A.A. Knopf), 1963, [Italian ed., Milan (Il Saggiatore), 1964]; *Rock Art in Central Arabia*, Louvain (Institut Orientaliste), 4 vols., 1972-75; *L'art rupestre du Negev et du Sinai*, Paris (l'Equerre), 1979, [Italian ed., Milan (Jaca Book), 1979], [German ed., Bonn (Lubbe), 1981]; *I Camuni alle radici della civiltà europea*, Milan (Jaca Book), 1982, [French ed, *La Préhistoire des Alpes*, Paris (Payot-Jaca Book), 1986]; *The Mountain of God*, [French ed., Paris (Payot-Jaca Book)], [English ed., New York (Rizzoli)], [Italian ed., Milan (Jaca Book), 1986]; *Har Karkom In the Light of New Discoveries*, Capo di Ponte (Edizioni del Centro), 1993; *World Rock Art. The Primordial Language*, Capo di Ponte (Edizioni del Centro), 1993; *Valcamonica Rock Art: A New History for Europe*, Capo di Ponte (Edizioni del Centro), 1994; *Les racines de la culture*, Capo di Ponte (Edizioni del Centro), 1995; *Il museo immaginario della preistoria. L'arte rupestre nel mondo*, Milano (Jaca Book), 1995 *I segni della storia*, Roma (Di Renzo Editore), 1997; *Esodo tra mito e storia*, Capo di Ponte (Edizioni del Centro), 1997; *L'art rupestre dans le monde. L'imaginaire de la préhistoire*, Paris (Larousse), 1997; *Höhlenmalerei*, Zürich (Benziger), 1997; *La religion des origines*, Paris (Bayard Éditions), 1999; *Har Karkom. 20 anni di ricerche archeologiche*, SC vol. 20, Capo di Ponte (Edizioni del Centro), 1999; Editor, *40.000 anni di arte contemporanea. Materiali per una esposizione sull'arte preistorica d'Europa*, Capo di Ponte (Edizioni del Centro), 2000 (ed. Fr. *40.000 ans d'art contemporain. Aux origines de l'Europe*, 2003); *The Riddle of Mount Sinai*, Archaeological Discoveries at Har Karkom, Capo di Ponte (Edizioni del Centro), 2001; *Gobustan, Azerbaijan*, Capo di Ponte (Edizioni del Centro), 2001; *La struttura elementare dell'arte*, Capo di Ponte (Edizioni del Centro), 2002; *Lo stile come fattore diagnostico nell'arte preistorica*, Capo di Ponte (Edizioni del Centro), 2002; *Arte preistorica. Una rassegna regionale*, SC vol. 24, Capo di Ponte (Edizioni del Centro), 2002; *Introduzione all'arte preistorica e tribale*, Capo di Ponte (Edizioni del Centro), 2003; *Aux Origines de l'art,* Paris (Fayard), 2003; *La Civiltà delle Pietre*, Valcamonica, una storia per l'Europa, Archivi, vol. 16, Capo di Ponte (Edizioni del Centro), 2004, *L'art du Tapa. Étoffe pour les Dieus, Étoffe pour les Hommes*, Paris (L'Insolite), 2005, *Har Karkom. A Guide to Major Sites*, Capo di Ponte (Edizioni del Centro), 2006; *L'odysée des premiers hommes en Europe*, Paris (Fayard), 2007; *Capire l'arte rupestre*, Capo di Ponte (Edizioni del Centro) 2007; *The Civiliszation of Rocks. Valcamonica, a History for Europe,* Capo di Ponte (Edizioni del Centro) 2008.

Professor Anati can be contacted through the Centro Camuno di Studi Preistorici, Città della Cultura, 25044 Capo di Ponte (BS), Italy. E-mail: ccspreist@tin.it; anati@msh-paris.fr.